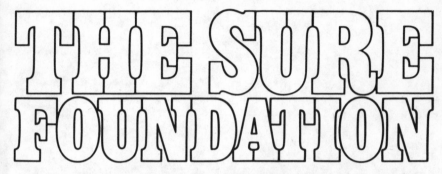

THE SURE FOUNDATION

Jim Bakker Presents A PTL Club Daily Devotional Guide

With Dr. C. M. Ward

Edited by Jeffrey Park

PTL Television Network
Charlotte, North Carolina 28279

Dear Faith Partners,

My Bible tells me (and the signs today are obvious) that we are living in perilous times. And God's Word says that in these days Satan will try anything and everything to try to steer believers away from God's will.

We have had this daily devotional guide, authored by one of America's foremost ministers and my favorite preacher, Dr. C. M. Ward, prepared especially for you our PTL Partners, that our lives may be strengthened and established in God's perfect will. If you will join me this year in these daily discoveries from God's Word, I believe we will be established together and strengthened to reach out to others worldwide for Christ that He might soon return for His Bride, the Church.

In warmest Christian love,

Jim Bakker

Jim Bakker
President

The AUTHOR:

Editor's Note:

Any builder can tell you that if you want to build a tall building, you must first dig down to set a firm foundation. Jesus told his followers that their house (lifestyle) must be built upon a rock to withstand the storms of life. Paul wrote to the Colossians that they must be "rooted and built up in Him (Christ)." The writer of the book of Hebrews exhorted believers that they could not go on to perfection without first laying the foundation of Christ. Therefore every new believer today needs a foundation for building upon his faith in God.

In the Book of Habakkuk, the Lord speaks: "write the vision and make it plain upon the tables, that he may run that readeth it." This is the purpose of this devotional: not only to provide daily inspirational reading, but instruction in the basic doctrines of faith in Christ. The selections are written in clear and simple English and garbed in the everyday experiences of Christian life, so the reader can easily apply them to daily living.

The bulk of the devotionals in this book were edited from the radio sermons of Dr. C. M. Ward,

(cont.)

known to millions around the world for the past twenty-five years as the voice of the weekly "Revivaltime" broadcast. Doctor Ward is described by his peers as one of the most eloquent, articulate, and relevant ministers of our generation. While he has served for many years as an evangelist, and his love for soul winning is supreme, C.M. also spent many years in pastorates in both the United States and Canada. As a pastor, he hated evil and loved to instruct his sheep in godly living and warn them against the pitfalls of Satan. This unique combination in C.M. of evangelist and pastor enables the messages of this book to naturally flow with the love of God from the point of salvation to the solid foundational principles of faith.

The introductory messages to each topic are written by popular guests of the PTL Club, who each share a favorite Bible verse and its meaning in their lives. Dr. Ward's own favorite verse is self-explanatory and shares God's promise and our hope for every reader of this book: "Thou will show me the path of life; in thy presence is fulness of joy; at thy right hand there are pleasures for evermore." —Psalms 16:11

CONTENTS:

JANUARY:
The Love of God

"For the Son of man is come to seek and to save that which was lost." —Luke 19:10

The Sure Foundation

> *"NEVERTHELESS the foundation of God standeth sure, having this seal, the Lord knoweth them that are His. And let every one that nameth the name of Christ depart from iniquity."*
>
> —II Timothy 2:19

That word, "nevertheless" means so much. Regardless of situations, disappointments, mental illness, problems, failures, inequities, or reverses, we have a sure standing point—a solid foundation.

What is the foundation of God? It is all that He stands for and is His nature. It is creation, salvation, spiritual growth through the Bible and healing now. How does it help? It enables us to stand and maintain a dynamic balance in life.

Dr. Clyde Narramore
Author, Christian Psychologist

The "seal" (meaning inscription, guarantee, or decree) tells us that the Lord knows those that are His as well as those not His. He has chosen us and called us to depart from iniquity so that we can receive His blessings.

The Thunder of His Power

"...how little a portion is heard of Him? But the thunder of His power who can understand?" —Job 26:14

George Otis
Author

Our God is so vast in His power and understanding and love. We know of only a microcosm of that which is to be understood of His way. Paul talks of the unsearchable riches of knowing God.

The adventures and excitements that this world offers is nothing compared to the High Adventure of knowing God. It is thrilling to know that I have a God, who is so great, holy and wise that each day, even throughout eternity, will hold new excitement and new joy of learning new things of His greatness and goodness.

He Cares For Us

"Jesus Wept" —John 11:35

These two little words speak more about caring for people and their problems and griefs than most people say in a life time. I am what I am because Jesus cared for me. Jesus wept for you and He wept for me; He gave me a hymn about that.

I believe the thought of Him weeping over the world should make each of us sorry and filled with regret that we made Him pay the price that He did — The Cross. And then thankful that He did it for us.

Hank Snow
Country & Western Singer

God's Faith In Man

*"And God said, Let us make man in our image,
after our likeness: and let them have dominion over
the fish of the sea, and over the foul of the air, and
over the cattle, and over all the earth, and over
every creeping thing that creepeth upon the earth."*
—*Genesis 1:26*

Man's entire hope rests upon his Creator. Without a center or foundation in God, man is left in confusion and anarchy. In God, man finds the
faith of His creator. God created man and said, "It is *good*." Of all the
creatures, of God's creation, only man was created in God's likeness.

Only man can share in the creative, eternal responsible nature of God.
God said, "Let him have dominion." God believes in man and gives him
the authority to take dominion over his creation. God says, "I have furnished the raw materials, created the universe out of nothing, but now you
must take dominion. There are children to be born, civilizations to be
founded, laws to be discovered and applied, buildings and churches
erected, pictures to be painted, songs composed, oceans sailed, and mountains tunneled."

As God told Abraham, "Though man has no faith in you, with my
help, you can do it. You can become that nation, that family of man that I
will bless forever." We that have the heritage of Abraham through Christ
can look forward in faith and hope today because God believes in man, in
each of us individually.

Let us ask God to help us to know His faith in us and move forward in
confidence today to do His will.

The Surprises Of God

"Unto you it is given to know the mystery of the kingdom of God"   —Mark 4:11

The great Creator of the world is the master of the unexpected. Just look at nature. No matter how many winters we've lived through, every spring is exciting. God made it that way. He gets His fancy designs out, His color brush, turns on the music and washes everything clean. There you are, it's spring and you feel like a million!

In all nature, God makes His designs so elastic that they are a constant stream of surprises. For instance, God takes a birch tree, spring touches it, and it is burnished. Summer kisses it and it is green. Winter strips it and then decorates it in a filigree of silver. God keeps nature exciting, wonderful, and packs it full of punch and interest.

God does the same unexpected things in human lives. That's why the Bible is so interesting and full of intrigue. Why did God save Hagar, the mother of Ishmael and root spring of the Arabs after she was kicked out by Abraham? Who would have chosen little freckle faced David among all his handsome brothers? And then Peter in prison, along comes an angel and an earthquake. God's plan for our salvation by the sending of His Son, born in a humble stable, rejected of man and dying on a cross is perhaps the most surprising of all. God is the master of surprise and the dramatic.

That is the way He seasons all of our lives. Our joys surprise us and our griefs take us the same way. We may be having a blue week, but next week may be just the opposite. But God is working out His plan, which includes many surprises. When we think of our own plans and the things we are going to do, stop a minute and think of the surprises of God. Surprising things will be happening if for no other reason than that God is God. He is the Master of the unexpected.

The Marvelous Creation

"I will praise thee, for I am fearfully and wonderfully made: marvelous are thy works; and that my soul knoweth right well." —Psalm 139:14

So many things we take for granted. For instance, we should be thankful that we do not have universal joints at our elbows and knees. What could we lift or how could we walk if these joints did not have a "stopper" on the back side?

How thankful we should be because our teeth are made to match. We had nothing to do with it, but our loving, caring God designed it that way. The teeth are arranged in just the right way. We could hardly chew corn on the cob with molar teeth, or a steak with wisdom teeth. And wasn't God kind to place our noses on upside down, so we don't drown in the rain, and blow our hats off when we sneeze?

What if we had to grease up our joints like an automobile? In His kindness, God made our bodies with a "one shot system." We put food in our mouth, and we're strengthened and still get lubricating fluid in all the joints of the body.

God has placed our eyes in deep sockets, protected by overhanging ledges of bone and eyebrows to catch the dust and perspiration. He has placed the heart, the most precious of all organs, within its bony prison, protected by the ribs and arms. The important blood vessels of the body and the principal nerve trunks are placed safely on the flexor or inside places of the arms and legs. A wise and understanding Sovereign God knew the hazards on the road of life and arranged special protection for these parts which are so essential to life.

Even without the wealth of medical science today, David could see that he was fearfully and wonderfully made. The splendor of it pierced David's soul and it should ours. All of this divine care for our bodies should lead us to want from His gracious and loving hand the provision He has made for our souls.

The Intolerable Commonplace

"But Naaman was wroth, and went away and said, 'Behold, I thought, He will surely come out to me, and stand, and call on the name of the Lord his God, and strike his hand over the place, and recover the leper.'"
—II Kings 5:11

Naaman was the four star General of Syria, who was a leper. His rage is so entirely natural it hardly requires an explanation. He was looking for a spectacular cure—something very fancy and unusual. He had determined that there must be magic to it. After all, he was a big customer; back at the palace, his doctors would sing their incantations and perform their three ring circus of mystical bunk. After this build-up, the Jewish prophet's message to his expectant soul is, "Go wash in Jordan!" What an outrage to be treated as a commoner and General Naaman, who could control an army but not his temper, went away in a rage.

This same story is repeated in the New Testament. The Jews felt sure that the Christ, the Messiah, would flash on them with sudden glory. And then Christ was born in such lowly fashion and humble upbringings, all too ordinary. The Jews were angry, feeling cheated as Naaman and they turned away from Jesus in rage.

The story is repeated today. People look for God in religion with all the trimmings, they want it spectacular. And God says repent, confess your sins, forgive and humble yourself to others. And many say that's too ordinary.

The disappointment of Naaman is common. They come to Jesus because they are cursed with the leprosy of sin and they have heard of Him. But they are disappointed when the message comes simply, "Believe on the Lord Jesus Christ." They want it more difficult, something they can work at to gain merit. The great offense of the cross is it is such a simple way. "Except ye become as a child." But the beauty is that God can take the simple and commonplace and fill it with such glory. He wants to do that with you and I.

Where Are You?

"And the Lord God called unto Adam, and said unto him, 'Where art thou?'" —Genesis 3:9

When we get ourselves in deep trouble, usually we are not particularly interested in somebody asking us how we got in that condition, or telling us that we goofed. The question we want answered is: How do we escape the difficulty or problem?

When Adam disobeyed God and hid himself in the garden, *God came to Adam to show him* the way out. If people can only realize that this is God's attitude. Christ came, not to condemn the world but that the world through Him might find salvation. God is in the saving business. TRUE RELIGION is showing a person how to rise out of trouble. God was the first one to stand by His creature, to be there to find a way to help Adam.

"Adam—where are you?" That is the question we all must answer. Knowing where you stand is a pre-requisite of how to get out of your difficulty. God wanted Adam to answer this so He could help him find his way home once more. *Wherever you are, there is help for you!* If we will face the facts and determine exactly where we stand, we will find a solution to our problems. That is why the Bible says God will not allow us to be tested above or beyond what we are able to bear, but will with every temptation make a way of escape. There's always a way out. There's always an answer.

However, you can't go someplace until you realize you are already somewhere. We must get out of the fog, our mist, our pipe dreams. "Come to yourself," as the prodigal did. That's the first step toward a solution to your problem. Jesus said that the man who is well needs no physician. If you are sick or needy, realize it. That's the first step toward getting better. Jesus said He came not to call the righteous to repentance but the sinner. You'll never realize how quick a change for the better can and will come until you look up into the face of God and say humbly, "God be merciful to me, a sinner." "Adam—where art thou?"

Let us ask God to help us to recognize our need and present ourselves to Him so He can show us the way home.

God Guides Wise Men To Christ

"And lo, the stars went before them."
—Matthew 2:9

Trails are interesting things. Let us consider the trail that God made to lead the wise men to the birth of Christ. If we were to take an imaginary flight through space, we would find the nearest planet thirty-seven million miles away, and the nearest star twenty-five billion miles away. Recently scientists observed the explosion of a star in space. Actually the star had exploded over five years ago, but it had taken that long for the light (travelling at 186,000 miles per second) of the explosion to reach earth.

Yet God prepared a star whose light would come and shine over Jerusalem just at the proper time of Jesus' birth. The men of the Old Testament from Moses to David and Isaiah understood that the stars were a trail of God's handiwork. From Genesis to the end of the Old Testament, we find the writers are on the trail. Where does it all lead? To Christ in the manger. The one great hope that beats and throbs through the Old Testament is the Messianic hope.

Just as for the wise men, there are great rewards for following God's trail that leads to Christ. First, there is a great light on that trail. In this world of uncertainty and surrounding darkness, "I know" is a mighty thing and "I have felt" is an unbeatable argument. Second, the trail has a great goal. So many people today live listless lives because they have no goal, no divine end toward which they strive. The strength and zeal for life comes in our high calling to follow after Christ. Third, the trail leads at last to God. Oh, the privilege of walking *in the light.*

God has given each of us a trail today that leads to Christ. In His perfect plan, we can trust His way.

A Picture Of A Man

"Behold the Lamb of God..."
—*John 1:29*

A restless little daughter was disturbing her father. To amuse her and keep her busy, he tore a map of the world from the newspaper he was reading and cut it into small pieces. "Here's a jig-saw puzzle, dear," he said; "now run along and put it together."

The youngster, whose knowledge of geography was slight, went to work on the map and soon had it assembled. Her father, aroused by her clamor of triumph, was astonished at the feat, and asked, "How did you do it so quickly?"

"There's a picture of a man on the other side," she replied. "I put the man together and the world came out right."

How simple but profound. No matter how much this world of ours is upset there is a *picture of a man* that comes back to us that will make it come out all right. Most of us are like the child. Our knowledge is too slight to enable us to make the world come out right. Our salvation is to concentrate on the Man.

But what a man is our Christ! "All things were created by Him and for Him: And He is before all things and by Him all things consists. And He is the head of the body, the church: who is the beginning, the first born from the dead; that in all things He might have the preminence. For it pleased the Father that in Him should all fullness dwell." (Colossians 1:16-19).

The fullness of creation and all God's nature is in the Man, Christ. When we make Him Lord, our world is together and we have victory and peace with God and man.

The Gladsomeness Of Jesus

*"God, thy God, hath anointed thee with the oil
of gladness above thy fellows."*   —*Psalms 45:7*

These prophetic words refer directly to the Lord Jesus Christ. This Man of Sorrows, Savior of Calvary, was the happiest man who ever lived. Most of our modern religions have not portrayed Christ that way, but it's true. Jesus called himself a bridegroom and even his enemies called him a "wine bibber", hardly the picture of a gloomy person. How did Jesus maintain this even through the darkest hours—this unworrying and radiant heart? It is profoundly helpful to meditate on this. Let me advance some suggestions.

First, He never swayed from His appointed task even when things were rough and friends urged Him to be careful. He kept on and set His face steadfastly to Jerusalem. He always knew where He was going. One of the best things about doing what you know you should is that you're always glad you did it. *Do your duty and it leads to gladness.*

Second, Jesus lived in the abundance of life. He always had a full day. There were no dull days in His life. He shunned laziness like He shunned the devil. He could not stand anything "dead" around Him. If He got in a dead church service, He would break it up with the unusual, a miracle or something. He continually drew upon the boundless life within His Father's heart—a gladness the world could never take away. He said, "This joy no man takes from you."

Third, the deepest root of Jesus' gladness was that He never doubted God. There is nothing like faith to keep up your spirits. Jesus was tempted to doubt just as we are or more: a homeless wanderer, betrayed by friends, nailed to a cross. But to trust as He trusted was *victory* and that kind of moral victory brings a radiance of joy.

To live as Christ, in faith unfailing, is the victory that overcomes the world. The victories of Christ were won for us. A Christian does not so much win his victories as he does to appropriate the victories of Christ. Live as He did—trusting, keeping the heart open to the inflowing tide, and even in the dreariest hours, you'll find a singing heart.

His Eyes

"His eyes were as a flame of fire."
—Revelation 1:14

When Saint John was an old man, he had a vision of the ascended Christ. Now remember, John had seen Him upon the earth and lived with Him. And the thing that instantly struck him as he sees His Lord again in that vision was that His eyes were as a *flame of fire*. More than one Bible character has borne witness to this impressive characteristic of Jesus. In the Gospels, the father of the epileptic boy cried, "Master, look upon my son." Just the look of Jesus could do so much.

There was the look of detection. When the poor woman with the issue of blood pressed through the crowd to touch His garment and was healed, Jesus turned and *looked*. Under that gaze, she knew that she was known. In all that big crowd she was singled out by the penetrating eyes of Jesus. There was the healing power of God in His eyes.

Then there was the look of anger in the story of the man with the withered hand. The Pharisees and hypocrites didn't want anybody helped if they weren't the folk to do it. The Lord looked on them with anger, being grieved at the hardness of their hearts. Jesus was angry. His anger flamed and burned at the wrongs men commit against their fellowmen. We, too, would shrink to face our Lord on Judgment Day if we selfishly stood in the way of someone that needed God's help.

There was the look of disappointment by our Lord to Peter after he denied Christ. But there was also concern in that look. There was the look of the love of God that gripped Peter in his weakness, and held him, and would not let him go. When we disappoint our God, He looks and cares.

Finally, there is the look of trust and perfect confidence in God. When Jesus fed the multitudes, He made the crowd sit down and took the loaves and fishes. Before He blessed and brake, He *looked* up. One look upward to draw for His need on God's unfailing reservoirs, and our Lord was ready for everything that mighty hour demanded.

The eyes of Jesus are a flame of fire and they are looking on us.

A Cure For Heart Trouble

"Let not your heart be troubled: ye believe in God, believe also in Me." —John 14:1

Believe in God—This was the great, earnest theme of Jesus' teaching. That faith must be at the very base of any successful and happy life. Without it, it's impossible to make sense out of the riddle of the universe in which we live.

Now from all outward appearances, Jesus' disciples "believed" in God. But it is the working value of a man's faith that counts. The disciples believed but their thought of God was too vague to be of value. He was but a "general truth"—His presence, His great plan for their welfare, His individual love, were things beyond their appreciation. *And Jesus had come for that purpose*—to give men a close-up, individual view of exactly what God was like.

The truth of God was too big for the disciples to comprehend and yet without it, life could not go on for faith must rest in God. That's why God Himself had to find an adequate expression in human form. Christ is the middleman between God and men. He brings truth down to our conception. He renders God intelligible—not merely some mind billions of miles away that thinks and plans but a loving heart close up to me that feels and cares. This is the Father whom Christ came to reveal, and whose heart He bids us look.

Soon thereafter, the death and resurrection of Jesus proved as nothing else could, the divine fatherhood of God. It kills forever in the heart of the true believer any dread of life or fear of death. Fear, that great enemy of true living, is dispensed within the Gospel, the Gospel that God is love, revealed in the picture of Jesus Christ, his life, death, and resurrection. Faith in God—a God you can know and love, is the true cure of heart trouble.

Down In The Dumps

"WHEN THE DOORS WERE SHUT where the disciples were assembled for fear...Then were the disciples glad, when they saw the Lord."
—John 20:19, 20

After the crucifixion, the disciples got together and they booked a room—a room called despondency. They were not the first or last to book that room. Job had been there. There was the depressing day when he dragged his feet and sat down and cursed the day wherein he was born. The mighty David had sat in that room talking to himself: "Why art thou cast down, O my soul? And why art thou disquieted within me?" David had the blues there and so did Elijah—so bad he wished he could die.

Here were the disciples-door locked, shades drawn in fear, their joy gone. In their room of despondency, they had a bed of restlessness. In a corner was the couch of hopelessness and in the center the table of remorse with chairs of defeat. The only window was the outlook of despair. All this furniture crept in because one thing was missing—Jesus. His presence had always lightened and sweetened the atmosphere. Now he was crucified and gone, along with their hopes. What a difference the presence of Jesus makes.

The disciples were despondent (and we too sometimes for the same reason) because they forgot the promise of Jesus: "I will never leave you nor forsake you." Their misunderstanding of Jesus' mission had steered their mind in a wrong direction, just as happens to us when we look to circumstances. It led them to disappointment—their wrong secret hopes had perished. But Jesus had not.

In spite of closed doors and darkened windows, He came (and will come). His presence changes everything. The disciples are glad! There is one certain cure for periods of despondency that get into our lives...that is to get into the presence of the Lord. "In His presence is fullness of joy."

Let us look up from our moods and worry and burden to see the King Jesus...happy to be with us, chasing away the blues.

The Cross And The World

"God forbid that I should glory save in the cross of our Lord Jesus Christ, by whom the world is crucified unto me, and I unto the world."
—*Galatians 6:14*

The Cross stands between two worlds. It makes the dividing line between the kingdoms of this world and the kingdom of Heaven. *They have nothing in common!* A real Christian and a sinner are two different people. They cannot be one and the same...no more than you can be a Russian citizen and an American citizen at the same time. You can't swear allegiance to both! "If any man love the world—the love of the Heavenly Father is not in him."

What does it mean to love the *world*? The Greeks had several words for world and as used here, it refers to the world system and this world spirit ("get-all-you-can") that the New Testament warns about. It doesn't refer to the world of nature that God created but the corrupt world system of which satan is prince. Jesus came to this world and there was no place for him; that world crucified Christ. *To be friend of one is to be the enemy of the other.*

St. John describes the world system as, "the lust of the flesh (sensuality); the lust of the eyes (covetousness); and the pride of life (vanity)." This attitude toward life is wholly against God and seeks only the kingdom of this world and the glory of man. When Christ entered this world, He revealed the rotten living, the greed and pride and selfishness of this system. Rather than adjust and yield, the world crucified our Lord.

No wonder the world hates and persecutes the true Church. The symbol of the Church in this world will always be the cross. He that bears it must remember that he bears the mud and reproach of the world. A Christian is in the world, but not of it. He is on one side of the cross and the world is on the other.

The Cross And Love

"He that spared not his own Son, but delivered
Him up for us all, how shall he not with Him also
freely give us all things."   —Romans 8:32

Many years ago, Dr. John Jowett, the great theologian, was driving with his pastor friend, Dr. Joseph Parker, through one of the loveliest glens in Wales. At one point in their journey, they observed that a small clearing had been made upon a wooded slope and that a naked scar stared down from the height. Jowett recalls, "To the ordinary observer, it was only a big red gash bleeding there on a lovely hill, but to my friend, it filled with vision and at once became a minister of grace." Pointing to it, Dr. Parker reverently said:

Hath He marks to lead me to Him
If He be my guide,
In His hands and feet are wound prints
And His side
Forever here my rest shall be
Close to thy bleeding side
This all my hope and all my plea
For me the Savior died.

History will forever record that the vast majority of sacrificial deeds and lives offered for the good of the fellowmen have been those of Christian men and women. We think of David, Paul, Martin Luther, Florence Nightingale, George Muller, David Livingstone, Abraham Lincoln, and Martin Luther King—men and women with strong convictions that stood by them no matter what the cost. But all these lives shrink under the magnitude of *God's commitment to men demonstrated on the cross.* It was the supreme love of God shown on the cross that rather inspired the convictions of these men and women.

A very foolish woman told her pastor, "I'm not going to have children." When asked why, she said, "My husband loves me now, and if we had children, I'd have to share that love." How foolish! The more you love, the more will you love. If we will respond to God's love and love Him with all our heart, we will love our fellowman with a greater and growing love. The cross is love triumphant—a never ending supply!!

Pardon

"And let him return unto the Lord, and he will have mercy upon him; and to our God, for he will abundantly pardon."
—Isaiah 55:7

In 1829 George Wilson was sentenced by the United States court to be hanged for murder. President Andrew Jackson pardoned him, but he refused to accept it and the Supreme Court was called in to decide. Chief Justice Marshall gave the decision, "A pardon is a paper, the value of which depends upon its acceptance by the person implicated. If refused, it is no pardon." George Wilson was hanged.

At Toulon where the galleys were kept, a German Prince visited the arsenal. The commandant, as a compliment to the visitor's rank, offered to set at liberty any prisoner whom he selected. The Prince went round the prison and conversed with the men, meeting only with universal complaints of injustice and false accusations—everybody to blame but themselves. At last, he came to one man who admitted his imprisonment was just. As you would expect, the Prince selected him, saying, "This is the man I wish released—the one who owned up to his guilt."

Then in Kentucky, Samuel Holmes, awaiting punishment for murder, was visited by a friend, Mr. Young. Moved by Holmes' condition, Young appealed to the Governor for a pardon. In respect to Mr. Young who had been cited for great bravery, the Governor granted the pardon. With the document of freedom in his pocket, Young visited his friend but first asked, "Sam, if you were fully pardoned, what would you do?" Holmes responded, "I would go and kill the judge and the man who witnessed against me." Without a word, Young mournfully left, tearing the pardon in shreds.

These examples speak of the pardon for our sins that God has provided for us in Christ. We are pardoned, but it is effective only if we receive it, admit our sin and guilt, and are sorry for our sins. There is no need for us to die in our sins. There is a pardon issued for you with your name on it. The rest of it is up to you.

Common Sense
And The Atonement

*"But we also joy in God through our Lord Jesus
Christ, by whom we have now received the
atonement."*   —Romans 5:11

Before we can really enjoy the Christian life and joy in God, we must accept the fact that we are guilty. We literally base our hope of eternal life on an innocent man having been punished in our stead.

Yet we would not consider such a thing in our courts of justice. Suppose a murderer has been found guilty and sentenced to hang. But the judge says, "The man who has been convicted is guilty, but in his place I will order another man to be executed." Never! We carry out our justice on the principle that it is better that one thousand guilty men should go free than one innocent man suffer unjustly.

But suppose I loved that murderer as much as my own life, and volunteered to die in his stead, and by thus dying for him, I satisfied the demands of the broken law and in addition to expiating the man's crime, also supply him the means of a complete moral and character rebirth? If I could do that, wouldn't you call that a glorious and noble transaction? That is impossible with man. But, *that's exactly what Christ did for me!*

Christ by His death made it possible for men to be reconciled to God. He prayed in His agony, "If it be possible, let this cup pass from me." But it was not possible. *Only Christ could pay the price for our salvation.* Though some may insist, what about the good man, the African who never heard, those who lived before Christ, for each of us, the crucial question remains, "Will I receive what Christ has done for me? Will I join the myriads before the throne of God that cry with joy, "Salvation to our God and the Lamb that was slain."

Finished

"He said, It is finished..."

—John 19:30

This is the most wonderful sentence in the Bible. When the words were spoken on the Cross it did not seem as though any victory was won—except for the evil powers of darkness. These words came from a marked, forsaken, broken, wounded, bleeding man. As the crowd left, no one seemed to care, yet that last cry was heard by Heaven and Hell. It wasn't a cry of defeat; it was a glorious cry of victory.

First, it means the sufferings of Jesus are finished. Jesus lived in a human body, became acquainted with all my grief and then He suffered for me physically. Death by crucifixion was punishment invented by cruel people in order to inflict the greatest degree of suffering in dying. The terrible thirst, bones pulled out of joint—He bore that torture for me. But Jesus will never suffer again, it is finished.

Second, never again will He be humiliated. Can you think of greater humility—His lowly birth, living with no material assets, dying in shame. It meant all of that for Jesus to assure my fallen nature. He became the very target of my sin. All the foulness that my fallen nature is capable of erupted in savage fury upon Him.

Third, never again will He endure such loneliness. Jesus was the friendliest person who ever lived. He loved children, old folk and everybody. But He was misunderstood, even by those closest to Him, there was no one He could really become "close to". But that hour is passed.

The mission of the redemption of mankind is complete. The victory is won. Today we see the last, dying kick of the forces of Hell. Jesus is victor—and the devil knows it. We need not struggle and live in turmoil when in Christ we share the victory, the victory of "it is finished."

Believe Also In Me

"Ye believe in God, believe also in me."
—John 14:1

A recent survey shows that 99% of all Americans claim to believe in God. In fact, 87% of those interviewed were *absolutely certain* there was a God. The survey suggests a strong, positive faith in God and might suggest that America is a Christian nation. Not quite! Jesus said, "Believe also in me!" That which *activates* our faith in God is our personal acceptance of His Son—the Lord Jesus Christ as our Savior.

To simply believe in some Supreme Being—located somewhere—we know not where and doing something—we know not what...*will never be enough—never!* For when you say you believe in the existence of God—you haven't made any greater acknowledgment than *devils* make. In the book of James we read, "Thou believest that there is one God-thou does well-the devils also believe, and tremble." Mere acknowledgment of the existence of God is worthless unless it affects conduct.

The Bible tells me that God is fully and completely revealed in Jesus. God alone becomes real to me as I see His outworking through Jesus to reach and save this fallen world of wrecked and ruined sinners. *To deny Christ is to deny God!* And faith in Jesus is predicated upon our acknowledgment that we are sinners and need saving. To disbelieve this is to make the mission and ministry of Jesus of none effect.

A real faith in God will lead us to Jesus and faith in Christ will lead us in a personal way to the cross and then to the open tomb of His resurrection—where we are changed by a "new birth"—a new horizon—*BORN AGAIN.*

Substitutes

"Having a form of godliness but denying the power thereof..."   —II Timothy 3:5

Many are settling for a substitute. Now not all substitutes are bad. We can substitute saccharin for sugar, margarine for butter, rayon for cotton, Crisco for lard, machine power for man power, even one man for another in sports, stand-ins in movie parts, and even one another in life for love's sake (when we fulfill the law of Christ by bearing one another's burdens).

Then there are things for which there are no substitutes, for example, the Christian home and marriage. God says it is a divine institution. It is the supreme human relationship. The husband and wife are to be one, and marriage is to be for life. Today, the devil tempts with the substitutes of living together, and even homosexuality. Neither of these substitutes are satisfying, fulfilling or lasting.

Then there is no substitute for the church. Many have tried with social movements, fraternal organizations, clubs, etc. True, the Church is imperfect, but its contribution to society and every individual is imperative. In society, it is a decay preventing force, even as salt. For the Christian, it is largely charged with the responsibility of feeding and maturing the saints, building and perfecting the body of Christ.

Most important, there is no substitute for God. Men have tried substitutes like loyalty to the state (from Caesar to communism), technology and man-centered science, money, and even religious observance (worshipping the image of God rather than God). In each, worship is a form. But vital Christianity is not mere form, it is a *force*. Such a force that a mere handful of people in the early Church shook Jerusalem and the waves went out to the whole world. That same marvelous power can become ours, not by culture, wealth or education, but by the immediate touch of God. There are no substitutes.

Seeking The Best

"The kingdom of Heaven is like unto a merchant man, seeking goodly pearls."
—*Matthew 13:45*

In these last days, God is reaching down to save all kinds of people. Listening to a former Las Vegas night club entertainer give his testimony of conversion, I was interested in what he had to say. He said, "I am conscious that for the first time in my life, I am doing something that is worthwhile." How well that speaks of the purpose of being a Christian and living a kingly life with a sense of value.

The Gospel writer describes it as those who are "seeking goodly pearls." It's making life count. The Bible also speaks of those who treasure their "paste gems" and pass up the goodly pearls. They are described as "lovers of pleasures more than lovers of God." Judas Iscariot is the classic example of one who wasted his opportunity and passed up the goodly pearl.

The Apostle Paul wept about a friend of his, a travelling companion, who came to a place in life where he passed up that which was worthwhile for the shoddy. We read these pathetic words: "Demas has forsaken me, having loved this present evil world." Think of that man's opportunity! He had the privilege of the fellowship and training of the Apostle Paul, but preferred the swish and whirl of the world and his life went down in moral defeat.

It takes most of us many years to discover that the really good things—the big things—are inside and not outside the man. Paul had no jealousy, only pity for Demas. He knew it is, "godliness with contentment that is great gain." That must be sought above and earned in the struggle of faith. *But it's the best!* The Christian life puts in the zest to seek the very best!

Something It Pays To Know

"I KNOW whom I have believed, and am per-suaded..."
—II Timothy 1:12

It pays to know. Once a Virginia farmer, vacationing on the Atlantic Ocean and unable to swim, dropped his billfold containing thousands of dollars into the ocean. Before either life guards or the Coast Guard could reach it, it disappeared forever. Not *knowing* how to swim cost this man his life savings.

All of us do not know things that could cost us. We do not know what tomorrow has in store. We do not know when we may be afflicted with sickness or disease. We do not know why innocent people are called upon to suffer for the sins of others. We do not always know why things which we desire are denied or why other things we would avoid are thrust upon us. The list could go on and on.

And while the things I do not know far outnumber the things I know, nevertheless, I am glad that I know this: "I know whom I have believed..." I know God! I find my Heavenly Father perfected and revealed in Jesus Christ. In Him my questions have been answered and simply, I know God is a God of love because His love is manifest in the death of Christ on the cross for our sins. The things I know about God are not hard to know. Anyone may be assured of them.

I hate to lose my money, all of us do. Nothing makes you feel worse than to lose something of value. But if we lose some money or a valuable, we can usually work and recoup our loss. But if I lose my soul, what then? Jesus put it this way: "What shall it profit a man if he gain the world and lose his own soul? What shall a man give in exchange for his soul?" Can you answer that today? If we do not know Jesus as our Savior from sin (because of our refusal), we will be a lost soul for all eternity. It pays to know—Him!

Servant Or Son?

"Make me as one of thy hired servants."
—Luke 15:19

This little line comes from perhaps the best known story in the Bible—the prodigal son. This statement is part of the conclusion of the young son when he had "come to himself."

The story is familiar. After requesting and receiving his inheritance and squandering it on riotous living, he found himself bankrupt in a hog pen and there he decided to do three things: (1) go home; (2) admit his wrong; and (3) make this seemingly manly proposition to his father: "make me as one of thy hired servants." He would get back in the right environment, turn over a new leaf, and work for a living. He would pay his way and not be under obligation to his father. He didn't want anything free, just a chance to prove himself. He had made a mess out of life, but he'd get busy and show his father that he could straighten up.

Good conclusion, right? Wrong! And unfortunately it's the same conclusion many people come to today. In making his conclusion, the prodigal son hadn't taken into account that all he had, had been given to him by his father. And his father delighted in sharing and helping him. What if the father had not welcomed him as a son and restored his inheritance but had accepted his proposition? The young man would have never understood the key to life—the power of love. His "new leaf" would have faded fast if the burden was not lifted by his father's love.

Many today realize their fault and guilt and turn back to the Church. Do we offer the same love as the father did or do we accept their proposition to be a hired servant? The only true members of God's family are those who have received the gift of God. Salvation can never come through human effort, but only by God's grace. The only way we'll get to Heaven is through the door. Jesus paid it all in His blood—that we might be grateful sons, not servants.

Saved By Prayer?

"I tell you, this man went down to his house justified..."   —Luke 18:14

This verse comes from the familiar story of the publican and the Pharisee who went up to the temple to pray. The publican's prayer, "God, be merciful to me a sinner" is perhaps the best known in the Bible.

Jesus' response to this prayer is wonderful, "Justified". The word means given a clean bill of health—cleared of all charges. Can this one sentence prayer do the same for you? Let's see what went into it to bring about that justification.

First, he sensed a day of retribution ahead: "God be merciful." He knew his guilt and felt he deserved punishment. Until we know of a surety that we are going to be punished for our sins we are not likely to quit sinning. Because He knew the publican sought grace, it meant a decision. It meant receiving an answer—forgiveness.

Then, he was conscious of his sins. "I am a sinner." Only God can save sinners. He can't save good people. We may feel we haven't done anything terrible, so why do we have to acknowledge our sin? Let's look at the Sermon on the Mount and see the inward standards of God's best, "Are we meek, hungry, and thirsty after righteousness, merciful, pure in heart, a peacemaker." Against these standards, we can all confess, "God, help me a sinner."

Third, he was broken in spirit. One can be conscious of sin and not turn away from that. Godly sorrow, the Bible says, brings repentance and effects salvation. His sorrow turned him to God and not himself. Turning over a new leaf won't cut it. The only effective cure is to put our entire trust and confidence in the finished work of Christ.

The publican accepted the plan of God and came *down justified*. This man came away with his desire. He didn't leave the altar until he received it. We can have it, too. Let's not settle for anything less.

Cock Crow

"And immediately...the cock crew."
—Luke 22:60

Many on the night of Jesus' betrayal heard the shrilling summons of the rooster. But for the disciple Peter, there was something in that note which was inaudible to anyone else. Nature was sending him a message of warning, reminding him of his cowardice and boasting. One crow and Peter's memory was alive.

Jesus, who knows our nature perfectly, used Peter's memory as the servant of restoration. In the dark hour of temptation, Peter had forgotten everything: his loyalty, love and infinite indebtedness to Jesus. The night found him cursing and denying his Lord. And you would have thought nothing short of a lightning bolt could arrest that panic stricken heart. It was not the sound of the rooster, but the awakening of his memory that reached Peter's heart that dawn.

God sent the cock crow not to just awaken Peter's memory of the bitter past, but also as a hope of tomorrow. The timing was perfect: the brink of dawn, a new day. Jesus could have said, "before the torches go out." But no, He chose the harbinger of the morning, a token to tell Peter that his night was passing and a new dawn of hope and opportunity lay ahead.

The combination of memory and hope is a powerful one. That is what our Christian sacraments are about: remembering His death until He comes. In not just the sacraments but in everyday experiences, God will awaken our memory with the same simple message. There's a new day of promise facing you. Believe it and walk out upon His promise.

New Birth

*"Which were born, not of blood, nor of the will
of the flesh, nor the will of man, but of God."*
—John 1:13

I was always told to be good, but you might as well tell a black man to be white. We are a bad lot, the whole of us, by nature. It is astonishing how the devil blinds us, and makes us think we're so naturally good. We get all fancied up for the photographer and send the pictures to our friends. But suppose he took a true picture of our soul, would we send those around?

A man was told the water in his well was bad. "Well," he said, "I'll see to that," and he painted the pump. A lot of people try to make the well right by painting the pump. But what they need is to go to the source. Make the fountain good and the stream will be good. Let the heart be right, and the life will be right. The trouble is inside; what man needs is a new birth under new management.

That new birth comes from above. How do you get it? By receiving God's Word into your heart. Christ says, "The words that I speak unto you, they are spirit and they are life." You take the Word of God into your heart, and there is the germ, there is the life. If I take my watch and plant it, I don't get any little watches. Why? Because the germ of life isn't there. It takes the germ of life to produce new life. Put in the good seed of God's Word, and then pray to God that the dew of heaven (the Spirit of God) may rest upon it, and you will have good results. That word becomes alive and makes you partaker of the divine nature.

When you have that new divine nature inside, you don't have to worry about "painting the pump." It will be easy to serve God for "His yoke is easy, His burden is light." Why? Because the source is pure!

The Certainty Of Heaven

If it were not so, I would have told you..."
—John 14:2

On one occasion, the late Professor Huxley was watching a glorious sunset from an Alpine height, when his companion asked him: "Can you behold such a sublime scene as this and not feel there is a God?" Huxley replied: "Oh, I feel it—as much as any man. And I can rejoice in it if you don't tell me to prove it." But the moment one tried to bring the reasoning with which Huxley dealt with the matter of the hereafter, then he said: "I am an agnostic. I don't know." There are thousands like him. They have never allowed the warmth of a personal experience with Jesus Christ to satisfy their longings forever about heaven.

On the other hand, the promise of the return of Christ is clear and certain and His statement regarding the preparation of many mansions is unmistakable to those who know and believe Him. One translater puts our text: "If our separation were to be eternal, I would have forewarned you." Therefore, Heaven is sure to the child of God, because the promise is sure.

First, Christ's precious death obtains it. It was for this He came. He said, "I am the Way"—the way unto the Father. Then, Heaven is certain for Christ's priestly presence sustains it. He has gone to announce our coming and sustain its nature. A missionary was testing the little native boys' faith with the question: "If Jesus went to hell, would you follow Him?" The boy brightly replied: "Oh, there is no hell where Jesus is."

And then, Heaven is certain to believers because Christ's sure, valid promise contains it. Jesus spoke much about Heaven and the believers reward to it. Either He was true or the great fraud of history. If King David could cheer on his men to take Jerusalem from the Jebusites with the assurance that he would dwell there and they share his dwelling, how much more should we be comforted by our Lord's words about the New Jerusalem.

Resurrection Now

"If ye then be risen with Christ, seek those things which are above—where Christ is..."
—Colossians 3:1

Risen With Christ, what do these words mean? Certainly Christ was resurrected. But He is immortal in Heaven and we are still mortal on earth. Either this text is trying to tell us something of profound import or it means nothing at all.

First, we must understand that events can speak to the world and its condition. For example, an apple fell and a thinker watching it fall, asked why it fell that way. That event opened a new vista into nature and the meaning of the world and space. In Philadelphia, Franklin flew a kite in a thunderstorm and filled a bottle with a tiny flash of lightning. That event sparked a new source of light and power such that today the force of electricity toils for us in myriad ways.

Similarity, the resurrection of Christ is more an event in history. It reveals a higher way of life that would have remained unknown were it not for His birth, life, death, and resurrection. The above verse says there is now a new kind of living possible, a new power that can uplift and energize our mortal state. Just as electricity opens new standards of life to those who grasp its truth and use it, to those who grasp the import of Jesus' resurrection, there opens a whole new life of joy, hope, warmth and light.

The resurrection of Jesus is the ultimate victory over hate, fear, illness and death. Jesus is the transforming elemental energy in the world. It was for us that He died and rose. So for us this resurrection is emancipation, it is transformation, it is regeneration, releasing the tremendous reservoir of life within. "Out of our innermost being shall flow springs of living water." "If God be for us, who can be against us?" This is resurrection life *NOW!*

Good Cheer

"But straightway Jesus spake unto them, say-
ing, BE OF GOOD CHEER; it is I; be not afraid."
—Matthew 14:27

Not only here but throughout the Gospels the word, *Cheer,* stands out in the ministry of our Savior. Many people would argue this statement but the New Testament records that He was the most cheerful person who ever lived: "thy God, hath anointed Thee (speaking of Jesus) with the oil of gladness above thy fellows:"

The religions of the world are filled with contemplative philosophy, self-denial and stoicism' but Christianity is the "gladdest" religion of all. And where there is gloom and boredom and staleness and ecclesiastical fog, it is not real Christianity regardless what it is named.

Jesus came into this world to bring cheer. He never intended man's faith to be a strait-jacket. And the fact that He was the most cheerful person who ever lived, does not detract one iota from the sorrows He bore. The sorrows only deepened His desire to communicate to mankind the joy of relationship and service to the Father.

Jesus encountered more obstacles, discouragements and temptations than us all but He didn't let them get Him down. Paul answers this paradox out of his own experience: "As sorrowing, yet always rejoicing." Despite the worst troubles and human misery, Jesus never lost faith in God's crea-tion. There was that something ("anointed with the oil of gladness") that just flowed from Him that lifted folks' troubles and made them glad. No one could come into touch with Jesus without having his burdens lifted.

God today wants to give us a life of cheer in Him. Not just a vaccina-tion of religion with its rules and ceremonies, but a real relationship of ser-vice and friendship with God out of which true cheer comes.

Is There A Difference?

"Then shall ye return and discern between the righteous and the wicked; between him that serveth God, and him that serveth Him not."
—Malachi 3:18

It was a dark day when Malachi was called to the prophetic office. The priesthood had become unspiritual and mercenary. Israel followed its leaders into worldly life, and religion had become largely an empty form. Social vices went unrebuked, and family life was cursed by divorce and unfaithfulness. Government had become corrupt. Wicked men were in power and the poor were opposed.

Therefore, a spirit of unbelief prevailed, common opinion said the proud were happy and that it was a vain thing to serve God. People scorned prayers as wishful thinking. There seemed to be no difference between the Temple faithful and those who never attended. Against this background of skepticism, Malachi brings our text. He proclaims that when the days of judgment come, God will spare the faithful man even as a man spares his own son. Then you will see there is a great difference between him that serves God and he that doesn't.

The problem of skepticism over saint and sinner was not new to Malachi's day. Even the devil resented the insinuation that he was not as good as Job. And he set out to prove it. Satan claimed the only difference between himself and Job was due to the better treatment Job got from God. The devil still repeats that lie, "Will a man serve God for nought?" And He will lie saying, "Christianity is only a racket."

God's word tells us that there is a great difference between the world's two classes: the saint and the sinner, the forgiven and condemned. Sometimes the differences are not so outwardly apparent. Sometimes sinners inherit or develop good constitutional traits like patience or generosity. Sinners may be taught correctly and hold good beliefs but "hold down the truth in unrighteousness." It is in the heart where the differences are clear.

Christians differ from all others in their aim in life—to please Christ. Therefore, they have an inner peace and unique oneness with God because Christ dwells "within". And finally, their identification as a child of God differs-they recognize the authority and will of God-while the sinner is a slave. God's people are children of the light. Let our light shine today.

FEBRUARY:
Deciding for Christ

"...If any man will come after me, let him deny himself, and take up his cross daily, and follow me." —Luke 9:23

Following Christ

"...I count all things but loss for the excellency of the knowledge of Christ Jesus my Lord: for whom I have suffered the loss of all things and do count them but dung, that I may win Christ."
—*Philippians 3:8*

Many people have approached me and said, "Tom, boy you are lucky getting fame in Hollywood and all that." I can say that I am truly grateful to God for the opportunity to use the ability He has given me before so many people, but it is nothing compared to the deep inner peace and joy of knowing Jesus.

Tom Netherton
Singer

The worldly fame, popularity and good pay are all fleeting satisfaction and are not really ours but gifts from God. But the love of God is something that lasts, that none or nothing can take away and is available to us all whether we're a singer or a construction worker. I enjoy being a "regular" person and being with "regular" people.

Much of what we share and enjoy together is because of our fellowship in Christ. That is what is really satisfying!

For God SO

"For God so loved the world, that He gave His only begotten Son, that whosoever believeth in Him should not perish, but have everlasting life."
—John 3:16

Keith Miller
Author

Like most people, I often heard this verse in Sunday School. But when I came to know Jesus personally, its truth came alive in my heart — the goodness of God, the wonder of His love!

The world comes into new perspective before this truth. It shines with hope and births new life. The gift of God in Christ for all mankind is the foundation for all the Gospel. Religion on any other basis will falter but God's love stands and shines forever.

Jesus, The Faithful Witness

"(grace & peace) from Jesus Christ, who is the faithful witness, and the first begotten of the dead, and the prince of the kings of the earth. Unto him that loved us, and washed us from our sins in his own blood, And hath made us kings and priests unto God and his Father; to him be glory and dominion for ever and ever. Amen." —Revelation 1:5-6

These two verses tell us who Jesus is, what He has done for us and what we are through Him. We need to know that Jesus is Lord of all and conqueror over all evil because it is through *His* power that we are victorious. "Greater is He that is in us than He that is in the world."

We need to know that He has washed us from all our sins so that we can come before the throne of God in faith, pleasing God in our worship as priests and partaking of His strength and nature to bring kingly service to His kingdom on earth.

Kenneth Copeland
Evangelist

Facing The Judge

"It is appointed unto men once to die, but after this the judgment." —Hebrews 9:27

Anthropologists say that there are three propositions that have been pretty generally held by men everywhere in all ages. The first is that there is a God; second, that man continues to live after this life; and third, that men are going to be called to account—that we are responsible for our actions.

For example, the Egyptians in ancient times when they had embalmed a body, had it presented before a court of 42 judges. These men made strict inquiry as to the conduct and character of the deceased. If he were found wicked and unworthy, he was deprived of honorable burial and his body thrown into a ditch. If he were found to be good, the body was given an honorable burial, in a cemetery by a lake which could be reached only by boat at the approval of the judges.

People have always believed in a judgment day where things will be settled right and forever. And the Bible from beginning to end confirms this. Jesus summed it up: "There is nothing covered that shall not be revealed and hid that shall not be known." Judgment Day begins down here but it will be finished in Heaven.

Human life in itself is a story of judgment. The fact that men die is evidence of judgment. The way they die is exactment of judgment. Sometimes it appears here that the judgment of life is not fair—heavy on some and light on others. But we must remember, judgment is only begun here and not finished. Jesus often spoke about *harvest*. There will, as He said, be a gathering—a winnowing and a final and lasting disposition.

The Good News is that God offers to settle judgment out of court! Receive His forgiveness.

A Quick Settlement

"Some men's sins are open beforehand, going before to judgment and some men—they follow after." —I Timothy 5:24

It seems our text is trying to tell us that there are two ways to handle trouble—either to keep running away from it as long as you can or meet it face to face and get it settled. We can get things settled down here or there'll come a settlement sooner or later.

God offers us the greatest deal I know of-the privilege of sending your sins on before you-the opportunity of making a *quick settlement*. Many, even church people, have been deceived to think that eternal life and the kingdom begin when they get to heaven—that the accounting has to be done then. The time is *now*.

Jesus said, "He that heareth My Word and believeth on Him that sent Me—*hath* everlasting life, and shall not come into condemnation—but *is passed from death unto life.*" Paul adds, "There is therefore *now* no condemnation to them which are in Christ Jesus." As the Bible says, there comes a judgment for all of us after we die. But the Good News is that we don't have to wait until that judgment to deal with them. We can confess them *now*—bring them out in the open before God and be forgiven. Have them blotted out from our life and his record through the atoning blood of Jesus.

If we take God's offer and settle it now, we won't have to meet it on Judgment Day. God's Eternal Court is *now* in session and Jesus, the Righteous Advocate, is ready to appear on our behalf with His precious blood. This is the provision we can make for eternity.

Sin To Sin

"Woe...(to them) that take counsel—but not of Me—and that take cover with a covering but not of My Spirit—THAT THEY MAY ADD SIN TO SIN."
—Isaiah 30:1

The story goes there was an American exploration party in Africa that suddenly came upon a group of natives eating a meal of human flesh. When they interrogated the chief, they were surprised to have him reply in perfect English and found that he had been educated in the United States. When the leader of the expedition asked him how it was possible that after being educated in America, that he could still eat human flesh; the chief replied, "I now use a knife, fork and spoon."

Civilization can be a cover but it alone will never take the pagan out of a man. And the Church today faces the same problem with "religion." In the parable of the mustard seed, Christ predicated that the Church would become a favorite "roosting place" for all kinds of worldly men and women.

There is only one bonafide entrance into the Church of the Living God, and that is by the New Birth. Our message must not be "come, join the church," but "come, be born again." Then we will get back to the biblical pattern that only those "such as should be saved" shall be added to the Church.

Many in the scriptures from Joab, to the sons of Eli, to Ananias and Sapphira, all tried to use the Church for a covering for their sin. Instead they found severe punishment. God has a remedy for sin; He has a covering—just as He provided in the Garden for Adam and Eve. It is only through the cleansing blood of Jesus. If our covering is any other thing, the Bible speaks "Woe..." and we can translate that "Whoa"; stop and come to Jesus and receive His mercy.

Near-Sighted Nazareth

"Is not this the carpenter, the son of Mary...And they were offended at Him."
—Mark 6:3

As a preacher, I have heard many comments on sermons after service, but never one like this. Usually if a man becomes famous, his hometown is so proud and gives a royal welcome when he returns. But the townspeople of Nazareth were saying in effect, "Nobody can be great who has ever lived next to us. Nobody can be famous whose family we know." They failed to see the reflection on themselves which these words implied.

When the Man of Galilee returned to quiet Nazareth, He really upset things, blowing across the tranquil life of those villagers as a mighty wind. The people who had known Him for years and traded at His shop must have gasped in their wonderment and admiration. They would be astonished both at His teaching and miracles. Unfortunately, they stopped there. They admired but didn't receive and admiration is not enough to bring us to salvation.

Because they stopped at just admiration, pretty soon their near-sighted view of Jesus became indignation. They thought His teaching was great and all, but to impose that teaching on them—"How ridiculous and from this carpenter!!" They could not see greatness in the commonplace of life.

The result of their near-sightedness—lost salvation. "He could do there no mighty work because of their unbelief." Unbelief can tie the hands of Omnipotence. God will never force His way in. Without faith, God cannot and will not work. So Jesus quietly went on His way to other villages. What shall we do? Let us fling open the gate and receive Him in fulness.

If Thou Knewest!

"If you knew the gift of God."

—John 4:10

From the familiar story of Jesus with the Samaritan woman at the well, we get perhaps the most profound and saddest statement of all time: "If thou knewest". How much we miss by ignorance!!

What sailors missed until the compass was invented! How many women sewed themselves blind before Elias Howe gave the world the sewing machine. How many tortured sufferers before anesthesia. How many deaths from tuberculosis because we didn't know how to cure or prevent it. How many are dying today of cancer because we don't know how to deal with it. How much people have missed by not knowing.

In a prison on death row lay a man awaiting execution. If only he could get the governor's ear, he would plea for mercy, he would explain. The warden brought a visitor through the corridor. The visitor stopped, asked a question or two, received swift, curt answers and went on. The next day, the condemned man learned the visitor was the governor. "If I had only known."

The gifts of health, wealth, friendship and mercy we miss by ignorance are legion. But these are not earth's best possessions. These are indeed gifts of God, but there is *The Gift of God*...and multitudes miss it by not knowing. I have never known a person who sincerely gave his or her heart to God who hasn't publicly confessed, "Why didn't I do it before"..."If I had only known."

The Gift of God is Christ, Immanuel (God with us). His eternal presence in our lives as Counsellor, Comforter, Guide and Guard, Sweetness and Light, Succour and Deliver. This is the *gift* of God. He simply awaits our consent. Let us say yes and receive.

The Calls Of God

"Because I have called, and ye refused; I have stretched out my hand, and no man regarded; but ye have set at nought all my counsel, and would none of my reproof: I also will laugh at your calamity; I will mock when your fear cometh."
—*Proverbs 1:24-26*

This is an awesome text. God is our Benefactor but if we refuse His calls, He will be our Judge. "Because I have called." No one can deny that God tries to save us from hell.

God calls us by His Spirit. Since Pentecost, His Spirit is resident. He touches every conscience. Though His presence is often resented and resisted, it can never be ignored. This would be a comfortless, godless, helpless, and hopeless planet were the Holy Spirit absent. He ministers the mercies of God. Every good desire and every hunger for righteousness are implanted by the Spirit of God. When you push it away or ignore it, you grieve Him. The call of the Holy Spirit demands a reply.

God calls us by His Word. The Bible is everywhere and there is a call on every page. When you hold God's book in your hand, it outweighs the world. It speaks when governments tumble. It is there when your friends forsake you. God's warning and His promises to you are there in black and white.

God calls us by His providences. Some rule the affairs of men. Why is one taken the other left. It isn't that I'm lucky or worthy but He tells me He gives His angels charge to keep me in all my ways. God speaks to us by letters, by our pastor, by narrow escapes, by people who cross our path, by sickness, by TV and radio. The danger is our negligence. We must respond and it takes a personal decision. Say "Yes" to His call. Remember, you are either at peace or at war with God. What will it be?

Catching The Wrong Bus

"Forsake the foolish, and live; and go in the way of understanding." —Proverbs 9:6

Recently a newspaper carried the story of a man who boarded a bus, intending to go to Detroit; instead he wound up in Kansas City. *He had caught the wrong bus.* Such things go on habitually in human life. There's nothing wrong with most of our intentions. Nearly everybody desires good things. But many of us end up in an entirely different place than we started out for. Our destination and our desires get all tangled up!

The Prodigal Son did not start out for the pig trough. He didn't want rags, loneliness, hunger. He planned for happiness, freedom, and adventure. Somewhere—something went wrong! Life is full of this experience. It's one thing to desire a happy home, a respectable character, a good reputation, but too often we let it go at that. The old saying goes, "if wishes were horses, beggars would ride." The question is: "Are we on the right bus?"

Jesus never soft-pedaled this fact. He said, "Because strait is the gate, and narrow is the way, which leadeth unto life, few there be that find it." It is easy to wish and hope for the best and then do nothing about it. *But it is another thing to be willing to pay the price.*

We will never get the precious things in life by a loose, wishing way of living. Sooner or later, we must reach a point of decision. And the price of any destination that is worthwhile is self-discipline—"the straightened road" that Jesus talked about. And what is any worthwhile life without loyalty. That "narrows" you down. Loyalty to a purpose or friend can bind you down. But there's glory in it for those who pay the price.

The liberal says, "there is no right or wrong", just simply inhibitions to shed. Neither the Bible nor our conscience will buy that bunk. The Gospel tells us there is a right way, the way of Christ who said, "I am the way."

Can I Get To Heaven On A Pass?

"We know that we have passed from death un-
to life.."   *—I John 3:14*

"Can I get to heaven on a pass?" The young fellow asked me one time.
I surprised him with the answer, "Yes, that is the only way you can get
there. There are no paid admissions." "But," he said, "it doesn't sound
reasonable." No, but then God didn't consult us in arranging His plan of
salvation and let's be grateful He didn't.

Paul wrote the entire book of Romans to show that no man could
possibly buy his ticket to Heaven by his own efforts, goodness or morality,
only by trusting in the shed blood of Jesus Christ. Listen, "there is no difference, for all have sinned and come short of the glory of God." "Being
justified *freely* by His grace"..."a man is justified by faith without the deeds
of the law"..."Being justified by faith."

The Bible leaves no question about the issue. The only way to Heaven
is by faith. That does not mean any old kind of faith. Some people say that
just believing is important, no matter what it is in. Saving faith is *faith in*
His blood—Christ died for me. "No man comes to the Father but by me."
"Neither is there salvation in any other—for there is no other name under
heaven given among men whereby we must be saved." (Acts 4:12)

The wonderful part of God's plan is that we can be sure of our ticket.
If we were depending on our merit or goodness, we could never be sure.
But salvation is an outright gift: "the gift of God is eternal life through Jesus
Christ." And it is a gift for all. Jesus said it is for "whosoever"—that means
me and it means you. Have you got your pass?

Rich Man

*"But God said unto him, THOU FOOL, this
night thy soul shall be required of thee: then whose
shall those things be, which thou has provided."*
—Luke 12:20

The context of this railing is the rich farmer who prospered bountiful-
ly and thought to store up his wealth for a life of ease. Now, there is no
businessman who would call this man a fool from a business standpoint.
And Jesus says nothing against the man's morals. We can assume he was a
sober, clean decent sort of man.

Neither was this man stupid with his money. He knew how to farm
and got his crops under cover. He enlarged his barns. Intelligently, he
knew if you don't have space for your crops, don't waste it, save it!
Moreover, he had sense enough to know when he had enough. He wasn't
grabbing for more.

But Jesus said that he was a fool! And so is everyone else like him.
Why? First, he thought material things would satisfy. He said, "Soul...eat."
Eat what? His corn or hay? The only things that the soul can feed on and
be satisfied are the things that are imperishable. "Man's life consists not in
the abundance of things which he possesses. It is not things upon which
you feed, it is the bread of life come down from Heaven."

Second, he didn't recognize his dependence on God. He took credit
himself and gave no thanks to God. "The fool hath said in his heart, 'There
is no God.'" He had lost his God-consciousness, forgetting that his breath,
his limbs, his mind, were all because God gave and God loved.

Third, he prepared for life down here but neglected to prepare for
eternity. We can make plans for our days here but how much more important for that long unending tomorrow. How can we judge a few years here
against eternity. When we concentrate our thoughts on things here and
shut the door of eternity from our view, we are *making* the most foolish
mistake ever. Eternity means more than time.

Forgetting God

*"Afraid of a man that shall die...and forgettest
the Lord thy Maker."* —Isaiah 51:12, 13

Forgotten is one of the saddest and most lonesome words in any man's dictionary. Being forgotten is perhaps the cruelest thing that can happen to you. Personally, I prefer a man, every time, who opposes me rather than a man who ignores me. There's no greater insult to God than to forget Him—to love and plan and work—as though He didn't exist.

Self-confidence, busyness in the affairs of this life and material abundance are all common reasons why people forget God. But perhaps the greatest reason comes from our text above: "Afraid of a man that shall die and forgettest the Lord thy Maker." The fear of man destroys the nobler fear of God. For two commanding fears cannot occupy the soul at one and the same time. One fear will drive out the other. The fear created by a cracking whip will drive out the fear of a shying horse when he sees some unfamiliar object in his path. If a fire breaks out on a wintry night, the fear of the flames can drive out of the soul the fear of the frost. It seems as though one fear draws to itself the energies of the mind, and other fears are left without any sustenance.

So it is with "fear of man." It drains to itself the mental energy and devotion which ought to feed the fear of God. *You cannot serve God and mammon.* If the barometer we consult for our guidance is the opinions and conventions of man—God will be nothing. Whether it is our work, our standards, our speech, our witness, it will be either God or man that directs. The Bible says: "The fear of man is a snare." So many are so scared of what folks will think and say about us that we just put away all thought of God. The answer?! God's Spirit is faithful! "He shall bring all things to your remembrance..." Let the Spirit of God have His way.

Who Is Responsible When God Hardens A Heart?

"God hardened his heart"

—*Exodus 7:13*

If God hardens a heart, how can that person be responsible for sin? In our text we read that God hardened Pharoah's heart. If this is the case and the consequence of this hardening was rebellion against God, then God was responsible and it would be unjust to hold Pharoah accountable and punishable for his sin. Right?

This question illustrates how God works and deals with man. What kind of man was Pharoah? First he was not a man who wished to obey God. When Moses presented his case, the Pharoah insolently spoke: "Who is the Lord that I should obey His voice?" Even after the signs of God, Pharoah continued his insolence and deceits.

It is the signs, miracles, judgments, displays of God's power and existence that either soften or harden the individual to whom they are directed. If the Pharoah had chosen the right attitude (as Saul of Tarsus did) it would have led to his repentence and salvation. Therefore, the fault is not with God who proclaims "that He is not willing (desirous) that any should perish-but that all should come to repentance."

It is God's universal method...if a man chooses error He will give them up to error. II Thessalonians 2, says if a man chooses to deceive, he will be deceived to believe a lie. When we speak that God hardened Pharoah's heart , we must understand that you cannot coerce the will by force. As the saying goes, "You can lead a horse to water, but you can't make him drink". Pharoah chose deceit and found its own reward.

The same case is ours. Those who reject forgiveness cannot be forgiven. To resist the light that the Holy Spirit brings to us, is to deliberately choose darkness. For we as Christians, a "hardening of the heart" is deliberately resisting and despising the truth. The Bible says this is blasphemy against the Holy Spirit and it has its own reward. Choosing to deceive will reap deception. God gives us good food, but we must eat it.

The Backslider And His Savior

"I will heal their backsliding; I will love them freely: for my anger is turned away from him."
—Hosea 14:4

Recently a woman came to the church altar where she knelt broken in spirit and sobbing in penitence. She cried, "Lord, here is my heart, I give it to Thee this night.!" Then she continued, "O, God have mercy upon me, a sinner!" She repeated these words over and over in deep emotion-and yet no peace came-no joy came! There was nothing wrong with her prayer. But there was something wrong with her faith. A trained personal worker came to her and insisted that *she bring Christ crucified and risen into her supplication.*

The worker urged, "say for *Jesus'* sake." But overwhelmed by the sense of her sins and driven only by the enormity of them, she refused at first. Then at last, almost suffocated with sorrow and distress, she feebly said, "Have mercy on me for the sake of Jesus." When she repeated several times, unbelief fled away and faith triumphed; and the peace of God, which passeth all understanding filled her happy soul.

This example illustrates that it is unbelief that attempts to torture the human soul. Unbelief will always set out sin and failure before us, like it did David, "My sin is ever before me;" What will bring relief? What is the cure? David found it in prayer. "I have set *the Lord* always before me." This is the victory: *"The Name of Jesus is above every name."* Name the disease! Name the failure! Name the sin! And Christ's Name is above it-more powerful-more conquering-more eternal! All in the name of Jesus!

We need not be driven under by failure. Send your thoughts to Calvary. Make your thoughts work for you instead of destroying you! Feast your mind in the fathoming love of God in Christ Jesus. If you are going "to lose your mind"-then "lose" it at the Cross! There you'll find victory.

The Backslider—His Misery

"Thine own wickedness shall correct thee...and thy backslidings shall reprove thee" —Jeremiah 2:19

The backslider is one who ceases to go forward. He has lost momentum. He is being swept back down the broad road of destruction. The awful price of the backslider is the loss of joy and peace in exchange for misery.

The New Testament has this to say, "Knowing that he that is subverted, and sinneth, being condemned of himself." (Titus 3:11) A backslider carries within himself the awful knowledge that he is giving comfort and aid to the enemy of his soul. He is constantly condemned. He cannot convince himself. He is a fugitive from his own conscience.

This is the misery of a backslider! His conscience is awakened by the Spirit of God; and this God-given faculty upbraids him continually. Where is he who has sufficient fortitude to sustain, unflinchingly, such a visitation? The Bible says, "The spirit of a man will sustain his infirmity, *but* a - *wounded* spirit *who can bear?"* A backslider is a spirit whom sin has wounded.

That is why the backslider is either the unhappiest person in the community or is hiding from himself under the cover of booze, drugs, or the like. But you cannot really get away from yourself. The cure is to look to your Heavenly Father even as the prodigal son did, "I am no longer worthy to be called thy son." Yet the Father waits to be gracious-"while he was yet a great way off, his father saw him." *Never limit God's eye of mercy.* He delights in bringing forgiveness and mercy to the backslider.

Many of us do not realize that "there is no good thing in us" until we "slide back" as it were. God our Father awaits our reconciliation to Him through Christ in love and mercy. So why wait?

Prepare To Meet Thy God

"It is appointed unto men once to die but after this the judgment." —Hebrews 9:27

There is an inevitable meeting—one that each of us are going to—a meeting with our God. The Bible tells in unmistakeable, plain language that some day at the great white-throne of God the books will be opened and men will be judged "out of those things which were written in the books according to their works." Now no one will tamper with these "books" or bribe the judge; it is one trial that will be on the "up and up."

At anytime there may be just one step between us and that judgment and there is something we must prepare! We must prepare a lawyer, an advocate, someone who will speak for us and plead in our behalf. Or do we think that we can speak for ourselves? Do we cringe from the Sunday preacher and avoid the look of the policeman and expect to stand under the gaze of the very presence of Almighty God. We will never be able to plead our own case!

There is only one accredited counsel in the court of Heaven and He is available to us. "We have an advocate with the Father, Jesus Christ the righteous." He has been assigned to the human race and we either take Him or stand alone. For there is absolute merit in what He did on the cross of Calvary and any member of the human race can claim a share in that great victory. The blood of Jesus Christ cleanses from *all* sin and the record becomes clean. Heaven will be a place for those "who have washed their robes white through the blood of the Lamb." Pure and white, not guilty!

That can be our record or we can stand alone. The choice is ours!

Repentance

"Except ye repent, ye shall all likewise perish."
—Luke 13:3

In this "born again" age, repentance is still a word that you hear little about. Yet, it is the essential ingredient in producing the Christian new birth experience.

Nearly everybody knows the simple meaning of the word, "repentance"—it means to change your mind. It's a complete change of views, disposition and conduct with respect to sin. The Holy Spirit is the author of "godly repentance" and with it, He begins to move in a man's soul.

Repentance begins with *conviction of sin*—acknowledgement of guilt—sorrow for wrongful acts. This, however, is just part. Hell is full of people that are sorry for sins-Cain, Ahab, Judas and others. Repentance is more.

Repentance brings self-condemnation. You stop making excuses and defending your sins and evil habits. You see that only yourself is to blame: "I am a sinner, I am guilty." This brings you to the mercy seat of a faithful God. Your pride is gone, excuses vanished, spirit of rebellion broken and you are brought face to face with God's claims on your life.

Then repentance includes a hatred of sin, forsaking it and a determination not to repeat it. If you truly repent, there'll come a dislike for the thing you have repented of. Many depend on feeling for their repentance, their savior is their experience and not Christ. We are saved by facts not feelings. We don't have to feel hate for evil; we can see the truth and choose to hate the evil. Feelings will come as we walk into the light and understanding of God's truth.

If you have truly repented, your heart will be come tender and sensitive to sin, you will have inner peace, and you will know that something has happened to change your natural mind.

Going My Way

"Toward Jerusalem"   *—Daniel 6:10*
"Toward Sodom"   *—Genesis 13:12*

The contrast here is as big as black against white. These two Old Testament characters were headed in opposite directions. Daniel opened his windows *toward* Jerusalem and Lot pitched his tent *toward* Sodom. Here are the life-stories of these men in a nutshell. It also suggests the question for us, "What direction am I travelling?" What is the big magnet in my life? What is my heart set on?

I'm sure Daniel's wish as much as yours or mine was to stay out of the lion's den and to stand in good grace with the king. He had a good job and wanted to keep it. He knew the value of his position. But when it came to making a choice between it and his God—he "opened his windows toward Jerusalem" in the sight of the whole town. He let everyone know where he stood on questions of right and wrong. He didn't go out of his way to offend, but he never "ducked" the issue of right.

Lot, likewise, knew what Sodom was. It had a wide open reputation for sin. And Lot had the voice of his conscience to consider. He had been brought up right and knew the warning he heard. But there were those keen commercial instincts and the love of money. Opportunity for easy money lay in Sodom and Lot made up his mind that this was for him.

It is one thing to make mistakes, we all do. Peter once denied his Lord with curses. But that denial was not a fair sample of his attitude toward the Master. We may turn off course awhile but Christ knows the "toward" of our heart. The love of God is a love that looks more at what we aim than at what we reach. Our Heavenly Father is a Father who looks, not at the fall only, but at the road we were travelling on when we fell. God will help us up but we must choose the right road!

Pay As You Go

"The Kingdom of heaven is like unto a mer-
chant man, who...when he had found one pearl of
great price, went and sold all that he had, and
bought it."

—*Matthew 13:45, 46*

Jesus always will have the respect and admiration of the world's merchants. Again and again He put life into commercial figures and taught that everything we choose has to be paid for. If you choose the highest-says Jesus-you must pay for it or if you choose the worst—the judge (says Jesus) will "deliver thee to the officer, and thou be cast into prison. And thou shall by no means come out til thou have paid the last farthing." Whether we choose the best or worst, we pay for it.

Hitler chose to be Hitler and he paid the price. Toscanini chose to be Toscanini and in self-dedication and self-discipline, he paid for it. The godly man pays a price to live righteously; "If a man would follow me, let him deny himself and take up his cross and follow me." But the ungodly man also makes a sacrifice—the costliest kind—in giving up everything that most renders life worthwhile. Esau wept bitterly about the sacrifice he made to sell his birthright for a mess of pottage.

The choice we have is when we pay. The devil says: "Never mind about the bills-take it now and pay for it later!" God says: "This is what it will cost-pay now-it's worth it." Remember Huckleberry Finn's words, "what's the use you learning to do right, when its troublesome to do right and ain't no trouble to do wrong." That idea shared by the crowd comes from the fact that to do wrong costs nothing in advance-paying for it comes afterward.

Note the contrast. Bryon wrote before he died: "My days are in the yellow leaf; The flowers and fruits of love are gone; The worm, the canker, and the grief are mine alone!" Paul wrote: "I have fought a good fight, I have finished my course. I have kept the faith henceforth there is laid up for me a crown of righteousness." The choice is ours: pay now or later.

The Unmerciful Servant

"So likewise shall my heavenly Father do also unto you, if ye from your hearts forgive not every one his brother their trespasses."
—Matthew 18:35

This conclusion comes from the familiar story of the servant forgiven of his debt of 10,000 talents ($25 million) by his lord, yet was unforgiving of the debt of 100 pence ($40) by his fellow-servant and was therefore delivered to the tormentors. The picture is clear and strong. It is a picture of eternity. Our God is a loving, forgiving, merciful God but *He means business!*

Jesus gave us many illustrations to hammer home this truth. He tells us of the rich man and the beggar Lazarus. The rich man was self-righteous and self-satisfied and irresponsive to the needs of others around him. The surprise of his life came when he woke up in Hades.

Then Jesus told of the man who came to the wedding feast without the wedding garment (provided free by the host). His sin was presumption, lack of reverence. He wasn't going dressed up, he thought his own clothes were good enough. He didn't realize how self-centered, ungrateful and out of place, he'd be in his own garments. He didn't want to miss the feast but he wanted to go on his own terms. He, too, was surprised when he was thrown out into outer darkness.

The five unwise virgins also wanted to attend the wedding feast. Their sin was they didn't recognize their need. They thought they were good enough; so content in their own ways that they missed it.

Our God means business. His way is the only way. If we are going to partake of His goodness, we must share it; if we are going to count on being redeemed ourselves, we must show ourselves redeemers. Let us never become self-sufficient, presumptious or content but realize we are eternally debtors to the infinite grace of God.

Choose You This Day

"Choose you this day whom ye shall serve..."
—Joshua 24:15

Everyday we encounter many choices. We must either make up our minds or our minds will be made up for us. History is filled with examples of the importance of decisive action. When Alexander the Great was asked how he conquered the world, he answered, "By not wavering."

In our scripture context, Joshua had brought the entire nation of Israel together for decisive action. In delivering Israel from Egypt and placing them in the beautiful land of Canaan, God had given them not only an inheritance but a responsibility. In indecision and indifference, the people were sinking into idolatry. Joshua told them this could not continue, they must decide who they would serve and which way they would go. To not decide, was really a decision for the enemy. Joshua tells the people he and his house had decided, they would serve the Lord.

Today, you and I must decide. We too, face an enemy, the prince of this world, the power of darkness. To not decide, is to decide to slip into the darkness of the world. Time decides for the man who will not decide for himself. The Bible says we must make our calling and election sure. We decide when we confess Jesus is Lord, when we stand for deciding what type of world we desire to live in. We are also deciding our eternal destiny.

Every day, every moment the swing of the rope of opportunity for choosing good and the greatest things of life becomes shorter and shorter. Let us not wait for the next swing. "Seek the Lord while He may be found—call upon Him while He is near." Choose now!

Command Thou Me

"Ask me of the things that are to come concerning my sons, and concerning the work of my hands command ye me."   Isaiah 45:11

How do we command God? We see this verse dramatized in a book in the New Testament. In Luke, chapter seven, we view the centurion's faith, John the Baptist's doubt, the sinful woman's gratitude and the resurrection of the widow's son. Here Christ is commanded by the undying needs in the souls of men and women.

The centurion came to Jesus about his dying servant. His case suggests that the sense of need, inspired by love, invariably commands Christ. Certainly, he was a good man and understood authority, but he is recognized for sensing need for which there could be no help outside of God. Christ emphasized the truth that there could be no divine help to those who have no sense of need. God enjoys meeting our needs as much as the mother who bends over the cradle to respond to her child. God says, "Before they call, I will answer."

John the Baptist's situation is the example of faith beset by doubt. John, the rugged fearless preacher, through long evil months in a lonely, filthy prison was sapped of strength and strained in his soul. His questions got too big to contain; he inquired of Christ, "Art thou He that cometh, or look we for another?" Can faith, harassed by doubt, command our Lord? Jesus' answer is big and clear, "In that hour He cured many diseases and plagues and evil spirits." He wants to help if we only will ask Him.

The sinful woman's gesture of gratitude is clear. Penitence and gratitude command Christ. He forgives sin and gives rest to the weary. Then when Christ looked on the grief of the mourning widow, it seemed hopeless but not too late. There was no room for Him and death on the same road. God is never late and "he that was dead sat up", and, "He gave him to his mother." Our need, whether great or small, can command Christ if we but come for His help, love and mercy.

You Are Invited

"Come Unto Me..."

—*Matthew 11:28*

Today we live in perhaps the most skillful and high pressure advertising society in history. The kind of cars we drive, the clothes we wear, the places we go are largely determined by advertising. Our lives are full of appeals. And so is the Bible. From the third chapter of Genesis ("Where art Thou, Adam?"), right through the Bible to the book of Revelation, we find the appeal of the Spirit of God to lost humanity to turn back to God.

We see Moses appealing to Israel, after the destruction of the golden calf, "Who is on the Lord's side? Let him come unto me." Joshua appealed to the nation to make a definite decision: "Choose you this day whom ye shall serve." Later, King Josiah calls for a public assembly after reading the book of the law to Israel, and called the people to stand in assent to a covenant to keep the law of God.

Jesus made numerous invitations. He said to Peter and Andrew: "Follow me and I'll make you fishers of men. He said to Matthew, the bootlegger, "Follow Me." He invited Zacchaeus down out of the tree. And he told his disciples, "Go out into the highways and hedges and compel them to come in, that My house may be filled." The book of Acts is filled with examples that His disciples did just that—inviting and persuading all they encountered to follow Christ.

The book of Acts is still being written and the same invitation extends to us today through God's Word and all who truly preach the Gospel. We are invited to come to Jesus. We must make a decision with that invitation. It calls us to action. Have we responded to God's appeal today?

Fighting God

"If it be of God, ye cannot overthrow it; lest haply ye be found even to FIGHT AGAINST GOD."
—Acts 5:39

In the context of our scripture, the Jewish Council was furious with the disciples, Peter and John, who had filled Jerusalem with preaching of the Gospel and were boldly placing the blame for the crucifixion on members of the court. The court was ready to "liquidate" these troublesome followers of Jesus. But Dr. Gamaliel had a cooler head and reminded them that Christ was not the first to make great claims. If He were an imposter, His cause would fade away, but otherwise they would be fighting God.

What is it to fight God? It is to *resist* the Will of God and it is largely the story of humanity. Every one of us at some time has fought against God. Jesus alone could truly say: "I do always the things that please Him (God)." The conflict of resisting God began in the garden with Adam and Eve and continues today. Fortunately, God does strive with man to know His will. Otherwise, we would be lost eternally?

What are some of the consequences of our fighting against God? First, to fight God is to fight oneself. When one is at war with God, he is torn by an inward conflict. Second, we lose that *inward peace* which is the "birthright" of the children of God. Jesus had given us peace but if we resist we lose both peace and its consequence: joy. Third, we lose a power that might be ours. No man can conquer an outward foe when divided on the inside. And fourth, when we fight God and ourselves, we find ourselves fighting others. Under conviction, Balaam tears into a rage when his donkey bucks a little. Even so today it is common to see a person under conviction get "mean."

God will help one who honestly "kicks against the pricks" as He did Saul of Tarsus. Our fighting against God can lead to repentance and with that salvation. But let us not be stubborn, when God shows us the truth. Stubborn resisting in the face of truth is as the sin of idolatry.

Biological Urge

"All unrighteousness is sin."

—I John 5:17

In a recent federal government investigation into organized crime, one of the defendants argued that his big-time gambling activities was simply an outlet for his "biological urge." A President of our country was removed from office, not as much for what he personally did wrong, but for taking the wrong lightly and covering it up.

Liberalism and modernists have labored diligently to make light of sin, advancing such theories that sin is a "biological urge", a physical disease, a mental infirmity, or a "figment of a theologically perverted imagination." Modern man has willed to be "liberated" from his religious bonds. Today we see the harvest of that liberation—corruption in government that reaches to the highest office, such cheating and deception that honest laborers bend under the load of taxes to pay other people's way, and a soaring crime problem that produces murders and rapes every hour of the day in our country.

The billions of dollars spent yearly to eliminate human problems only seem to create new ones so more new programs are asked for every year. All because we have resisted calling a spade a spade, and sin—sin. The rule book, the Bible which has held true through history, tells us that all unrighteousness is sin. That means in plain vanilla that everything that is not right is wrong.

The shortest distance between two points will always be a straight line. Going around the bush will never get us ahead or will calling sin by any other name do more than confuse the issue. God has made a way of victory over sin through the cross. Let us fact it, deal and walk in victory not confusion.

Getting Rid Of Self!

"If any man will come after me, let him deny himself..."   —Luke 9:23

Many of you will agree that your biggest enemy is yourself. Self-will is a tiger that roars its head against the will of God and can seem hopelessly strong. Yet the first step in a *consecrated life* (a life of blessing) *is an unconditional surrender to the will of God.* How can we learn to yield?

All of us have seen at some time or other the pretty and selfish girl surrounded by wealth and admiration until she was wholly spoiled. Her whole being is perverted by a refined selfishness. But we see that same girl after years as a selfdenying, loving wife and mother, devoted to the happiness of her husband, sharing his poverty, toiling for his comfort, with a love that never wearied and a heart that never grew cold or tired, nursing the little children that have come in her arms.

What may we ask cast that idol of self from the throne of her life? The answer is nothing but love! A noble, beloved human friend came in and took the place that self occupied. So the love of Jesus, when truly revealed by the Holy Spirit, wins the heart and makes us content without the things that once we demanded, because His smile is our sunshine and His love our heaven.

Our self-seeking for happiness is never ending and never satisfying. But when, as Abraham laid his Isaac on the altar, we lay down our life, then we find, as Abraham did, that what we gave we have, and what we would have kept that we should have lost. "For he that saveth his life shall lose it, and he that loseth his life for My sake shall keep it unto life eternal."

Are You In Tune?

"Looking unto Jesus, the author and finisher of our faith..." —Hebrews 12:2

An instrument must be tuned before it is played. A violinist first tunes the A string to international pitch which is A-440—meaning the A above middle C is vibrating 440 times per second. Once the A string is tuned to A-440, the other strings are tuned from it. When all its strings are in tune, the violin can be played harmoniously with other instruments tuned to the same pitch. Otherwise, discord would result.

We, too, are either in tune or out of tune. Our happiness and health depend upon this. Christ is the "Middle C" for living-for we tune to Him. If we are not in proper relationship, we cannot get along with other folk or circumstances around us. We either vibrate in harmony or in discord. Christ called this harmony love. Everything responds to love. Science says even plants and flowers respond to those who love them. As Jesus showed in the prophetic lesson of the fig tree, a curse can wither a tree.

Everything shrivels and wilts in the midst of unpleasantness, amid discord and wrangling. These destructive, harmonious vibrations are seen when hate, anger, resentment and fear are present. Even small children and pets in the room feel the discord and chill of such actions and try to get away from their presence.

A mother sent her newly born baby back to the maternity hospital because she was emotionally upset and her husband had deserted her. Although the baby got meticulous care, he failed to gain weight and became seriously ill. A volunteer "mother" came and held the child in her lap for feedings, stroked his head, and sang softly to him. The child responded almost immediately and soon returned to good health. What he needed above all else was love.

The conclusion is that our lives should be in harmony with Christ so that in turn we may be in accord with our friends. Every day, we are either a healthy or unhealthy influence on those about us. Love is the New Testament keynote.

MARCH:
The Assurance of Salvation

"Verily, verily, I say unto you, He that heareth my word, and believeth on him that sent me, hath everlasting life, and shall not come into condemnation; but is passed from death unto life." —John 5:24

God's Riches

*"My God shall supply all your needs according
to His riches in glory by Christ Jesus."*
—*Philippians 4:19*

Bill Basansky
Evangelist

This verse sums up the fulness of the riches of God's goodness that I have in Christ. I've already learned that I'm born of God and loved by God. He answers my prayer and I'm a "conqueror" through Christ. His intercession in heaven and the Holy Spirit within encourages me and establishes me in who I am.

What really gives me joy, vitality for life and keeps above my enemies, is this wonderful assurance that God is going to meet all my needs. He backs that provision with all the riches and glory of His dear Son.

Called to His Purpose

"And we know that all things work together for good to them that love God, to them who are the called according to His purpose."
—*Romans 8:28*

This verse has progressively become my favorite scripture as I have had it's meaning steadily unfolding throughout my life. I never had any problem with the first part of the verse but I found myself asking God, "How can I be *sure* that I'm called according to Your purpose?" God said, "Henry, do you know that you're born again?" "Sure, Lord, You've given numerous scriptures that leave no room for doubt on that one." (I John 1:9, John 1:12, Romans 10:9, etc.) "Yes, Lord, I *know* that I belong to You." "So, You mean that this promise is for anyone who loves You and who is Your child and belongs to You?!! — That was *Good News* to me!

Henry M. Harrison
Co-Host of PTL

God is actually forming all things, all situations to work them together for my good...Individual circumstances have been extremely painful — even heartbreaking — but knowing that God is forming them together and making my life something beautiful through these situations is joy unspeakable!!

Delighting in Him

"Delight thyself also in the Lord and He shall give thee the desires of thine heart." —Psalms 37:4

Harald Bredesen
Author, Pastor

I believe this is the secret of the Christian life. If we seek the goodness of God and find delight in Him, then there is no difficulty in doing His will.

Many of us have grown up with a stain-glass window, disinterested view of God. When we get past that to discover the one true God, who is kind, loving and interested in us, we find ourselves delighting in Him and wanting to do His will. Our "shoulds" become "woulds."

Not only does God give us what we desire then but he gives us our "desires." He changes our desires to His and His are always right and attainable in Him. That is victory! And our Christian life can be victorious daily when we simply delight in Him.

Life Through The Blood

"For my flesh is meat indeed and my BLOOD IS DRINK indeed."   —John 6:55

This is one of the Bible's deep mysteries, the feeding by faith on the sacrifice of the Son of God—assimilating the Life Blood. To the inner man, it is nourshing, refreshing, strengthening and cleansing.

To the Mosaic Jews, this statement by Jesus was startling. Under the old covenant, drinking of blood was prohibited. But Jesus brings a new covenant, "This is my blood, take, drink of it." Even as in our body, drink cleanses and refreshes the system, the blood of Jesus shed at Calvary is efficacious for soul cleansing and refreshing to all who would assimilate its power by faith. Jesus goes on to describe three blessed effects in appropriating the power of Christ's work on Calvary.

First, the gift of eternal life: "Whoso eateth my flesh and drinketh my blood *hath* eternal life." The tense is present—right here (not merely beyond the grave):vigorous, strong, abundant life filling the soul. All the sin that would destroy and choke the life of the soul is gone through the blood of Jesus.

Second, there is the abiding presence of the indwelling Christ. "He that eateth My flesh and drinketh My blood dwelleth in Me and I in Him." Christ suffered for us; He shared His life with us and as we receive with thanksgiving this truth, He comes to dwell with us. Through forgiveness in His blood, sin can no longer separate us from God. A moment by moment faith in His blood ensures us a moment by moment presence of Christ within.

Third, the empowerment to Godly service: "He that eateth Me shall live by Me." Jesus' sacrifice works in us so it can work through us to others. When a brother sins, no longer do we sit in judgment upon him. Through the fruit of grace, we can identify with the erring brother so as to make his sin our own and bear it in spirit before God.

We ought to partake of Christ's work, then, for our life, for strength in our soul, and for service to others.

Victory Through The Blood

"They overcame him by the Blood of the Lamb..."
—*Revelation 12:11*

You hear many people today praying for victory over this sin or that one. Nowhere in the Bible are we promised victory over sin. God has promised something better—death to sin, destruction of it through the blood of Jesus. Every blessing that has come to the sons of men has been secured by the blood of Jesus. Christ's blood provides victory over the three great enemies of the Christian—the world, satan and death.

We see the devil's attack on the believer in many ways: as the "birds of the air" to take away the seed (Word) that has been planted; as a serpent to deceive; as a lion terrifying by his roar; as an angel of light to counterfeit; as the accuser of the brethren; as an adversary to resist; and as the father of lies. In each case, the believer can defeat the devil when he attacks. How? By taking the offensive in prayer with confidence before God by His blood. Only a living faith in the power of the blood can provide the assurance for victory.

The world is anything that comes between us and God—the lust of the flesh, the lust of the eye, the pride of life. The world holds many charms, but there is a treacherous hook in those charms that only Christ can free. John proclaims victory here: "This is the victory that overcomes the world, even our faith." Faith in what? Paul said, faith in the Crucified One and His blood.

The last great enemy to the Christian is death: "O death, where is thy sting? O grave, where is thy victory? Thanks be to God which giveth us the victory through our Lord Jesus Christ." The lives of James, Paul, Luther, Bonhoffer, Elliott and thousands of others, martyred for their faith, yet rejoicing, speak boldly that the victory over death is won. These have found peace (eternal) with God through trusting in His blood.

Forgiveness Through The Blood

"In whom we have...through His blood, the forgiveness of sins, according to the riches of His grace." —Ephesians 1:7

Forgiveness is one of the most beautiful words in our language. It is a word of hope and cheer. It is also the only gate by which we enter into salvation. Many would like to be saved through building their own character, some belief in religion or philosophy, or good deeds. But God says, "Except ye repent (receive forgiveness), ye shall all likewise perish."

The nature and extent of God's forgiveness through the blood of Jesus is best illustrated in the forgiveness of King David. This mighty king and man of God, was rich in spiritual experience, yet he committed the gross and terrible sins of murder and adultery. The sin of one so renowned in the service of God was far more unpardonable than if he had been ignorant of God's grace. But even he found forgiveness from the Lord. Later, he wrote: "Blessed is the man, whose *transgression is forgiven* and whose *sin is covered*...to whom the *Lord imputed not iniquity.*"

The Mosaic Law made no provision for David's sin. By Law, he had to die. So it cost God something to *forgive* David's *transgression*. Just like King Darius when he put Daniel in the lion's den against his own wishes to maintain his reputation, God's Word was at stake. It cost God the death of His Son, to bring us forgiveness and yet maintain His righteous attitude against sin. How wonderful when Nathan told David, "The Lord hath put away thy sin."

For more that a year, David tried to *cover* his *sin* by deceit, drunkenness, cruelty, murder, religious exercise, remorse, etc. But still his sin was uncovered—to God. Only the blood can cover! "Though your sins be as red as scarlet, they will be as white as snow." Unlike much human forgiveness, God washes away and forgets our sins through the blood of Jesus.

God did not impute David's *iniquity*—did not count it against him. People often, just like Pharoah, will follow you out of Egypt. How difficult it is for a man with a criminal record to get anywhere. Man may count me a sinner but God doesn't. He treats me as though I have never sinned. Through Christ's blood, He forgives, covers and forgets.

Access Through The Blood

"Having, therefore brethren, boldness to enter into the Holiest by the blood of Jesus...let us draw near..."

—Hebrews 10:19, 22

Whether it be business or politics or social status for many, much of their efforts are aimed at getting into the "inner sanctum". But for the believer, our right to enter God's "inner sanctum", the Holy of Holies, lies in the blood of Jesus. Through His blood, we can come before the Father's throne as confidently as approaching our best friend.

First, the blood of Christ cleanses our conscience: "the Blood of Christ cleanse your conscience from dead works to serve the living God." The conscience marred by sin can at best do dead works, it is concerned about upgrading itself. The blood of Jesus sets our conscience free to wait upon the living God to do His will.

Second, the blood of Christ establishes and affirms the Word of God: "He took the blood...and sprinkled the book." A covenant is only valid so long as both parties are alive. It is exactly the reverse in the case of a will. No will can be executed until the testator dies. The New Covenant is Christ's last will. His death brought about its execution and the Holy Spirit is the executor.

Third, the blood is established in Heaven: "He sprinkled with blood...the heavenly things." The writer of Hebrews says, "the blood of Christ speaks better things than that of Abel." This is because Abel's blood spoke from the earth while Christ's blood speaks to us from heaven. If we could enter Heaven itself, we should find at every hand, tokens of the blood-shedding on Calvary. You'd hear the song of the Lamb, see the throne of the Lamb, the book of the Lamb, the blood of the Lamb, and the marriage of the Lamb. It is the great theme and victory of heaven.

That is why we can boldly enter with no worthiness of our own. Let us make use of the blood as we come within the veil to pray and stand together with Christ for His Kingdom.

Redemption Through The Blood

"Forasmuch as ye know that ye were not redeemed with corruptible things,.... But with the precious blood of Christ, as of a lamb without blemish and without spot." —I Peter 1:18-19

Trading stamps have caused a revival in the use of the word, redemption. But they don't give us much clue to the meaning of our redemption in Christ. Yet it is a vital part of our salvation.

The word, *redemption*, has in the past had reference to a slave market, "a lock shop," or held for ransom. What is required was payment of a price. Redemption meant to purchase out of the market, to liberate. It suggested a deliverance from something terrible. The scriptures tell us that Christ has redeemed us "from the curse of the law," "from all iniquity," "from guilt" and "of our body." These are our dungeons, chains and task masters from which Jesus frees us.

While part of redemption is "deliverance from" the other part is "purchase to": "Ye are not your own, ye are bought with a price." We have been purchased so we no longer belong to the world, devil or ourselves, but we belong to Christ. A Zulu convert put it well, "The Cross of Christ condemns me to become a saint." We are no longer our own souls, bodies, time, talents, possessions or money. The cost of our redemption was the life and blood of Christ, that we might live upon Him.

The scope of our redemption is to all life: "redeem us...a people for His own possession zealous of good works." Our redemption from the curse of the law, means freedom and a positive life unto righteousness. And that redemption includes our entire being as the Spirit brings new power to our mind and will and body for Christ's use. Then when He shall appear, our redemption shall become totally complete as our mortal bodies take on immortality.

Assurance Through The Blood

"HOW MUCH MORE shall the blood of Christ, who through the eternal Spirit offered Himself without spot..."   —Hebrews 9:14

We naturally judge a sacrifice by the value of the one who makes it as well as for the cause for which it is made. Is it the blood of an animal that has met its death? Is it the blood of a human being? That is more valuable. Is it the blood of some distinguished person? Is it shed on the behalf of others? We worthily honor the blood-stains of Martin Luther King Jr. among others. The more distinguished the victim, the more moving and stirring will be the effect of the sacrifice. And the sacrifice at Calvary was not just a distinguished human, it was the blood of the Son of God.

The author of the Book of Hebrews writes to the point that Jesus is better. In our text, he observes that the sacrifice of Jesus is better. The blood of Christ draws its greater efficacy and power by the following:

First, it is a blood sacrifice prepared by God Himself: "a body has Thou prepared me." Jesus was a lamb slain from the foundation of the world. It was for this cause that Jesus came into the world born of the Holy Ghost. Jesus could offer perfect blood because of His divine seed.

Second, it is the blood of one who perfectly did the will of God. "Lo, I come to do thy will, O God." Christ was not merely born into this world in order to offer Himself as an atoning sacrifice for me and die, but He lived and labored to accomplish the will of God. His perfect life constituted the fulfillment of the Old Testament law that the Lamb should be without blemish. He was born of a woman that we might be born again of God. He shed Himself of the Divine Nature that we could be partakers of it. He became a servant that we might be free of slavery and joint heirs as sons of God. And He worked that we might not want—toiled that we might rest and became naked that we might be adorned with robes of righteousness.

Third, it is the blood of one offered for a sacrifice for sin: "by the which will we are sanctified by the offering of the body of Christ once and for all." Jesus not only died, He died a voluntary suffering death. It was offered for sin. The life Jesus so willingly offered to endure such a suffering lingering death should give us boldness indeed. The rent veil, the broken body, the poured out blood—this is the surety of the New Covenant.

Consecration Through The Blood

"I beseech ye therefore, brethren, by the mercies of God, that you present your bodies a living sacrifice, holy, acceptable unto God, which is your reasonable service." —Romans 12:1

This thing of consecration has been confusing to many of us. It has been erroneously described to be the condition of receiving the Holy Spirit. But the Bible declares the *gift* of the Spirit is received by faith. In the book of Romans, known as the Gospel according to Paul, consecration comes *after* the gift of the Spirit. We cannot consecrate until we have the unction (power) within to do so.

Therefore, consecration is not of the self-life but rather out of the Spirit's power within. Paul affirms this in the verse before our text: "For *of* Him and *through* Him (and) *to* Him are all things." The power of consecration is *of* Him. A woman in one of my congregations had this experience to clarify this truth. Her husband wasn't saved and she often prayed, commiting him to God. One day the Lord stopped her prayer and challenged her that He really would take her husband from her. She felt the strong "No" well up within her heart and realized her previous words were just lip worship. But as she waited in humble confession and earnest desire before the Lord, she experienced a strange calm willingness to yield even her dearest to the Lord. She then realized this *holiness* of the heart was by God's power and not her own. This is the living sacrifice. By the mercies of God, we identify ourselves with Christ who made the perfect offering. The Holy Spirit within us enables us to trust God for His goodness.

The acceptability of our consecration is *through* Him. God calls for something more than willingness to surrender. He demands it be holy and well-pleasing to Him. How? Through Christ—the altar sanctifies the gift. Only what we offer in faith through his shed blood is acceptable.

Then, the object of our consecration is *to* Him. Whether we live or die, it is to Him. Our life (reputation, finances, success or goals) should speak to others of His life. He has given us our very life and hope—to *Him* belong all the glory and praise. This is consecration.

Conclusion On The Blood

"Let us draw near with a true heart in full assurance of faith, having our hearts sprinkled from an evil conscience, and our bodies washed with pure water." —Hebrews 10:22

The message of the Holy Spirit rings clear when the blood of Christ is mentioned: to "listen to the Blood that speaks," to offer "the better sacrifice," to fear lest we "count it a common thing," to "remember Him" through the blood's symbols, "to eat His flesh and drink His blood," and "to proclaim to all the forgiveness of sins through His blood."

Therefore, appreciation of the blood of Jesus is the really true standard by which we measure our spiritual state; God will hold us responsible for our heart's attitude toward the blood of His Son. And if we are to have a proper attitude, what does it require?

First, we must come boldly and draw near to the throne of grace: "Let us draw near having our hearts sprinkled." Sadly, some only know the "outer court" life of Jesus—His earthly ministry. Others draw nearer through the blood and know His "holy place" life—the risen Christ. The amazing fact is that we have the *right* to know Him that best way. Jesus is the mediator—the go-between—who gives us the blood-bought right to enter in with Him to the Holy of Holies. To do so we must exercise a living faith in our Redeemer. We must believe Him completely. Unbelief is the paralysis of the soul!

The exhortation of our text is this—have *boldness* to enter into the holiest by the blood of Jesus. Go from faith to faith. Know personally His authority. Then, testify and proclaim its power. "Let us consider one another to provoke unto love and good works."

David said: "I have *believed*; therefore have I *spoken*." This boldness is only possible for believers through Christ's redemptive blood, but this wonderful redemption is not just for our own pleasure and profit. We are compelled to think of others. If the angels in heaven are always engaged in these heavenly songs—angels that have never needed the merits of atoning blood—how much *more* should we sinful, rebellious mortals overflow with songs of gladness and thanksgiving? Let us draw near having boldness to enter into the holiest by the blood of Jesus!

The Defender

"And He is the propitiation for our sins."
                                        —I John 2:2

The word, "propitiation," means an atonement or an expiation. Here it means that Christ does something that my failure can not undo. He undertakes my case. For I wouldn't have a chance without His intercession for me.

More than just an advocate to see that I'm not hailed into court without an adequate defense, "in Christ Jesus" I am innocent until proven guilty. Just as He pleaded successfully for the dying thief, the woman taken in adultery and for Saul of Tarsus, He pleads for me—not with words, but with wounds. The fact of facts is this that Jesus Christ died for me. God cannot and will not ignore that death, providing that I do not, when he hears any charge presented against me.

Beyond his death, Jesus is our great High Priest. From the Old Testament, when Aaron entered the Most Holy Place, he was bound to carry the names of Israel's tribes on his shoulders and breast. They were placed upon his shoulders in token that he bore the burden of their wickedness and infirmities. They were placed on his breast in token of his love and care for them as their High Priest. Jesus is our High Priest: "We have not a High Priest which cannot be touched with the feeling of our infirmities, but was in all points tempted like as we are, yet without sin." He died to make *satisfaction*. He lives again to make *intercession*. We are on His shoulders. We are near His heart. He takes my name. He pleads for me and you!

An Advocate

"...if any man sin, we have an ADVOCATE with the Father, Jesus Christ the righteous."

—*I John 2:1*

The judicial system in America is an adversary system and every accused person is entitled to an advocate, whether guilty or not. Joseph Nye Welch, the famous Boston attorney, speaks of his role, "When a client comes to me with a case, no matter how unpopular, no matter how black the past, no matter what doubts I have to his guilt or innocence, I must give him faithful service and do my best for him, without judging him." Another prominent lawyer speaks on the issue of defending the guilty, "A lawyer serves society best by defending all accused persons whether guilty or innocent."

Where did this present day idea of advocate come from? It came right from our New Testament—our advocate with the Father, Jesus Christ. Why do I need an Advocate? *Because I have a great adversary.* The New Testament tells me that the devil accuses me "before God day and night." He goes right up to God and says about me, "God, is that one of your Christians doing that thing?" Everyday I need someone to plead my case—to say, "My Father, I took all that into account when I died on Calvary." Well has the writer said:

"I hear the accuser roar
of ills that I have done
I know them well, and thousands more
Jehovah findeth none.
Though the restless foe accuses
Sins recounting like a flood
Every charge our God refuses
Christ has answered with His blood."

Jesus Never Fails

*"And when they lifted up their eyes, they saw
no man, save Jesus only."*   —*Matthew 17:8*

They tell the story of the country fellow down in Georgia. He found himself at midnight in the middle of the graveyard. He got scared, started to run, fell over a couple of tombstones and scratched himself unmercifully getting through the bushes. The next morning someone said to him, "Don't you know a ghost can not hurt you?" "Maybe so," he said, "but they sho can make you hurt yourself." Feelings can be a fickle thing and not always to be trusted.

In the familiar account of the transfiguration from which our text is taken, Peter wanted to build three tabernacles to house his mountain top experience. That did not work. Wonderful as Peter's experience was, Peter possessed something better. He had Jesus and when the experience passed away, he still had the Lord. All else may fail; but we still have Him. And He fills our hearts with the love of God.

Some of the Bible characters who saw and were part of the some of the most supernatural experiences, wound up with nervous breakdowns. Their feelings failed them. Elijah, the Old Testament prophet, folded up under the juniper tree and wanted to die. John the Baptist feeling so low in prison voiced his doubts on Jesus' Messiahship. David the Psalmist felt empty and completely alone. Paul said, "No man stood with me." Their feelings got them down. We all have experienced this. But remember in the midst of fears and evil forebodings, we are not alone, Jesus abides.

Feelings may fail; civilization may fail; friends may fail; the church may fail; but Jesus does not fail. Jesus did not reprove John the Baptist for his low feelings. He said the best thing about John when John had said the poorest thing about Jesus. He "knows our frame and remembers that we are dust." We can trust our feelings to Him.

The Power Of The Resurrection

"That I may know...the power of His resur-
rection." Philippians 3:10

Paul never doubted that Jesus was alive. That fact had changed his life. His message was: "If Christ be not risen...we are yet in our sins." Only clear, unavoidable facts could have so convinced this stubborn, dogmatic man. The "Sonstroke" Paul experienced on the Damascus Road had turned his life upside down and completely around. The certainty of Christ's resurrection released a new life, a new power in Paul. Paul recognized this and sought to know (experience) the fulness of that life-giving power.

First, the resurrection revealed the power of evidence. It was the seal of heaven upon the entire plan of salvation. Jesus had made tremendous claims—more than any other man. He claimed to be God, to forgive sins, to be immortal. It took the resurrection to substantiate these claims. In it, all that Jesus claimed was guaranteed and ratified by God. The disciples and Paul now had a bonafide gospel to preach. The resurrected Christ sent them out as authoritative witnesses. Death had been conquered.

Then, the resurrection brought sustaining power. Paul and the disciples faced death for their message. They would receive imprisonment, floggings and torture. But in the midst of this brutality, they knew Jesus was with them. They had seen Him come and go through closed doors. His living, helping presence was always there to strengthen and sustain. "Lo, I am with you always."

Finally, the resurrection is an exalting power—a hand that reaches down for us to help us upward. As brave and courageous as Paul was, he would never have made it without help from above. He knew Christ was there undergirding, leading him on to finish his task. Over and over, his confession was "I can do all things through Christ which strengtheneth me."

Where would we be without His strength? We can draw new power for life today—because He lives!

Forty Days Of Blessed Realization

"I am with you always, even unto the end of the world." —Matthew 28:20

The God we serve today is a knowing and understanding God; he knows our weaknesses and how to provide strength. God in Christ knew man's difficulty in seeing and comprehending the miraculous. So in His grace and mercy, Jesus gave mankind forty precious days after He had completed His mission on earth—the forty days after His resurrection.

Until the resurrection the disciples supposed that when Jesus died, He was no longer with them at all. Even the resurrection did not totally remove this impression from their minds. Therefore, one of the primary endeavors of Christ during his last forty days was to cultivate the truth that He was with them still and always.

In the forty days after His resurrection Jesus communicated other important truths to the disciples. First, his lingering in fellowship with the disciples and others showed that His sorrows, His enemies, and the imperfection of His friends had not deterred His concern and love for mankind. His miraculous appearances in bodily form showed He was in a higher state of humanity and could always be present with them, even though He was ascended. His indeterminate appearances gave them a constant expectation. He appeared both at prayer meetings and in "non-religious" settings to help them fish. In this way, they could feel that He was with them as they worked for their daily necessities. And he appeared to not just them, but to women and to laymen.

What was the result of these appearances to the disciples? First, they didn't need to linger or mourn around an empty sepulchre and after his ascension, they were never more joyous: "they returned to Jerusalem with great joy." Why? Because they were sure He was present and could still help them even though He was invisible. Christ, Immanuel, is with us today. May we live with their same confidence and expectation.

At Jordan

"And Jesus, when he was baptized, went up straightway out of the water: and, lo, the heavens were opened unto him, and he saw the Spirit of God descending like a dove..." —Matthew 3:16

We see in this picture of Christ's baptism at Jordan, His consecration to public ministry. When others were baptized in Jordan, it was a symbol of their need of cleansing. But our Savior had no sin to be repented of; he was rather surrendering to a life's work.

What were the consequences of this consecration? First, we see "the heavens were opened unto Him." Rather than referring to the material sky, I believe that meant a vision broke over His soul—the vision of his life's work. Just like when Peter was praying on the housetop, he too, saw the heavens opened and the revelation of the spiritual equality of Jew and Gentile. Our surrender to God's will, too, will bring a vision. And the largeness of our vision will depend upon the fullness of our surrender.

Then this dedication brought a new endowment—the Holy Spirit descended upon Him. Before Christ lay the highway of Messiahship and the long conflict with the powers of darkness that would lead to the Crucifixion. And for that task, God gave Him the needed equipment, the Spirit "without measure." When we yield to God's direction of our lives, God has the full equipment we need in order to take that direction.

Lastly, the dedication brought a *new intimacy*, the voice of the Father for all to hear: "This is my beloved Son." Jesus had always known the presence of His Father. But here was the audible witness from above. *What glorious certainty!* You've got to know that God is with you and that He owns you as His child, if you are going to be successful on any mission you undertake for Him. Jesus dedicated Himself for life or death. His coming up out of Jordan was offering Himself as a living sacrifice. This is the true picture of Christian consecration.

Holy Ghost Regeneration

"Not by works of righteousness which we have done, but according to His mercy he saved us, by the washing of regeneration, and renewing of the Holy Ghost." —Titus 3:5

This is the principal work of the Holy Spirit—to renew men—to make new men. The New Testament is filled with references to this work of the Spirit, from Jesus' response to Nicodemus' question (born of the Spirit) to Paul's repeated assurances to the church (the Spirit gives life).

One of the best examples in the New Testament which illustrates the work of the Holy Spirit in regeneration is where Jesus compares the new birth to the growth of a seed. Here the human heart is the soil; the seed is the Word of God; and the sower is the preacher. Jesus says it is the Spirit of God that quickens the seed (God's Word) in the human heart. Therefore, every sower is absolutely dependent upon the Spirit of God for the regeneration of souls.

Recently, newspaper headlines have carried stories of the dramatic conversions of men deep in sin—men like Nicki Cruz, Eldridge Cleaver and Charles "Tex" Watson. These men had an old nature which was so corrupt that to society they may have appeared beyond hope. But the Bible notes no special type of sinner—all have sinned. To anyone, the Spirit of God has the power to quicken the Seed, and bring forth an entirely new nature in that soul. Regeneration goes down to the deepest depths (dividing assunder of soul and spirit), transforming thoughts, affections, and the will of the whole inward man.

What else can pierce so deep into the soul and so enliven the core of man? Only the same Spirit that has raised Christ from the dead can make a man a new creature. Do you know His quickening power?

Sealing Of The Spirit

"God...who hath also SEALED us and given us the earnest of the Spirit in our hearts."
—*II Corinthians 1:22*

Under the Old Testament law, it was the custom of the priest who was responsible for service to select a lamb from the flock. He would inspect it with the most minute scrutiny in order to discover if it was without physical defect. If perfect, he would seal it with the temple seal, certifying that it was fit for sacrifice and for food.

Similarly, the Lamb of God, Jesus, presented Himself at Jordan for the Father's inspection. He must be a "a lamb without blemish or spot." The heavens open and God gives witness: "This is my beloved Son in Whom I am well pleased"; and then the Holy Ghost comes upon Him as *"seal"*— the seal unto (1) separation unto sacrifice and (2) service. "Labor...for that meat...which the Son of man shall give unto you—for Him hath God the Father *sealed*."

In this, we today share the same experience as our Lord: "In Whom having also believed ye were sealed with the Holy Spirit of promise." This sealing is no conversion, it is something that happens to the converted soul. In conversion, the believer receives the testimony of God and "hath said to his soul that God is true." It is in the baptism of the Holy Ghost that God sets His seal upon the believer that he is true. This is God's "Amen" to the Christian just as God did to Jesus at Jordan.

In our sealing, to what are we separated? Paul writes to Timothy: "Having this seal—(1) the Lord knoweth them that are His, (2) let everyone that nameth the name of the Lord depart from unrighteousness." This is what the Baptism of God's Spirit is in our lives—ownership and holiness. There comes a devotion to Jesus! God cannot and will not put His signature upon what is not His. It means something to bear this signature.

Just as the forehead of the Temple Priest had inscribed "Holiness Unto the Lord", the Holy Spirit puts his mark upon us—the righteousness of Christ. "In Him is no sin—whosoever abideth in Him sinneth not." God's sealing of the believer is His gracious communication of the Holy Spirit unto all who accept and commit themselves to His holy calling.

Follow His Steps

"Because Christ also suffered for us—leaving us an example, THAT YE SHOULD FOLLOW HIS STEPS."   *I Peter 2:21*

What steps did Jesus take? Let's look at His ministry from the start. "Jesus also being baptized—and praying—the heaven opened. And the Holy Spirit descended in a bodily shape like a dove upon Him." Jesus practiced what He preached and He preached receiving God by His Spirit. Before He ever began His public ministry—He sought and received the Holy Spirit. That came first!

So when Jesus went to pass on the ministry to his disciples, his command was the same: "Be baptized with the Holy Ghost." A ministry (or a witness or testimony) to be successful must have the Spirit of God behind it. The pattern in God's word is clear. Jesus told them, "As My Father hath sent Me, even so send I you." And when He had said this—he breathed on them, and saith unto them, "Receive ye the Holy Ghost." It is clear, if we are to be his followers, the sent ones, we must receive and be filled with the Holy Ghost.

The task before the follower of Christ is a supernatural one. Jesus used that supernatural power while on earth and He said, "He that believes on Me, the works that I do shall He do also and greater works than those shall he do." When Jesus came to earth, He came at our level. He got tired and thirsty and lonely like we, and to carry on, he used that power of the Holy Spirit—the same power that is available to us today.

Most important, Jesus used the Spirit of God to defeat the devil. When the devil tried to tempt, that anointed utterance as He poured out the authoritative Word of God put the enemy to flight—and brought Jesus to the people in the *power* of the Spirit.

Do we seek ministry? Would we be His follower? Let us follow His steps—in the fullness of the Spirit.

Is Salvation Free

"And whosoever doth not bear his cross, and
come after me, cannot be my disciple."—Luke 14:27

Here is a story for just supposing. The King of England is out taking a walk and encounters a tramp along the hedgerow. In compassion, he tells the tramp, "I want to help you so I would like to adopt you into my royal family and make you one of my sons."

In surprise, the tramp responds, "Your majesty, how much will this cost me?"

The king replies, "Absolutely nothing. It's all a part of my free grace."

So the tramp goes back with the king to the palace and looks about everywhere, enjoying all that is now his. While he is reveling in the good things about him, in walks the valet and says, "Excuse me, sir, your bath is ready." As the tramp is about to protest, the valet says, "You are now a prince; it is customary for members of the royal family to bathe." In the tub, the tramp sighs, "I might have known there was a catch in it. The king told me it was free and before I turn around, I have to do what I never did before—take a bath."

So he begins to realize that if he is to enjoy this new found blessing as part of the royal household, there is a price to pay. It is nothing to get in, but it is something to stay in. Soon the tramp discovers there is a new suit of clothes to be worn, some new dinner manners, even a new diet of food to get used to. Again he says to himself, "So it's all free, is it? Then why do I have to pay such a price so as to act like a prince?"

The analogy is clear. Salvation is free but it costs you and I to be a disciple of Jesus. Our calling is high, to be kings and priests unto God. That means a new nature and new God-glorifying habits. We must walk worthy to live in His palace!

The One Thing

"One thing I do, forgetting the things which are behind and reaching forth unto those things which are before, I press toward the mark for the prize of the high calling of God in Christ Jesus."
—Philippians 3:13, 14

Paul was a "driven" man. His life reeked with commitment—the kind that makes champions and heroes. There were no "ifs" in his service; it was serving with all his *mind*, his *heart*, his *soul* and *strength*. Besides the fact that He was God's man for that hour, there were several reasons why Paul served with such strength and dedication.

First, Paul never ceased to thrill in having been chosen by Christ and having his ministry exalted. He termed himself "least of the apostles" but he glorified his calling. Therefore, his work never became drab or common-place. Whenever he thought of his mission, he would get a second wind. It held a continual measure of excitement and preciousness. We must set our goals high if we are to have such motivation.

Second, Paul's past was a spur to his present. He was determined to atone for all the bitter memory of his misdirected past. He used the word, "stretching", meaning an intense and strained effort. He saw the implications of the Cross for the believer and determined to have his share in the victory and glory of eternal life. He also had confidence that the "grace" that reached him could reach anyone. He would share the Good News.

Thirdly, he experienced a bigger kind of living: "...all things are yours.." If the Lord and Creator of all gave that which was most precious to Himself, His only Son, He will also share all things of His creation with us if we use them for His glory and not selfishly.

Finally, Paul learned to live with his problems. He stopped groaning over his thorn and started glorifying. Rather than looking at the problem, he looked to the answer. And found satisfaction in being nothing more than "a *servant* of the Lord Jesus Christ."

We, too, can claim the "one thing" in our life—to serve the Lord.

Symptoms Of Salvation

"Rejoice evermore, pray without ceasing, in everything give thanks: for this is the will of God in Christ Jesus concerning you."
—I Thessalonians 5:16-18

When a company has bad working conditions and allows (or even forces) its employees to dress shabbily, the public appraises that employer in the light of what it sees in the employees. The employee's appearance speaks badly for the owner and leaves wrong impressions. The opposite is true as well. When an owner puts good equipment in the hands of his employees and dresses them smartly, the public is inclined to think well of that employer's product.

It is just so with our Lord! What kind of religion do we have? The world will get a wrong impression of our Savior if it sees ungrateful, sad and uncommunicative Christians. It is the happy, prayerful and thankful Christian that honors his religion and his God.

Paul tells us salvation is a togetherness experience: "hath quickened us *together* with Christ...and hath raised us up *together* and made us sit *together* in heavenly places in Christ Jesus." The quickening of the new birth produces joy which raises us up to prayer where we find rest and thanksgiving. These three elements of salvation are inseparable.

The Gospel is Good News and if we lose any of these three elements we lose the "goodness", the "vitality" of our salvation. If we stop praying, we will soon stop thanking; and if we stop thanking, we will soon stop rejoicing. A gloomy Christian is simply one who has lost his sense of "togetherness" with our victorious, joyous God. Let us return and pray, rejoice and thank evermore.

Our Election

*"Wherefore the rather, brethren, give diligence
to make your calling and election sure: for if ye do
these things, ye shall never fail."* —II Peter 1:10

Some of the Bible's darkest hours are the result of God's people taking things for granted. Israel failed miserably in its battle against little Ai because they took for granted God's help. Saul, the handsome and popular first king of Israel, lost his throne because he assumed it was all right for him to "fudge" a little. The prophets record that Israel in times of prosperity took for granted God's blessings—and found themselves in captivity.

Christians always face the ever-recurring danger of taking things for granted. Faith is active—not static! Many denominational churches are dying for that reason. They have been content in maintaining a standard. The moment you stop pressing forward you are slipping backward. Christ rebuked the attitude of "what was okay for grandmother is okay for me" over and over. He said "If thou canst believe, all things are possible for him that believeth." He calls us to go on and "make our election sure."

Jesus knew and experienced that Good Friday followed right after Palm Sunday. If we in any way lean on our popularity or other opinions, there is great danger of falling. The Bible says that the "man of high-estate shall be brought low." The way we can solidify our calling is to humble ourselves to walk with God. Open our ears and heart to God saying with Samuel: "Here am I Lord—speak for thy servant heareth."

The other side is just as true. People may not give you the slightest chance of success. God says, "believe." From the Bible to the latest testimonies today, we see God saving and using the most unlikely of characters. God loves to show what He can do with little when it is completely given to Him. But there is no place for "fence straddlers, quitters and the timid" in His church. We must exert effort—give diligence—to make our calling and election sure.

Hidden Manna...A White Stone... A New Name

"To him that OVERCOMETH will I give to eat of the HIDDEN MANNA, and will give him a WHITE STONE, and in the stone a NEW NAME written, which no man knoweth, saving he that receiveth it." —Revelation 2:17

There is plenteous provision for victory in the Christian life. But our captain, the Lord Jesus Christ, lets us know they are given in battle. We must press into the fight to gain the rewards.

To the overcomer, Jesus promises first, "hidden manna." In the ark of the tabernacle was placed some of the manna which the Israelites fed upon in the wilderness. Jesus told us clearly, "I am the bread which came from heaven." Jesus Christ then is the sustenance of our spiritual life. Paul spoke of this: "Our life is *hid* with Christ in God." It is the inner man, the eternal soul, that Christ feeds and nourishes with faith, love, peace and joy.

Then, Jesus promises a "white stone". This refers to the *tessera hospitals*—a token of hospitality used by the Romans and Greeks. When one person was kindly received of another or a contract of friendship made, the *tessera* was given. The stone was divided into two by the contracting parties with each writing his name on half; they then exchanged pieces. The *tessera* was carefully prized, entitling the bearer to protection and hospitality—almost like a modern credit card. Likewise, the Savior exchanges hospitality with the sinner who repents: "if any man...open the door, I will come in...and sup..and he with me." There is two way fellowship; God gives us His Spirit as the earnest of the promised possession.

There is a new name in the stone. The Christian knows God by a new name, not as Justice or Avenger, but as Friend and as Father. Our passport to Heaven is our knowledge of Him. And God knows us by a new name. He doesn't see us as dirty, rotten in sin. He sees us in Christ. He has a plan for our lives. He sees us overcoming our sin and his hospitality guarantees his continual help to that end. Only God knows "your new name", your reward, but you must fight to overcome.

Behold He Stinketh

"He cried with a loud voice, Lazarus, come forth"
—John 11:43

Men like Nicodemus, the secret disciple and women like Martha, the cumbered servant, are so sketched for us that we cannot but perceive them to represent distinctive types of personalities—which recur in every generation. God has chosen living characters to teach us these simple pictorial truths. The brother of Martha, Lazarus, is such a one, providing us a remarkable illustration of *regeneration* and new life in *Christ*.

In John chapter eleven, when Jesus encounters Lazarus, he is dead, illustrative of our lost condition—dead in trespasses and sins. Modernists have other definitions for sin like immaturity, heredity and environmental necessity, disease, mental infirmity or biological urge. But God's Word says that sin is death: "In the day that thou eatest thereof thou shall surely die." Sin's death is in the soul, separation from God, something worse than physical death.

But Lazarus is raised at the command of Jesus: "Lazarus, come forth." Sin and hell must yield to the voice of the Savior. One day soon all that are in the graves will come forth at the voice of the Son of Man—one class to the resurrection of judgment and the other class to the resurrection of eternal life. People today that are dead in trespasses and sins may, too, hear the voice of Jesus saying: "Come Forth!"

As Lazarus was raised, he "came forth *bound* hand and foot with *graveclothes*." This is illustrative of our old habits and ways (like fear, pride, lust, love of money) that would try to bind our new life in Christ. To this, Jesus proclaims, "Loose him, and let him go." Jesus offers us life and freedom from sin's bounds: "He that the Son makes free is free indeed."

The result of Lazarus being raised from the dead is feasting ("they made Him a supper") and witnessing ("come they might see Lazarus"). The results of true salvation is joy, fellowship with other believers, and a changed life others can come and see and behold that Jesus changes lives—eternally!

Trying Or Trusting

"But we all, with open face beholding as in a glass the glory of the Lord, are changed into the same image from glory to glory."
—II Corinthians 3:18

Many people that I encounter say they would like to be good, but they get so tired of the struggle that they feel they cannot stand the strain. To them, life seems to be built on the down grade...and it's easy to slip and hard to climb. They labor at being good like the singer who strains his voice, so distressingly that the audience suffers with him. But then I've also known other folk whose goodness was spontaneous. It overflowed and seemed effortless. What is the difference?

In one of the European galleries, there is an old Greek statue of Apollo, a beautiful figure of physical perfection. It is interesting to stand aside and watch the casual visitor pass by. If anybody stands long enough before the statue, almost invariably he begins to straighten up. He is not trying and is usually not conscious of what he does. He is simply following a great law of life—*we grow like what we live with*. Christianity is rather caught than taught. We don't do the changing...This Unseen Friend...changes us. Henry Drummond translates our text: "We all reflecting as a mirror that character of Christ are transformed into the same image from *character to character.*"

Suppose someone approached Paul in heaven and said: "What a will you have! You started a persecutor and ended up writing the most inspiring texts in the world's literature." Paul would respond, "it was not my will. I lived with Christ. I had daily inner fellowship with Him. All that was finest in my life came from that. I was changed from 'character to character.'"

Paul said *he was changed*. He got a new nature. It came not by trying but by trusting in Christ, the great Transformer. We, too, can become that reflection of Christ as we look to Him daily, moment by moment.

Three Dimensions

"The length and the breadth and the height of it are equal." —*Revelation 21:16*

John saw the City of God and he saw that the length and breadth and height of it were equal. If we examine the character of its citizens, we see conformity to the same measurements.

The meaning suggested by the word, "length," is *line*. We speak of men being in this line of work or that line of work. It's the thing he does—his chief interest or profession. How far should he go? Why, as far as he can, of course. God wants His children to put their heart into everything they do: "whatsoever ye do, do it heartily as unto the Lord." That includes doing the best job possible in work, fulfilling God's original command to Adam to "take dominion over the earth."

But traveling in one direction is not enough. Length, without breadth, is simply selfishness. It's the tendency of some people "to go to all lengths"; they are only interested in their own line. The priest and the Levite in the story in the "Good Samaritan" were these kind of people. They were earnest and sincere but selfishly they didn't have time to consider anything else but their own mission. The Samaritan, who had breadth enough to stop and tend the wounded man, shows us much about Christian character. As far as we go for ourselves, we should go for others when we "love our neighbor as ourself."

Its not hard to see that the height of divine symmetry is faith—the uplift and response of the whole man to God. Man is the only creature built to "look up" instead of "down." Nothing transforms character like fellowship with Jesus Christ. The truest help that any of us can secure each day is the help that comes through prayer. And the man who is best fitted to meet the storms of life is the man who has put his trust in God and committed all his ways to Him.

Christian character is three-fold then. It is solid like the dimension of life itself.

Guaranteed

"Can a woman forget her sucking Child, that she should not have compassion on the son of her womb? Yea, they may forget, yet will I not forget thee. Behold, I have graven thee upon the palms of my hands; thy walls are continually before me."
—Isaiah 49:15-16

Jerusalem was in ruins. The Babylonians had ransacked it. They had wrecked its palaces, desecrated the great altar of God, and dragged down the walls that once encircled the city of God, and those are the walls of which God speaks to Isaiah: "thy walls are continually before me." What was it that God could see that Isaiah couldn't?

The walls were either a memory of the past or a dream of the future. They had no being or substance, no foundation in fact. But it was God who was speaking—*those walls were not ruined in his vision.* We see only the present facts but He sees His eternal plan and purpose. And the most blessed experience this side of heaven is to stand with God and have your eyes enlightened to see victory where there seems to be nothing but defeat and ruin.

Gutzon Borglum, the great sculptor, has given us many famous sculptures, but the work for which he is best remembered is the head of Abraham Lincoln which he carved for the Capitol in Washington. He cut it from a block of marble in his studio and the transformation of which filled his maid with superstitous dread. Oblivious to his work on the stone, she went on dusting as usual. But one morning she saw the unmistakable lineaments of the mighty President appearing in the marble. Running over to Borglum, she said in awe, "Is that Abraham Lincoln?" As he nodded, the old woman exclaimed, "How in the world did you know Mr. Lincoln was in that block of stone?"

How did God know Peter the rock was in Peter the unstable? Or Paul the apostle in Saul the persecutor? Because God not only sees the outside, but God sees the inwardness and possibility of man. Knowing this, he sent His Son to die for us, that we might become his intention. In Christ, He says, "I have graven thee upon the palms of My hands." The nailprints say, "I'll never forget." The Lord of life watches over us in love!

Haunted House

*"When he is come, he findeth it empty, swept
and garnished. Then goeth he, and taketh with
himself seven other spirits more wicked...and the
last state of that man is worse than the first."*
—Matthew 12:44-45

I don't know of anything that is more lonesome than an empty house.
There is only one that is more depressing and dangerous...that is an empty
life, from which noble thoughts have fled and all that is lovely and kind
has been exiled. In this text, Jesus gives us this picture. Here is a human being possessed of evil spirits. But this person had gotten rid of these evil
thoughts and habits. He had cleaned house and the old life was gone. But
into this empty life worse evils entered and the last state was worse than
the first. A sad conclusion and illustrative of some today who are "good
for nothing." Negative goodness and rule keeping is never enough. The
evils that have been driven out must be replaced by what is good,
honorable, the truth and the best. As Paul said, "Be not overcome of evil,
but overcome evil with good."

A mother once unexpectedly visited the dormitory room of her son at
college. She observed that on the walls of his room were risque
pinups...but she made no reference to what she saw. On her return home
she selected a fine copy of Hofmann's "Christ and the Doctors," showing
Jesus with the doctors of law in the Temple. She had it suitably framed and
sent it to him. On her next visit, the lovely picture was hung on the wall
and the pinups had disappeared.

In the days of the Catholic evangelist, Savonarola when he was
transforming the wicked city of Florence—there was a festival, during
which the children and youth were destructive, flinging rocks through windows and doing other mischief. Instead of condemning the youth, he suggested they march through the city singing "Make Christ King" and collect
alms for the poor. It worked and a revival of religion resulted. This is much
to be said for this gospel of replacement. Inhabiting the house with the
Spirit of God.

The Sense Of God's Presence

"the Spirit of man is the candle of the Lord..."
—*Proverbs 20:27*

The great painting called The Presence portrays a beautiful cathedral with its high altar, its long aisle and row upon row of empty chairs. It is not the hour of regular worship—but like all cathedrals—its door it open for anyone who might wish to enter and pray. A burdened soul has wandered in and knelt quietly and penitently at the back of the last row of chairs. As the penitent kneels in prayer, a second figure emerges through the doorway and stands directly behind him. It is Jesus come to give comfort and encouragement in the hour of distress and to assure the soul of His Divine Presence.

There is a *Presence* like that in our lives. I know when it is there and I also know when it is not there. The songwriter has described it beautifully. He calls it, "being overshadowed."

An Old Testament story confirms the possibility of such assurance. Moses had come a long way, leaving his delightful home in Midian to take charge of a disgruntled and stiff-necked race of people. Leading them to a permanent home far beyond Egypt, he had met with little success. One day when his nerves were about to break, he prayed: "If I have found grace in thy sight, show me now thy way...that I may consider that this nation is thy people." Back came the answer saying, *"My presence shall go with thee and I will give thee rest."* But Moses wanted to see more. "Show me thy glory," he pleaded. He needed something to steady him—to make him sure. And God said: "I will make all my goodness pass before thee." And Moses is put in the cleft of the rock—and as the glory of the Lord passes by, Moses gets a glimpse of it.

Moses is not different from us. We want the assurance of God's presence and direction. Oh, the beauty of the name of the Lord, *Immanuel* or "God with us." God's presence has come in Christ and now dwells with us by His Spirit. We need not be alone ever.

APRIL:
The Power of the Holy Spirit

"How God anointed Jesus of Nazareth with the Holy Ghost and with power: who went about doing good, and healing all that were oppressed of the devil; for God was with Him." —Acts 10:38

No-Ground

"Give no ground, foot-hold or opportunity to the devil." —Ephesians 4:27 (Amplified)

Rev. Ev Carter
Evangelist

We as believers in Jesus Christ should not give the enemy an opportunity to work a sense of defeat in us — in our thoughts, attitudes, desires, will or emotion. Neither should we give ground morally, physically, socially, academically or financially.

We are new creatures in Christ, washed and redeemed in His blood, so God has made all things in us. As a man Jesus in His humanity defeated Satan. Therefore you and I, in our humanness can accomplish this same reality when we like Christ begin to function in our wholeness, totally dependent upon Him, who is our source.

Satan must keep his hands off God's property and since we have become God's property by making Him Lord, Satan must take his hands off of us, too. Say, "NO GROUND, DEVIL!"

Walking in the Spirit

*"There is therefore now NO CONDEMNA-
TION to them which are in Christ Jesus, who walk
not after the flesh, but after the Spirit.*
—*Romans 8:1*

Thank God, He allows us to start our Christian life without condemnation. God has not condemned me for all the crazy and sinful things that I did in ignorance before coming to Christ. He, indeed, gave me a new and fresh start in life.

But once we become a Christian, I believe God expects us to walk our talk. Hebrews chapter twelve says we are surrounded by a cloud of witnesses who lived faithful to God and now they are observing our walk before God. This is a good reminder and encouragement to me to walk faithfully before Him.

Gary S. Paxton
Music Artist

The Power and Joy of Giving

"I have told you this so that you will be filled with my joy. Yes, your cup of joy will overflow!"
—*John 15:11 TLB*

"And my speech and my preaching was not with enticing words of man's wisdom, but in demonstration of the Spirit and of power: That your faith should not stand in the wisdom of men, but in the power of God." —*I Corinthians 2:4, 5*

Frances & Charles Hunter
Authors

FRANCES— Joy works! I love all the joy promises. The joy of the Lord is my strength. His joy is in me to encourage me and assure me of His victory. This is the reason I can constantly bubble over with joy. Hallelujah!

CHARLES— There is a genuine gift of preaching. But we have seen more lives changed through the simple miraculous demonstration of God's Spirit and power than by all the eloquent words we could speak in our own wisdom.

The Holy Spirit And The Believer

"So is also the Holy Ghost whom God hath given to them that obey HIM." —Acts 5:32

Few believers have problems seeing God the Father or Jesus Christ as Persons, but many ask, "How can you call the Holy Spirit a Person?" How do we know the Father is a Person? Because certain names and works are ascribed to Him, and He is a Being with a self-consciousness, intelligence and will. The same can be said of the Holy Spirit. The Bible ascribes to the Holy Spirit the works of creation, regeneration, teaching, guiding, comforting and santifying. The Bible also ascribes to God's Spirit the attributes of holiness, truth, goodness and love. These must belong to a personal being!

Jesus' disciples had the same questions. Just before His crucifixion, Jesus tried to explain to them about the Holy Spirit: "For He dwelleth with you, and shall be in you." At that time, the Holy Spirit dwelt with them and they felt His Presence. But Jesus tells them there will be a new and distinct relationship soon. The Holy Spirit will come—not as a *power* acting upon them from *without*—but as a *person* influencing them from *within*. At Pentecost, Peter could proclaim, "receive the Holy Ghost." And Paul could write, "Your bodies are the temples of the Holy Ghost."

To be fully used by the Holy Spirit, we need this understanding. There is a great difference between indwelling and infilling. Of those used by God, John the Baptist, Mary, Elizabeth, we read, they were "full of the Holy Ghost." Paul writes the Ephesians: "Be filled with the Spirit."—not just a privilege, but the obligation of every believer. When the Holy Spirit fills us, the Bible says, "He *quickens* our mortal bodies so we are no longer debtors to the flesh, bound to sin." This is the secret of a life of victory over sin. Then the Holy Spirit *renews* us. There are times when our infilling drains—we can be renewed. Like the seven branched candlestick of the Tabernacle that burned continually and so was to be replenished daily with oil, we can be renewed daily by the oil of the Holy Spirit.

Finally, the Holy Spirit *anoints* us to service. Jesus did everything in the power of the Holy Spirit: "The Spirit of the Lord is upon Me—because the Lord has anointed Me." If it was necessary for Jesus to be *anointed* in order to serve His God acceptably, can we think we can do otherwise? The same filling and anointing is available to each believer who simply asks, obeys, and receives.

The Work Of The Holy Spirit

"Now there are diversities of gifts, but the same Spirit." —*I Corinthians 12:4*

An older Christian was once asked who the Holy Spirit was. He replied, "I'm not sure but I believe its the glowing smile on the face of the dedicated Christian." This may not have been an accurate answer but it surely was a recognition of the Spirit's work.

The work of the Holy Spirit is central in the believer's life. First, the Spirit is the medium of our spiritual life. By the Spirit, we are "born again," "made partakers of the divine nature," "partakers into one body," and "made to drink into one Spirit."

He is the birthright blessing of every believer: "an earnest of the inheritance" until our redemption is complete. Just as one of the first words we learn to say in the natural is "daddy," so the indwelling Holy Spirit reveal our heritage in Christ as sons of God, causing us to cry "Abba (Daddy), Father."

In Jesus Christ, the Spirit dwelt *with* the Apostles. But after the resurrection, the Spirit was to be *in* them. The weakness of the disciples was apparent until endued with the power of the Holy Spirit. With the Holy Spirit within, the disciples had a new sense of God's nearness and a new realization of their resources in Christ. The Spirit came as their teacher, helper, comforter, abiding companion, glorifier of Jesus and representative of the Father.

Individually, the Holy Spirit exalts righteousness in the believers. He is the revealer of divine truth. He searches the deep things of God and passes His discoveries on to us. He takes the Word of God and makes it alive in our hearts, and in our divine and human relationships until it becomes "fruit"—the fruit of God.

The Holy Spirit As A Teacher

*"But the Comforter...shall teach you all things,
and bring all things to your remembrance, whatsoever I have said unto you."*   —John 14:26

Our text describes the two-fold work of the Holy Spirit: (1) teaching and (2) bringing to remembrance. The validity of the second part is clearly seen in the work of the disciples, in the accuracy of their report of what Jesus said and did—which we now call The Gospels. Written independently after Jesus death, there is such total agreement and accuracy of context; only the Holy Spirit could have done this.

The same power is available to each Christian today who expects it and looks to the Holy Spirit for it. The Holy Spirit brings to our mind the teachings of Christ and of the Word of God just when we need them for the necessities of life or Christian service. Oh, the joy, the hope, when in the stress and doubts of life, the Holy Spirit brings just the right word or scripture. In the following verse after our text, Jesus says, "My peace, I give unto you." So it is when the Holy Spirit brings the mind and message of Christ to us.

The teaching of the Holy Spirit is the privilege of even the humblest child of God. God never intended that we be dependent upon human teachers: "You need not that any teach you." This does not mean that we don't listen to human teachers. But no amount of mere human teaching will ever give us a correct, exact and full apprehension of the truth. We must be taught by the One who "guides us into all truth."

How does the Holy Spirit teach? Let's look at the scriptures. First, "He shall declare unto you the things that are to come." Even in these last days, the Holy Spirit is preparing us for His return. Second, "He shall glorify me for He shall take of Mine and shall declare it unto you." It is the primary work of the Holy Spirit to reveal Jesus and to glorify Him. When the anointing fell on the disciples at Pentecost, their one theme was Jesus.

Finally, the Holy Spirit reveals the riches of God: "for the Spirit searcheth all things, yea, the deep things of God." These are riches that the natural mind cannot comprehend unless the Spirit enlightens. It is the Spirit that reveals God's goodness. What a wonderful job the Spirit has; what a wonderful thing to have Him work in us.

The Helper

"The Spirit also HELPETH our infirmities..."
—Romans 8:26

The Holy Spirit is the one who helps us become what God has intended. As the converted convict testified, "I'm going to be somebody because God don't make junk!" If we are going to lead an active Christian life and produce the fruit of the Spirit, we must have Help!

Jesus' description of the Holy Spirit was "Comforter" meaning *supporter* or *strengthener*. He is pictured as One who went into the court room when a person appeared before a tribunal and stood at his side, giving him counsel, cheering his spirit, and advocating his cause. The mission of the Holy Spirit was then to cheer and strengthen him at whose side He stood. How the disciples needed such help when Jesus ascended to the Father! They were to appear before the world as His witnesses and declare the truth in Christ endeavoring to persuade others of the claims of Christ. They needed a Helper to put into their hearts the words, thoughts and purpose of Christ. To manifest Jesus to the world, they would need the very Spirit of Jesus himself.

We say of the man who has listened to the thrilling tales of a hunter until he is on fire to go where the hunter has gone, that the man has caught the hunter's spirit. A person listening to a missionary can catch the missionary spirit. So His Spirit would inspire them to do the work of Jesus! The Comforter was to be to them the *Great dynamic* that would motivate them and not let them give up until their mission was completed.

So when the day of Pentecost came and the Helper descended, these men and women sprang forth in confident action and witness. Soon their dynamic faith had not only turned Jerusalem upside down, but the waves of it went to all the world. No wonder they could write, "the Spirit helpeth our infirmities." And He still does today. Give Him your weakness and fear and let Him strengthen and support you in the Spirit of Christ!

How Does The Comforter Comfort?

*"And I will pray the Father, and He shall give
you another Comforter...even the Spirit of truth..."*
—*John 14:16, 17*

In the book of Luke, the Holy Spirit is used synonymously with "good things from God." The Holy Spirit is our comforter and He comforts us with the good things to us by God, including assurance of salvation, peace and our adoption as God's children.

In the gift of salvation provided by the Father through the death of His Son on the cross, the Holy Spirit has an important role. The King proclaims a pardon. That proclamation must have effect. So the Comforter speeds to the mourner's heart: "The Spirit bears witness to our spirit that we are the children of God," "Where the Spirit of the Lord is—there is liberty." The captive has found deliverance. The bound are set free. The assurance of the Spirit brings this comfort: "We are of God"; "heirs of God"; "born of God"; "followers of God as dear children"; "fellow citizens with the saints and of the household of God."

Then the Comfort of God brings peace: "Peace I leave with you." This is a peace that the world cannot give; it is a heritage of God from the time of Moses: "I will give peace in the Lord." And to David: "He that delivered my soul in peace." And to Solomon: "all her paths are peace." And to Paul: "fill you with joy and peace in believing that ye may abound in hope through the power of the Holy Spirit." Peace and joy is not supplementary to the Christian life but rather elementary! It is the kingdom of God—righteousness, peace and joy!

Thirdly, the Holy Spirit witnesses to our adoption into God's family: "for ye have not received the Spirit of bondage again to fear—but ye have received the Spirit of bondage again to fear—but ye have received the Spirit of adoption whereby we cry, Our Father." We only love because, by the experience of the Holy Spirit, we know that God first loved us. It is not our worth that enables us to call ourselves, "a child of God." It doesn't come through reasoning or education. The Spirit of God puts that cry there! He confirms the love that brings us to rest at the feet of our loving Father. What could be of greater comfort?!

Standing Between Two Friends

"If ye then, being evil, know how to give good gifts unto your children: how much more shall your heavenly Father give the Holy Spirit to them that ask Him?
—Luke 11:13

God's greater answer to prayer is the Holy Spirit! The Father knows of no greater gift to grant His children than the Holy Spirit—the one whose breath brought order out of chaos, who breathed into the dust and dry bones and they became alive, and who accomplishes all for God's Kingdom: "it's not by might nor by power but by My Spirit..." This same Spirit is the gift of love.

Because of this, it is the gift that satan will work hardest, and lie the most, to keep believers from receiving. In the context of our scripture, Jesus warns us of some of the doubts satan will try to implant: "you will get a stone"—it will be hard and difficult; "you will get a scorpion"—you'll be disappointed—without pleasure—you'll be stung; "you will get a serpent"—you'll receive something from the devil—harmful—bring pain—it's poison and fanaticism. Have you ever heard these suggestions about the fulness of the Holy Spirit? Now you know from whence they come.

But Jesus says this *"Gift"* will be to you like bread and meat; it will *satisfy* you. Jesus adds, it is received by asking in prayer; and by not a single off-hand prayer but by prayer with "importunity." This is persistant prayer and prayer that intreats not just on behalf of self but others. This is the prayer that brings the Father's gift—when we realize our own powerlessness and desire to reach out to others. Like the friend without bread for his guest in Jesus' illustration, without power and contact with God we won't have anything to give to a needy world. We can be the one that stands between two friends—receiving from our *Rich Friend* (the heavenly Father) to impart to a *Poor Friend* (others). We are saved to serve and share.

The Giant Tranquilizer

"This is the rest...this is the refreshing..."
—Isaiah 28:12

We live in a world of disturbances. Daily our minds are being attacked by influences of all kinds. Every day there is an emotional drain. We need a stabilizer. What will it be?

Over fifty Americans a day commit suicide. One of eight consult a doctor each week. Fifty percent have no diagnosable physical ailment whatever. Recently, for the first time, Americans are paying more for drugs than for doctors—nearly ten billion dollars per year. No matter what the ads say, this is no bowl-of-cherries world. It is a world of tension, congestion, and confusion.

Nearly everyone wants to know how they can be calm amidst the storms and anxieties of life. Meditation, "psychic cures" and sleeping pills are tried and used by millions with only temporary alleviation. How sad these futile attempts at happiness and peace. Trying to ignore a world of realism doesn't bring peace. God provided the true solution long ago.

Jesus said, "I won't leave you *comfortless*." So many think of God as a *disturber*; but He desires to come to us as a *comforter*. He offers to come in our lives in tranquilizing power to allay our fears—free us from pressure—strengthen us for the competitiveness of life—giving release from tension and bringing refreshment. This is the work of the Holy Spirit.

The literal Bible answer to today's problem of tension and pressure is more of God's Spirit. In our text, Isaiah beautifully describes the fullness of the baptism of the Holy Spirit "for with stammering lips and another tongue will He speak...this is the rest wherewith ye may cause the weary to rest and this is the refreshing..." God offers to freely fill us with His Spirit. This experience is so real—so empowering—so exhilarating and liberating, it releases an utterance you never learned. It releases the fears and tensions and you may be free and live a life of fullness.

Receiving The Holy Spirit

"How much more shall your heavenly Father give the Holy Spirit to them that ask Him."
—Luke 11:13

A little boy was asked what the Holy Spirit means. He replied, "I suppose it is what puts the 'umph' in Christianity." A good answer when we add the tri—'umph'.

The gift of the Holy Spirit is not just a special gift for special people in service; it is the birthright of every Christian. "But this He spake of the Spirit, which *they that believed on him were to receive.*" It is the divine plan and program for all people: "to all that are afar off"; that means us!

Knowing it is God's will, we must respond by accepting the Spirit. It is a gift and only given to those who ask. It is received by decisive action—and actually on a trade-in basis. We cannot receive *Himself* until we have given *ourself*. It is an act of love and there is no love between persons unless there is a mutual self-surrender.

Surrender is different from dedication. In dedication, you still remain in control; in surrender you let go. You now lead a "Spirit led" life even as the canvas surrenders itself to the painter, the violin to the musician, and wire to electricity. Dying to self and receiving the Spirit is like taking a railroad engine restricted on solid ground and putting it on the rails—binding the wheels to the tracks only to find freedom to move and new power.

Receiving the Spirit is the receiving of a blessing (good things). Therefore, we take hold of what we receive. We become a blessing; we become victorious because He is. Having given ourselves, we now have a right to take Himself. We respond: "He comes! I welcome with open heart His coming! It is done! We belong to each other!" Just as marriage is a once and daily commitment we make our surrender and acceptance something once and for all and yet continuous.

The Baptism Of The Holy Spirit

"Have ye received the Holy Ghost since ye believed?" —Acts 19:2

Some people today believe that you get all there is when you receive Christ as Savior—that you receive all the Holy Spirit you are going to get (or need) at salvation. Our verse in its context speaks volumnes to this teaching.

In the fifth chapter of Ephesians, Paul commanded the believers there to be (continually) filled with the Spirit." But when Paul first comes to the large, wicked city of Ephesus as described in Acts 19, things were different. He finds a puny church of just 12 members. They were not touching the city for God and obviously lacked something. They were "baptists" fundamental and orthodox in John's baptism. Paul's first question? "Have ye received the Holy Ghost?" And they replied, "We have not so much as heard whether there be any Holy Ghost." What these "baptists" needed was the *Baptism of the Holy Ghost.*

And what happened? "Paul laid his hands on them, the Holy Ghost came on them and they spake with tongues and prophesied." This was the start of a mighty revival in the city of Ephesus. Luke records that it lasted two years spreading to all of Asia, with many miracles and healings by the hand of Paul. The whole countryside got stirred because 12 "baptists" got stirred with the *Baptism of the Holy Ghost.*

Therefore, later Paul could write to a Spirit-baptized church: "Be (continually) filled with the Spirit." After we are filled by the Holy Ghost baptism, there is a continued feeling of being full of His Divine Presence to every believer.

The empowerment of the Spirit, *after* they believed, changed a puny group to perhaps the strongest New Testament community. The same transforming power of the Holy Spirit is available for our life and our church today.

Riot And Harmony

"And Be not drunk with wine, wherein is excess (lit. riot); but be filled with the Spirit; speaking to yourselves in psalms and hymns and spiritual songs, singing and making melody in your heart to the Lord." —Ephesians 5:18, 19

Psychologists have recently identified four basic needs of the human soul—love, security, recognition and adventure. All people endeavor to fulfill these needs in some way. If a person cannot find fulfillment in positive and legal means, he will often resort to whatever means possible.

The basic need for adventure and excitement is to break the dead level of monotony. We need stimulation. Few people are capable of enduring the colorless course of routine life without variation or relief at intervals. Our text contrasts true and false excitement. One ends in *riot*, the other in *harmony*.

In speaking of drinking, Paul chose a typical and pointed illustration of a false and injurious stimulation that was common to his day (as well as our own). He might just as easily spoke of drug abuse, sensual lust, dare devil risk-taking, crime or gambling. In each, the false excitement produces a temporarily pleasurable, but habit-forming experience. In its tyranny, the false excitement lowers the tone of character and strips it of its higher qualities.

Youth with their abundant energy and zeal are most susceptible to this false excitement which offers a short-cut to fulfillment. But there is no short-cut or artificial way to attain brillancy and abundant living. The apostle confirms that the end of false stimulation is riot.

Only the spirit of God can so channel and stimulate our inner man to produce excitement and joy that is in harmony with God, our world and our own nature.

Be Filled With The Spirit

*"For I will pour water upon him that is thirsty,
and floods upon the dry ground: I will pour my
spirit upon thy seed, and my blessing upon thine
offspring."* —Isaiah 44:3

The evangelist D. L. Moody was preaching to great crowds of people and was enjoying an unusual measure of success—more than most preachers today. But one night after a meeting two godly women called his attention to his need for the filling of the Holy Spirit. As a result of this admonishing and the prayers of these women, Moody searched the scriptures and his own heart until one day he was gloriously filled with God's Spirit. He later testified, "that from that day on my ministry was different—it was His not mine."

Instead of having a few people coming to Christ for salvation—they came by the hundreds and thousands and the power of God was upon him in a tremendous way. There was never a question on his part as to why God so marvelously blessed him. It was, so he said, the result of the "baptism of the Spirit."

If we were to examine the lives of the heroes of faith—Finney, Edwards, Torrey, Wesley, Sunday, we would find each a man who knew the power of the Spirit and lived continually in its fullness. As F. B. Meyer put it, "Before each day and before undertaking any new task for God, be sure you are equipped with a new filling of the Holy Spirit."

A literal if somewhat liberal translation of Ephesians 5:18 is "Be ye continually being filled up to the brim with the Holy Spirit." Paul tells us that our filling must be retained and renewed *continually* if we are to be a blessing to others.

The picture this scripture gives is not like filling a glass and emptying it and filling it again; it is the picture of putting the glass under the faucet, filling it and keeping the glass under the running faucet, so it continually over flows streams of living water flowing from our inner most being. This is the blessed and blessing Christian.

The Holy Spirit And

"...He shall baptize you with the Holy Ghost and with fire."
                                                            —Luke 3:16

Some people either out of misunderstanding or lack of faith struggle to receive the baptism of the Holy Spirit. And when they receive it they think they've got it all; they've arrived! In reality it is just the beginning.

The yielding to the Spirit brings a new flow of the power of God through one's life and many things follow and accompany this work of the Spirit.

The Holy Spirit and *joy*: "And the disciples were filled with joy and the Holy Ghost." There was such an outbreak of joy and gladness on the Day of Pentecost that the people didn't want to go home. It got so that the early church shared things in common with the visitors who stayed. The Holy Spirit brings joy because He is the revealer of Jesus. And Jesus is rejoicing today in the victory won on Calvary. That victory was won for us—we share in it.

The Holy Spirit and *fire*: "shall baptize you with Holy Ghost and with fire." The fire of the Holy Spirit purifies our faith with testing, purging and refining. As with Jesus, after your baptism will come testing: "the chaff He will burn with fire unquenchable." It may seem that the fire of God will consume you but it is purifying fire and you shall "come forth as gold and silver."

The Holy Spirit and *obedience*: "the Holy Ghost whom God hath given to them that *obey* Him." The work of the Holy Spirit gives us new sensitivity to the will of God. When the Spirit spoke to Philip at Samaria and to Peter on the rooftop about the Gentiles, reason had to go out the window—but they obeyed and revival broke out as the result.

The Holy Spirit and *prayer*: "prayer and supplication in the Spirit." The work of the Spirit affixes a new attention and concentration to our prayer. It is Him working in us. God will reveal to us His will and purpose in our Spirit-directed prayer.

It is the "Holy Spirit and..." that keeps us overflowing.

Walking In The Spirit

"Speaking to yourselves in psalms and hymns and spiritual songs, singing and making melody in your heart to the Lord." —Ephesians 5:19

There are all kinds of good books available today on the Spirit-filled life, how to walk in the Spirit and others. But perhaps the best material on "How do Spirit-filled Christians act?" is set forth in "the Book." In Paul's letter to the church at Ephesus after commanding them to be continually filled with the Spirit, he gives outgrowths of the Spirit-filled life.

Our text is the first outgrowth—*a happy life*. Gone will be the grumbling, murmuring and complaining. The Spirit sweeps those things out of our life. He replaces them with a song in our heart—a new song and a new joy. It is the earnest of heavenly life.

The *spirit of thankfulness* is next: "Giving thanks always for all things." As we praise the Lord with melody in our heart, the Spirit gives us a fresh realization of the goodness of God. With the Spirit in control, the pressure's gone, anxiety is gone, formality is gone, and everyting tastes good.

Paul gives the next positive proof as *"submitting yourselves"* one to another in the fear of God. The Spirit reveals the truth that it is not by might or mental power but by the Spirit that God's work is accomplished. It puts everybody with the Spirit into the ballgame. All can and will be used of the Spirit in humility.

Finally, Paul says the outgrowth of the Spirit-filled life is relationships in proper order: "Wives submit yourselves unto your own husbands"; "Husbands love your wives"; "Children obey your parents"; "Servants be obedient to them that are your masters"; and "Master do the same...forbearing threatening." The outgrowth of the Spirit-filled life is to every area of our life not just in church. Only when we are in right relationship with God and others can we give and receive love.

Paul concludes this will make us "strong in the Lord and in the power of His might."

Growth In The Spirit

"Ye were sealed with the Holy Spirit of promise,Which is the earnest of our inheritance until the redemption..." —Ephesians 1:13, 14

The power of the Holy Spirit poured out through Paul had transformed the puny church at Ephesus into a zealous, active body of believers. To be expected, there were growing pains. But the same Spirit that had lifted their vision and given them unction for God's work would also channel them in moving together in God.

First, the Spirit *gives union* amidst difference of views: "For through Him we both have access by the one Spirit unto the Father." Never before had Jew and Gentile mingled together—the Spirit would be the great "common denominator." The Spirit-filled life is one of sacrifice, self-forgetfulness and brotherhood. This would leave room for different opinions, different cultures and various intellectual views. But in the Spirit, they would be united in the supremacy of Jesus and Christ's concern for the lost and His pity for the poor. They could labor and love together.

Second, it would be the Spirit that *would feed* and *teach*: "Strengthened with might by His Spirit in the inner man." Paul's great concern was for the inner man. If he can only get that strengthened, the rest will follow. If the "spirit" is rich, the soul will be properly clothed for eternity. But if the spirit loses its savor, what good is it?

Third, there must be a *sensitivity* to the Spirit: "Grieve not the Holy Spirit." The Spirit is the great monitor of divine love. When the flow of love is cut off, the Spirit is grieved—even as the Father was grieved over man's sin. It was the divine in Christ to suffer for us, it was the undivine in us to make Him suffer. The Holy Spirit shares the divine with us—if we first do not share Christ's grief, we cannot share His joy.

Finally, the *supplication* of the Spirit will empower: "Praying always with all prayer and supplication in the Spirit." The Ephesians (nor us) would not be left to figure out their problems or even to pray indiscriminately about them. The Spirit would lead them into prayer in conformity to the will of God. The cry of the Spirit is "Thy Will Be Done." These are the lessons of the Spirit-led life.

The Spirit-Filled Life

"But the manifestation of the Spirit is given to every man to profit withal."   —*I Corinthians 12:7*

God wants every Christian to have not only the Holy Spirit abiding in Him and the comfort, guidance and daily help of the Spirit, but also the manifestation of the Spirit. It is the supernatural manifestation of the Spirit of God that is the spark to revival and renewal in the Church.

Charles Finney in his autobiography tells of the miraculous cure of an insane woman—she was instantly given the power to read the Word of God, though she never learned to read. It brought about a great revival in that community.

In one of the meetings of Dwight L. Moody, a man with a hip disease from his early youth was wonderfully healed instantly—at the age of 38. John Wesley reported in his journal instances of healing for his brother, himself, others and even his horse—all recorded as faith building in himself and others.

It is the same manifestation of the Holy Spirit in churches throughout the land that is bringing renewal in all the Christian denominations today. But no longer is the manifestation just for the great evangelist or preacher. It "is given to every man." The supernatural power of the Holy Spirit is available to work in and through every believer.

The Holy Spirit is only limited by our own manifestation. The Spirit manifestation is shut down when we manifest pride and human endeavor. The one precludes the other. Only when we fully yield to the Lordship of Christ can the Spirit work. He will work when we let Him!

The Administration Of The Spirit

"...the selfsame Spirit, dividing to every man severally as he will." —I Corinthians 12:11

The Holy Spirit, coming down to fill the place of the ascended Redeemer, has rightly been called, "The Vicar of Jesus Christ." To Him the entire administration of the Church has been committed until the Lord shall return in glory. His oversight extends to the slightest detail in the ordering of God's House—from the implementation of God's gifts to the government and the maturity of God's saints.

From the beginning of the Church, it was the Holy Spirit that appointed men in its ministry and government: "Take heed unto yourselves, and to all the flock in which the Holy Ghost hath made you bishops." Pastors and elders were given by divine appointment and not by some elective method or political maneuvering. In fact, all ministry was given of Christ: "And He gave some to be apostles, and some to be prophets, and some evangelists, and some pastors and teachers for the perfecting of the saints into the work of ministry, unto the building up of the body of Christ." All these offices were appointed by Christ but instituted through the Spirit whom He sent down to man: "We are builded together for an habitation of God in the Spirit."

Today, even as the disciples did in the appointment of Mathias as an apostle, man sometimes tries to get ahead of God and make his own appointment, all we have is a skeleton. Mathias is never heard from again, but two years later, God appoints a Saul of Tarsus, who would become the great apostle of the early Church.

The bodies found in the excavation of Pompeii were in a perfect state of preservation—and in the very postition in which death had surprised them but with the first blast of air, these dummies fell apart. The body (or church) may be perfect as far as the organs are concerned—prayer still offered, Bible still read, religious habits preserved—But without "the breath of God" it is just a corpse. When exposed to trial of temptation or final judgement, these corpses will be destroyed. Our dependence must be on the Spirit of God—the Administrator of all.

Discerning The Gifts

"Let the prophets speak two or three and let the other judge." —I Corinthians 14:29

Many ask how do spiritual gifts operate? Are the gifts and manifestations of the Spirit one hundred percent supernatural? When a person interprets a message in tongues, does that person interpret the message word for word?

There are two parts to spiritual gifts—the human and the divine. There are divine gifts but they operate through human channels. God's part is 100% supernatural but man's part is natural—subject to error and mistake. If prophecy and interpretation were 100% supernatural, they would be infallible and could not be judged. God recognizes the "human element" involved and commands in our text that these gifts be judged.

It is the Holy Spirit that inspires, energizes and moves the human instrument. The human shapes and gives expression to that divine energy. Therefore, interpretation is not verbatim translation but human phraseology to the divine message.

All prophecy and interpretation must be judged according to the revealed Word of God. Peter, who saw the glory of the transfiguration and heard the divine voice, says "we have yet a more sure word of prophecy"—the scriptures. God will never speak anything that opposes His revealed Word—even Jesus came to fulfill and not destory.

Paul further directs that any prophetic message will be either for edification, exhortation or comfort. Just as the teaching of God's Word, it offers (1) safety to ourselves and others, (2) glory to God and (3) edification of the Body.

The Gift Of Faith

"To another faith..."
—I Corinthians 12:9

There is a lot of discussion about which is the best of the spiritual gifts. The answer, I believe is simple—it is the gift that is most needed in that situation. There is one gift, however, that is needed and important continually. That gift is *faith*—for without it, we cannot please God.

All faith is given of God but the Bible distinguishes between saving faith and the gift of faith. Saving faith goes before salvation to the sinner and issues according to God's expected plan—in the fulfillment of promises concerning salvation. The gift of faith is received after salvation by the saint and issues in unexpected things—those which only faith expects.

The gift of faith is also distinguished from faith—the fruit of the Spirit, Faith, the fruit, is for the believer's character while faith, the gift, is for power. With faith, the fruit, God's children believe unto assurance and trust His Word in such a way that they obey His commands. With faith, the gift, saints believe God in such a way that God honors their word as His own and miraculously brings it to pass: "he shall have whatsoever he saith."

We see the gift of faith in operation in the scriptures in several ways. First, it can produce direct supernatural blessing in fulfillment to human utterance as in the case of Issac blessing Jacob. God will honor the word of faith as His own creative word. Then the gift of faith may be for personal protection in perilous circumstances. Daniel stopped the mouth of lions by faith and Paul shook off the venomous snakebite without harm by faith. We also see it providing supernatural sustenance in famine for Elijah and in fasting for Elijah, Daniel and our Lord. We see it receiving the supernatural promises of God by Abraham and Sarah. We see it producing victory in battle with the helping hands of Aaron and Hur, and finally, we see it setting the captive free as Jesus and the apostles cast out the evil spirits.

The gift of faith is still needed today to subdue the world and establish it for His Glory!

Tongues

"divers kinds of tongues..."
—I Corinthians 12:10

This gift of the Holy Spirit is the most widely discussed and controversial of all the manifestations of the Spirit to the Church. Apparently it was the same case in Paul's day—for he devoted an entire chapter to it while to most other gifts, he devoted but a phrase. Rather than trying to decide whether it's the greatest or least of the gifts, it is helpful to see what the gift is and its value to the believer from the scriptures.

The gift of tongues is the supernatural utterance by the Holy Spirit in languages never learned by the speaker. It is not understood by the mind of the speaker and usually not understood by the hearer. It has nothing to do with linguistic ability or man's intellect. In manifesting this gift man's will is active, as well as his spirit and speech organs but his mind is at rest. The Lord Jesus, Himself, instituted this miraculous gift: *"In My Name* they shall speak with new tongues."

The Bible gives speaking of tongues as the common initial scriptural evidence for the Baptism in the Holy Spirit. In every case except one recorded in Acts where believers were baptized in the Holy Spirit, the outward evidence was speaking in tongues. What sweet, assurance!

This gift enables man to speak supernaturally to God: "in the Spirit he speaketh divine secrets." There is deep in the believer's life that which finds expression and release in speaking in tongues. Only this heavenly language can provide emotional expression for the love within our souls in His presence so that we may fully "magnify God." This is a common error peddled about the day of Pentecost that those filled were preaching to the foreigners. They weren't speaking unto men but magnifying God. This magnification in the Spirit is for our personal "edification." It is an exercise of our spirit that helps in the redemptive upbuilding of God in our lives. As we pray in the spirit, it provides rest for the weary mind and nerves, "This is the rest and refreshing."

Finally, it is a valid gift along with the interpretation of tongues for the church to be edified. As manifested in the church, it is the direct appeal of the Spirit of God and is a supernatural sign to the unbelieving. This brings conviction and opens the spiritual ears for the word of edification in interpretation. Is there any doubt that this gift is profitable to all? "I would that ye all spake with tongues."

Use Of Tongues In Public Worship

"How is it then, brethren? when ye come together, everyone hath...a tongue..."
—*I Corinthians 14:26*

Much of the controversy today over the gift of tongues involves its use (and/or misuse) in public gatherings of worhip. There is still much misunderstanding although the Bible gives clear direction for its use.

The first misunderstanding is where the gift should be used. There is a private use of tongues for personal edification. But in public, the gifts of inspiration (including tongues) are given exclusively for the edification of the church—that company of believers, filled with the Holy Ghost. They have no mention or purpose in an evangelistic service.

The use of this gift is by faith. Some think that one must be physically "moved-on" by the Spirit. Paul warns that the gifts may be neglected, so we should "stir up the gift" that is in you—exercise it.

We can and ought to control the gift of tongues: "the spirits of the prophets are subject to the prophets." The Lord has placed upon us the responsibility for the due restraint as well as the due operation of the gift. Paul in I Corinthians 14 gives us clear guidelines: First, though all can speak at once in other tongues, we shouldn't. Second, there should be two or at most three messages in tongues and each *must* be interpreted. If there is no interpretation, the gift musy be withheld.

The confusion with the gift of tongues arises not from God but rather from man's neglect of God's word. But the encouragement to the church is that only where there is life is there danger of disorder. Paul says, "forbid not to speak in tongues." In other words, it is much better to learn even with mistakes to use the gift properly than to prohibit its use.

The final test of proper employment of this gift is always edification. "Let all things be done...unto edifying...decently and in order."

The Spirit Of Infirmity

"There was a woman which had a spirit of in-firmity eighteen years, and was bowed together, and could in no wise lift up herself." —Luke 13:11

Here in scripture was a case of eighteen years of helpless paralysis and deformity—just about a chronic a case as could be brought to the "Great Healer." As Luke, the physician, describes it, this woman was bound by something more than the paralysis of body—the spirit of evil that spawns with disease, that saddens and blights and tortures and torments God's creatures. No amount of sympathy and encouragement could break that grip—only the manifest power of Christ!

Jesus reveals the cause of this woman's disease: "Satan hath bound her." He charges the devil with her unhappiness and misery. We all need to know our enemy—he that "comes to kill, deceive and destroy." To this in-firmity, Jesus replies: "Ought not this woman being a daughter of Abraham be loosed from this bond?" That "ought" tells all about God's feeling toward healing. God wills to heal all who believe. The expression "daughter of Abraham" suggests faith, a faith which, like Abraham's, believed without sight, and in the face of seeming impossibilities.

Her faith produced results; Jesus declared the work done— "Woman, thou art loosed from thine infirmity." The word of faith broke the devil's grasp—he must obey the word of Christ. Jesus laid his hands upon her and completed the work: "She was made straight and glorified God."

This is God's will for all of us to walk tall, happy and glorifying God—free from the spirits of infirmity.

Healing The Hurts

"And he stood over her, and rebuked the fever; and it left her; and immediately she arose and ministered unto them."   —Luke 4:39

Is God interested in little hurts and ills of life? With so many careful and gentle actions, Jesus answers with a dynamic, "Yes."

Coming back from the synagogue, Jesus and the disciples visit Peter's mother-in-law, only to find her sick with a fever. Now this was a case of a very ordinary disease. Jesus comes to her and He doesn't offer her an aspirin or give her some orange juice and tell her to rest. He recognizes the agency back of the fever; He rebukes the fever, affirming that it is the blistering touch of a demon. Today with picturesque diagrams and explanations, commercials would tell of natural reasons why we get headaches and fever and why we need their product. But *Jesus would not rebuke a mere natural law.*

Something had opposed her will and dragged her down for when Jesus rebuked her fever, this mother-in-law was healed as she took Jesus' hand and arose. She took hold of the Divine Power that reached out to her and immediately the fever left. Like her, we must meet His help.

Then she really got the victory in what she did in her new-found strength. She "ministered" unto Jesus and the disciples. This was the best proof of healing and the best use of it, too. Whether we are saved or healed, it is unto good works. She got busy for Jesus.

Whatever our ill, whether unusual or ordinary, Jesus cares. In His name, we have power over the attacker of our body and soul. Rise to meet Jesus today.

A Suffering Savior

"Himself took our infirmities, and bare our sicknesses."   *—Matthew 8:17*

One of the worst and subtlest lies of the devil that is running around today says: "It is hypocritical to confess that you are healed if you still feel any pain or symptoms." Never once during Jesus' life did He confess or complain of sickness; yet during all His ministry on earth He was suffering our sicknesses. The Old Testament prophet Isaiah describes Him as "a Man of pains and acquainted with sickness."

How revealing was this Old Testament Hebrew! "But only *our* diseases did He bear and our pains He carried. Yet did we esteem Him stricken, smitten of God and afflicted." Our Lord did not take these enemies of our health and happiness in some theological or mystical way. He took them just like He took the slap across the face in the court of the High Priest by the officers. *He took them and did something with them literally.*

His whole ministry then was one of continued suffering until it culminated in the the Garden of Gethsemane in "bloody sweat" which is known to medical men today as a deadly disease. In Matthew 26:38, Jesus tells His disciples, "My soul is crushed with anguish to the point of death." That it was the bearing of our diseases which crushed Him, is confirmed by the exact translation of Isaiah 53:10, "It pleased the Lord to crush Him through disease." He was bearing our diseases *before* He went to the Cross and would have died a premature death there had He not been saved by the agonies of prayer: "having been heard for His godly fear."

Again before He went to the Cross, He bore our diseases for "it is by His stripes we are healed." In Isaiah the Spirit of Christ says again, "I gave my back to the smitters and My cheeks to them that plucked off the hair. I did not hide My face from shame and spitting." In Psalms again, "The plowers plowed upon My back, they made long their furrows."

Therefore, to claim healing in Jesus' Name today is not a theological argument, it is a real and literal provision of Jesus' suffering for us.

The Power To Heal

"...for I am the Lord that healeth thee."
—Exodus 15:26

One of my favorite stories of healing comes from my father who was a Methodist circuit rider in Western Canada. He was introduced to the miraculous healing power of our Lord today through the testimony of Dr. A. B. Simpson, a Presbyterian minister from New York City. Dad tells this story of Dr. Simpson's life.

Dr. Simpson had long been a dedicated minister of a large city church but had collapsed of heart trouble. Specialists had told him that there wasn't enough constitutional strength in him to last more than a few months. In the weakness of body and soul came the words of the song: "My Jesus is Lord of Lords: No man can work like Him." And with no one else to help or guide, He searched the scriptures until he became convinced that part of Christ's glorious gospel to all who would believe was divine healing. And that conclusion brought action!

Raising his hands to heaven, he made three vows. First to accept the truth of God's Word in regard to healing and not question it again. Second, to use this blessing for the glory of God and good of others by sharing it in any way possible. Third, to commit the rest of this life and strength to God's service and keeping. What happened as the result of these vows? Dr. Simpson says, "I arose and immediately I knew something was done. Every fiber of my soul was tingling with the sense of God's presence. I did not know whether my body felt better or not, but I was Healed."

Dr. Simpson's healing was tested only days later when he was invited to join a group hiking to a nearby mountain peak. It was a step of faith but in the climb, "Divine strength reached out to me if I would take it, claim it, hold it and persevere in it." Dr. Simpson labored for many years afterwards and was responsible for many godly revivals.

Divine healing is ours for the asking and claiming.

The Word Of Healing

"He sent his word, and healed them..."
—Psalms 107:20

In creation, God said and "there was." He *spoke* creation into being. The writer of Hebrews confirms, "that the worlds were framed by the Word of God." There is Power in what God *says*! The Bible is more than beautiful literature, poetry and doctrine—it is creative.

The famous saying goes, "the pen is mightier than the sword." But unless there is motive action behind the words, they are dead. God promises to move all heaven and earth to perform His Word. "I will hasten (look after, stand by) My Word to *perform* it." "There hath not failed one word of all His good promise." When God speaks today, all the creative power that spoke the world into existence again goes into action. God's Word today is just as powerful: "The Word of the Lord endureth forever."

God's Word becomes alive, takes action in the medium of faith. Faith is action: "Faith without works is dead." It does not talk—it always acts. It is substance; it is evidence.

God's Word says, "Let there be..."; "Rise and be healed..."; "Receive..."; "Extend.." What is our response to that word? Our attitude to the Word of God means everything. Remember faith acts. Rise to meet God at His Word. Release your faith into action.

Jesus said, "Nothing shall be impossible unto you." We have the authority to say and act upon: *"Let This* be done in Jesus' Name." This is creative faith.

Opening Blind Eyes

"The blind receive their sight..."
—*Matthew 11:5*

Josephus, the great Roman historian, records that blindness was a common afflication during the time of Jesus. Jesus perhaps healed hundreds or thousands of blind people: "He healed all that came to Him." However, three individual cases of blindness healed are described in the scriptures.

First, Jesus healed the blind man at Bethsaida as described in Mark 8. The first thing that Jesus did was take this man by the hand and lead him out of town—away from his own security. The man had to learn to trust Jesus in the dark before trusting Him in the light. Jesus then began the work of healing with a simple anointing to His eyes. The result was healing but only partial; he said, "I see men as trees walking." Perfect sight came only when he looked up—at Jesus.

The second blind man healed by Jesus is described in John 9. Blind from birth, he afforded Jesus the opportunity to show God's love and redemptive power to lost humanity. To accomplish the healing here, Jesus tested the man's complete obedience by anointing his eyes with a clay and spittle mixture and commanding him to wash in the pool of Siloam. When the man plunged by faith into the pool, he was healed. And then his healing was seriously tested by the Pharisee questioning but he kept the healing by his confession of faith.

Jesus' healing of the blind beggar Bartimaeus is described in Luke 18. Bartimaeus cried out to Jesus until he was heard. He may have been blind physically but he wasn't blind spiritually. He could see that Jesus was the rightful "Son of David" and the giver of mercy. His persistent faith brought the answer. He knew what he wanted and what Jesus could do for him. Jesus spoke the word, his sight was restored and he followed Jesus.

Here are three different means of healing—but all looking in faith to Jesus.

Hindrance To Healing

"If the prophet had bid thee do some great thing, wouldest thou not have done it? how much rather then, when he saith to thee, Wash, and be clean?"
—II Kings 5:13

Many people today are looking for divine healing—but on their own terms. Before the divine touch will come, the proud self-will must be dealt with—this is the message of our text.

Naaman, the mighty leader of the army of Syria, was a courageous and honorable man, but he had leprosy. He had heard that Elisha was a prophet of God and went to see Elisha to ask him to entreat God in his behalf. Without as much as a personal greeting, Elisha sends the simple and humble message by messenger to wash seven times in the Jordan and be clean.

How humbling! But the proud self-will of Naaman must die before his body could be healed. It was Naaman's servant that gives the wise counsel of our text. Proud old Naaman rebelled at the way of the Cross. He wanted (like many today) religion and healing to be carried on a higher plain and a social level in keeping with his station in life. But there is only one way to victory; that is the way of the Cross.

The faith of Naaman consisted in his doing just what the prophet told him. When he took God's way without gratification and persevered in it, a perfect cure came. He humbled himself, pressed on, and was healed.

Naaman's healing lifted his horizon. He took home two mule loads of Canaan soil to use in worshipping the Lord—just like we in our healing, receive the earnest of the Spirit—a part of heaven begun on earth. It's the soil of Canaan—a foretaste of Glory; the pattern of things eternal.

When the victory's won, self-will is no problem; the vision is moved much higher. O, the blessing of it.

MAY:
Communicating with Father

*"Praying always with all prayer and sup-
plication in the Spirit, and watching
thereunto with all perseverance and supplication for all saints;" —Ephesians 6:18*

Partners in Prayer

"Again I say unto you, That if two of you shall agree on earth as touching anything that they shall ask, it shall be done for them of my Father which is in heaven." —Matthew 18:19

The most wonderful thing in the world is to have that sweet assurance that God is able and willing to take care of every need we have. As part of a singing group that has been together for many years, our lives and those of our families have been knit closely together. We have not been immune to the trials and storms of life.

I think the group has experienced about every kind problem you can think of—financial, health, family struggles, attacks from satan, grief, etc. But through the years we've learned to lean on the promise of this verse and take

Ben Speer
Music Artist

each problem to God in prayer. God has answered prayer every time — sometimes they were big miracles and other times it was just something small but special. I believe that everyone who will believe this promise will also find God always faithful.

Wait on God

"But they that wait upon the Lord shall renew their strength, they shall mount up with wings as eagles; they shall run and not be weary and they shall walk, and not faint. —Isaiah 40:31

Stuart Hamblin
Singer, Writer

This scripture is precious because God indeed did lift me up and gave me new strength that I never knew was available. God's strength is much greater than anything the world can offer.

The Lord made this verse precious and gave me a song about it, so I could really thank Him for it.

The Mind of God

"But we have the mind of Christ."
—I Corinthians 2:16

What a tremendous thought! When we are in right relationship with Jesus, He thinks His thoughts through us through prayer, through the Word of God, through meditation, and through time spent with Him. God does move upon our minds as we give them to Him and He impresses His thoughts upon us. The Spirit of God will come upon your mind, take over your thinking power and through the Holy Spirit we are enabled to think the thoughts of Christ.

Robert Gass
Pastor

As our mind is the servant of the will, God does not do awaywith our thinking faculties: He harnesses them and works through them. You "have an unction from the Holy One and ye knew all things," for "it is God that worketh in you both to will and to do of His good pleasure." God not only works in our minds, but He consecrates our desires so our thoughts are directed properly and positively.

Communion With God

"And Abram fell on his face: and God talked with him..."   —Genesis 17:3

About the only thing that bothers worldly people more than the miracles of the Bible, is the idea that people actually have conversations with God. That is completely foreign to them. Our text states that God talked with a man and implies that a man talked with God. It doesn't say God talked *to* him but rather talked *with* him.

This is only one instance of many where God talked with Abraham. It is a common experience in the Bible. All the great biblical characters talked with God. So the question arises, "Does God still commune that way with men today?" What do we mean by communion with God?

The character and nature of God affirms this communion. God is a person and therefore, He can speak. He is a spirit and therefore, speaks to the spirit. The Bible record shows He loves man and desires companionship with him. His role is the father and that role would be meaningless were He not able to contact His children. And finally He is infinitely all-sacrificing, so His place of power does not prevent His condescending to men of low estate.

The nature of man affirms this same communicability. Man is a person and a spirit, created in God's image. That creation includes the power of speech inwardly as well as verbally. The Bible record of the glories of the Garden of Eden is not so much the beautiful landscapes but beautiful fellowship and communion between man and his God. Sin separated man from that communion.

Christ's atonement restores us to that communion and fellowship: "I will come in and sup (fellowship) with Him." The work of Christ was to bring us back into communion: "In these last days *spoken* unto us by His son." God is a speaking God unlike false gods. All our spiritual worship implies communion with God and therefore, includes waiting and listening for God's voice as well as speaking. "Be still and know that I am God."

Prayer

"But prayer was made without ceasing of the church unto God for him." —Acts 12:5

An investigative reporter is trained to always ask these three questions: Why? How? And what was the outcome? When we read and study the unsearchable riches of God's Word, it is often good to do the same thing.

Our text provides a great opportunity for an investigative look at prayer. The *why* of their prayer is first, they felt the utter need to do so. Sometimes we pray with reservations. If God does not help, we can manage in some way without Him. Our need is not sufficiently pressing, but this is not the case here. And second, they believed God. It was not praying for God to do something they could do or praying for their own desire, it was prayer for God's work—cooperative prayer.

How they prayed is significant. First, they united in prayer. Unified prayers are established. Pentecost came by unified prayer. Second, they prayed specifically. Their request was definite, so they could be expectant of the answer. And they prayed earnestly, without ceasing. God has always put a premium upon persistence: "The earnest, energized prayer of a righteous man." In each discourse on prayer in the Gospels, Jesus emphasized persistence. And finally they prayed *to God*. They fixed their eyes not on their difficulties but on the possibilities.

The outcome of their prayer was the release of the Power of God upon him for whom they prayed. Simon Peter was in prison and about to be executed by the same wicked Jewish leaders that crucified Christ. Simon was not always a brave man but their prayers brought the peace of God to Peter. And then they miraculously set him free. The angel drew him out of prison and safely back to the church. It was a time of rejoicing for all. It did as much for those who prayed as for Peter.

Prayer is still doing something for the world!

Why Pray?

"My house is the house of prayer..."
—Luke 19:46

A pastor friend of mine related this experience of his, where a young lady sent him money confidentially that she wanted lent to a boy friend of hers who was going through college and preparing for the ministry. She asked the pastor to keep it a secret. As time went on, she invested several thousand dollars in this young man's education and was determined that her boy friend was to know nothing of the real facts of the matter until after they were married. Her reasons were understandable. She did not want to be haunted by the thought that he may have married her out of a sense of obligation. She wanted his love only if it were a result of true devotion and appreciation.

Today we have many books, sermons, and exhortation about prayer. But the bottom line says the only real value in being a Christian is because you want to be one, and only real value of prayer is because you want to commune with God!

There are formulas for prayer, suggestions for prayer, and testimonies of prayer. But the greatest reason for prayer lies in the opportunity offered by the Creator of the universe to join with Him in His creative work. The person who prays for this reason comes to practice day by day the presence of God. God's concerns are his concerns. His way of life is such that it is in harmony with what he believes to be the will of God. He is united with God in a sense of service through which his spirit finds a fellowship with God's Spirit.

Books and sermons can only stimulate just as viewing a sports event can stimulate participation. One cannot learn to swim by just thinking and talking about it, or learn to play golf by watching it on TV. We learn to swim by swimming. The same is true with prayer. One never comes to appreciate prayer, to understand it, to make it a reality within his own life, unless one prays.

Even if prayer was nothing more than talking to oneself, it would be worthwhile—by the practice of putting one's mind on positive values. But it is communicating with a living and loving God. Let's find time to pray today.

He Prayeth

"Inquire in the house of Judas for one called Saul, of Tarsus: for, BEHOLD, HE PRAYETH,"
—Acts 9:11

The grace of God was perhaps never more gloriously displayed than in the conversion of St. Paul. The change that occured in him was so sudden and remarkable that the disciples of Christ at Damascus were afraid it was not real. To remove such suspicions, our Lord assures Ananias, their pastor, that Saul was indeed a changed man: "for, behold he prayeth." The one that breathed out threats and slaughter was now speaking forth prayer and supplication. *Behold he prayeth.*

How unusual that the Lord would pick this piece of evidence to convince Ananias of Paul's conversion. For Paul had always been a "praying" man. He had been a strict Pharisee. Therefore, he was one of those who "fasted twice a week" and "prayed standing in the synagogues and even on the corners of the streets." And they prayed over and over again, "thinking they would be heard for their much speaking." So prayer was not new to this Pharisee. But there was something very different in his prayers now from those of the past. In reality, he was just beginning to pray; before he had just been saying prayers. Now he was praying not to be seen of men but to be heard of God. Rather than lip service, Paul's prayers had become simple and sincere from his heart. Ananias would recognize the difference.

Saying prayers is still common today, drawing nigh with the mouth and honoring God with the lips, but the heart is far away. Nothing deserves the name of prayer unless it comes from the heart! It is not words that make prayer, it is our desires. Paul's prayer as a humble sinner for pardoning mercy got a quick answer. In the three days of physical blindness, his spiritual eyes were opened. He learned the law was spiritual and the goodness of God was the power of the Gospel.

This is the sign of every true believer: He prayeth from the heart.

Prayer Can Do The Job

"I exhort...prayers...for kings, and for all that are in authority..." —I Timothy 2:1, 2

Just before the end of World War II in early 1945, a group of Washington congressmen felt that President Roosevelt needed prayer because the future so greatly hinged upon his doing God's will. The group decided to send congressmen Walter Judd and Rufus Jones to see the President, but first, they all prayed. According to the secretary's report here is what happened:

"A picture of the President was placed beside a picture of Christ—in order for us to picture Christ speaking to Roosevelt. Men of different denominations knelt on their knees and offered powerful prayers for the President. The Holy Spirit came in such a mighty way, we all knew that heaven had heard and 'come down.' In another room the phone rang and the secretary of the President gave a long personal message to our host. All in the room took it as a signal that God had alerted the President in some way.

Congressmen Judd said, 'Prayer can reach Roosevelt better than our visit. Let us not attempt to give any solutions to the President. Prayer can do the job.'"

Do we believe that today? Prayer can do the job. In Washington today, congressmen kneel and pray in weekly prayer meetings for our President and all the leaders. These men recognize the utter need for God's direction and guidance for our land.

Do we have the same mind about our lives? Without prayer, we labor alone. Maybe we can get along in our job without any help in God, but our performance will not be nearly as capable as when we ask God's help and direction. The things which are impossible with man are possible with God—whether it be in national affairs or everyday matters.

Practicing What We Preach

"Men ought always to pray..." —Luke 18:1
"He prayed more earnestly..." —Luke 22:44

When we talk about the discipline of prayer, there are many theories and suggestions. But Jesus didn't give theories or suggestive doctrines. He lived it. So when He spoke on the subject, it was with authority, without doubt. His statements on prayer are positive and emphatic.

Christ faced the facts. He knew the nature of God and man and He knew the relationship between God and man. He knew man is not just a machine but is rather a free spirit under a friendly heavenly government that exists to help him. So He taught simply, "Men ought *always* to pray." Prayer is just like breathing. Even as breathing is a natural part of our physical life, so prayer is a part of the necessary and natural movement of the spiritual life. In breathing we don't go hunting for atmosphere, it surrounds us. So we are to accept God as Him in Whom we live, move and have our being and make prayer the natural, glad and constant expression of our relation to Him.

Our relationship with God is that of Father and child. Therefore, when God answers prayer, He is only doing the natural things as surely as an earthly Father will listen to the requests of his child and grant them when possible. "How much more will your heavenly Father give good things to them that ask Him?"

But prayer goes farther than asking; it builds friendship. Fatherhood is a matter of relationship and responsibility. Friendship is entirely free and voluntary. Jesus says: "You have a friend." In the illustration where Jesus tells the disciples that they should always pray, the conclusion is that if persistence can overcome human resistence, how much more will prayer to our loving Father be effective!

Cashing Checks

"Unto me who am less than the least of all saints, is this grace given, that I should preach among the Gentiles the unsearchable riches of Christ."   Ephesians 3:8

Recently a large city in our country reported that more than 10 million dollars a year were lost by businessmen in that city on worthless checks. Passing forged or worthless checks now accounts for one out of six felonies committed in this country. Banks and law authorities are seaching for new ways to stop this thievery.

In prayer, we sometimes too try to pass worthless checks. This little story illustrates the fact: "Some time ago a young woman gave her heart to God but soon her love for the Master cooled, and she found herself back in worldly ways and companions. Then suddenly, her father became critically ill and close to death. In desperation, she turned to the Bible and found the promise 'ask what ye will and it shall be done unto you.' That seemed a clear mandate, a check that could easily be cashed. But no answer came and her father passed away. This experience embittered the girl. She lost all faith and she later poured out her complaint to a minister.

But wisely he said to her: 'What would you think about someone who tries to cash a check that wasn't made out to them, but was made out to someone else?' Then he showed her that the promise she seized during her father's illness didn't belong to her. He read the *entire* promise: 'If ye abide in Me, and My words abide in you, ye shall ask what ye will...' She was not abiding in Christ so she had no legal right to expect her prayers to be answered."

There is always a condition to be met before a biblical promise can be realized. Heaven will never make payment on worthless checks. Just as bank requires identification before cashing a check, God asks for our credentials when we come to Him. We must come with His identification: "In Jesus Name—in Jesus authority." He has made the way for us and given us His endorsement when we come trusting in Him. There are riches sufficient for any demand in the account of our Lord.

A Strange Contrast

"(I) was IN the isle that is called Patmos...I was IN the Spirit..." —Revelation 1:9-10

There could hardly be a sharper contrast between the two environments of life described by these verses. For John, the one environment was Patmos a deserted, rugged, inhospitable little "Alcatraz" of an island, dreary and desolate. But along with this there was another unseen and yet vivid environment—John was living in a spiritual world, moving in heavenly places with Christ Jesus enjoying all the promises of God. It was in this latter environment that he was at home.

This picture is pertinent indeed to our daily lives. All of us find ourselves in one environment that is visible to the human eye; it may be an office, a sales lot, a kitchen or construction site. And then there is an environment that is unseen to any human eye. We may be in despair or expectation—in sin, chained by habit, or like John, *in the Spirit.*

When John awakened in the morning, across his vision broke stern unadorned hills, worked-out mines, total desolation. But in that same moment he was conscious of another environment. Here is the beauty of living—to be spiritually alive and conscious of that unseen atomosphere that is all about us when we waken to the duties of the day. It is the love of God and divine encouragement and new mercy that greets our morning.

The one environment was not the apostle's choosing, the other depended on himself. John's natural home was Ephesus. He loved it there and was greatly loved by the people but the mighty arm of Rome had exiled him to this desolate place. One thing Rome could not take away from him was the love of God. In this great love, John found liberty in the midst of his prison. So too, we have things we cannot choose—our parents, much of our physical appearance. But we can choose *how* we will live. We may be handcuffed outside but we may be free as a bird inside. There is an atmosphere available to us all that satisfies, that overcomes the ugly, the lonely, the emptiness. It is found "in the Spirit."

Anointed To Preach By Prayer

"The Spirit of the Lord is upon me, because He hath anointed me to preach the Gospel to the poor..."
—Luke 4:18

Many, many Christian young people are questioning what God has for their lives. They go to Bible school and/or seminary, get educated and refined and wait for their "calling." They wonder whether or not God has called them to preach. Dr. John Rice, the Baptist evangelist, spoke to the heart of this question, "It is not a question of whether you have ever been called to preach. It is a question of whether you have ever been *anointed* to preach, whether the power of God is on you and whether you are filled with the Holy Ghost. That's the issue."

Before the Spirit baptism at Jordan, Jesus was a good man. He was always at church, read the Bible and was subject to His parents. But he never preached or won any souls. After Jordan, the Gospel writer proclaims, "Jesus returned in the power of the Spirit into Galilee and there went out a fame of Him through all the region round about." What had happened? The Spirit of God filled him and now He was anointed to preach.

It is one thing to go to church, pray, read your Bible and even have a family altar; it is another thing to accomplish things for God's kingdom. Our religion needs an anointing. There's an enduement from on high that has been and always will be the key to success.

The New Testament Church discovered the way to get this enduement—*they Prayed*. Even after they had been filled with the Spirit, they gathered and prayed. Chapter Four of Acts gives this account: "When they prayed; they were filled with the Holy Ghost and spoke the word of God with boldness."

If we want to have confidence and boldness in our witness and in our work, let us pray for the "anointing."

Praying In The Spirit

"But ye, beloved, building up yourselves on your most holy faith, PRAYING IN THE HOLY GHOST."
—Jude 20

It is well said that we are getting down to business when we pray. It is not so well said to say that we are in the praying business. Man is a "praying animal." The Bible says that, "O thou that hearest prayer, unto thee shall all flesh come." Unsaved men even pray. All nations pray. There is a universal sense of need and weakness that leads men to cry out for help to a Higher Power. But there is one kind of prayer that is needed most: "Praying in the Holy Ghost."

Prayer in the Holy Spirit is believing prayer. Unconverted people have no part in this praying for no one can pray in the Spirit who is not indwelt by the Spirit. In Old Testament times, people prayed according to the Spirit as they were controlled by Him. But Jesus proclaimed a new privilege to believers: "He hath been *with* you. He shall be *in* you." This is our opportunity today of being filled with the mighty Spirit of God.

When we "pray in the Holy Spirit," we are directing our mind, our spirit, our body, toward God. The Holy Spirit is gentle and will never coerce our will. So we must direct our will to God before the Spirit can pray in us. Also, we must release our sin and pride before the Spirit can pray. He is easily grieved by sin. So we must first ask the Lord to forgive and cleanse us, so the Spirit can be free to pray in us by His mighty power.

As we humbly direct our will to God and yield our mental and physical facilities to the Spirit, the Spirit will pray through us to bring us needed strength, needed direction, and confidence, worthy of praise and divine love. This is being built up in holy faith.

How To Relax

*"When thou prayest, enter into thy closet, and
when thou has shut the door..."*   Matthew 6:6

Row upon row of beautiful trees were uprooted and destroyed in a wind storm. The reason? The water was too near the surface, so the trees did not have to put their roots deep down to find water. Therefore, the tragedy occurred.

Prayer is a deep thing. It reaches through the surface tension of the body and mind to the heart and spirit. There, it communes with the living God, strengthening the soul to weather the storms of life.

To enter this deep communion, we must say to the *brain*, "you are now in the presence of God. Let go and listen. He speaks and I will listen." To the *eyes*, "close and inwardly see nothing except Him unto whose presence you have now come. He touches my eyes and they are no single." To the *nerves*, "relax—your God comes with good news—the news of redemption."

As I enter into prayer, I recognize my mind is being renewed. It no longer rests on itself. It comes into assurance beyond itself in the presence of God. Its antenna reaches up for His love: "my soul, wait only upon God. For my expectation is from Him." "The Lord is good unto them that wait for Him—to the soul that seeketh Him." The mind learns to relax and refresh itself in God's goodness—nothing that comes from God in prayer will harm or injure. The Lord is good.

Prayer is a secret companionship for the believer. There is no fear of disappointment: "He who believes in Him will never be disappointed." In prayer, we learn a deeper happiness than that based on fleeting happenings. That is shutting the door. We find happiness with Him, so even in the storms when the things about are stripped away, we can go on because He is still there with us. "And I will bring the blind by a way that they knew not. I will lead them in paths they have not known. I will make the darkness light before them, and crooked things straight."

Two Sources Of Strength

"In quietness and in confidence shall be your strength..." —Isaiah 30:15

In our modern electronic world, we are constantly bombarded and surrounded with noise around us. In fact, in a recent survey with young children, one of the most frightening noises to them was *silence*; we have become so bathed with noise.

But quietness is not just a luxury but a necessity in a normal life. It restores depleted vitality and builds up a resistive power. But its greatest value is to take us beyond our surface living to the root source of our life. The deep things come from pondering and meditating and getting alone, giving God an opportunity to commune with us. This is the message of the Bible writer: "Be still and know that I am God."

There is a close relationship between quietness and confidence. One is not likely to exist without the other. The blustering, boastful, self-promoting persons lack confidence. They whistle in the dark to try to convince themselves. But the confident man naturally avoids useless effort to attract attention.

Unfortunately, many have never learned quietness. From childhood, they were never taught to be patient and to ask for things quietly and in turn. They grew up competing with television and other sounds for parents attention. In these kinds of lives, there is no peace and no quietness.

Jesus gives us our example for strength. His life called for exceptional activity, traveling from one end of the country to the other many times on foot. Speaking to multitudes and performing many miracles. In the midst he regularly sought the reviving power of quietness in the lonely mountain and solitary shore.

We need to get quiet in Him. We can find help and strength in His presence. Get alone somewhere with God today! You'll come away better equipped for life.

Casting Your Care

"CASTING all your care upon Him; for He careth for you."
—I Peter 5:7

I am convinced that most Christians do not know how to adequately give their problems and worries to God. They don't know the strength of the word *Cast*. The dictionary defines it as: to throw, hurl, shed, to condemn (such as cast into prison); to form or shape in the mold. So it would be quite proper to translate our text: "Hurling all your worry upon Him," or "Condemning all your cares upon Him," or "Molding all your worries upon Him." Isn't that wonderful? I especially like the last one. So many times we let our worries bend us out of shape and control our lives. Peter, by the Holy Spirit, says "Take control—shove all those worries into God's mold." Channel them, control them in Him and they won't be worries any more.

Dr. Norman Vincent Peale, the great positive thinker, tells how he learned to live without tension from a redcap: "My train was late and with ill-tempered impatience I grabbed the porter as I got off and said, 'Bring these bags quickly, I'm in a terrible hurry.' When the porter followed in his calm, easy style, I started steaming. But he calmed me, 'This is no way to make time.' With a big smile, he continued, 'You can do a lot in a short time if you just go along, easy-like at it. And besides, you'll live longer doing it.' I slowed down, got the things I needed done in time, enjoyed it more and learned an important lesson."

Our Lord offers us a care-free life today. Because He cares He gave us His Son. He knows our needs and He cares. Jesus, the mighty counselor will be happy to listen to your secret needs with sympathy and in confidence. Not only will you receive ease of mind and heart, but bodily health. "They that seek the Lord shall not lack any good thing."

Unanswered Prayers

"Ye have not, because ye ask not. Ye ask and receive not, because ye ask amiss, that ye may consume it upon your lusts." —James 4:2, 3

The young people have a term for this kind of talk. It's called, "telling it like it is." James says flatly, "Some people don't pray" and "others pray selfishly and don't get answered."

It is strange that any man, any believer, can live without prayer. It is something you cannot put a value on. You can only say, "try it." But then there is unanswered prayer. Why does that occur when God promises, if we ask, we will receive?

First, prayer is sometimes answered when we think it is not. "No" and "wait until later" are just as much answers as "yes." In our ignorance we may have asked for what God could not wisely and consistently give. We learn in our Christian experience that God sometimes closes doors for our good, and the good of others.

Second, prayer is not always unanswered when not answered immediately. There is a difference between clamour and faith. God says if we have patience we will receive the reward. We can not rightly tell the Giver, "how, when and where." We must trust His judgment. It's never easy to wait, but it is good for us. God is never too late or too early.

Third, we often count prayer as unanswered because the answer is not in the manner we had anticipated. God often has better plans for us. Paul learned that on his passage to Rome. God answers more than "we think or imagine."

But sometimes prayer is really unanswered. When we pray selfishly, (in our name and not His) there is no room for God to move. It is like asking God to be selfish. Then there are times when we don't pray honestly; God knows the desires of our hearts and we cannot play games with Him. And finally, "if we hide iniquity (rebellion) in our heart, the Lord will not hear us." Our conscience will stand in the way of God's answer every time. When we pray sincerely and patiently, God does give "to all men liberally and upbraideth not."

Victorious Praying

"And it came to pass, when Moses held up his hand, that Israel prevailed: and when he let down his hand, Amalek prevailed... And Aaron and Hur stayed up his hands..."   —Exodus 17:11, 12

In John Bunyan's great analogy of the Christian faith, *Pilgrim's Progress*, Christian encounters the adversary, Appollyon. Christian did not seek the quarrel; Appollyon went out to meet him and Christian could not avoid the encounter: "Appollyon straddled quite over the whole breadth of the way." So it is with us. The *way* out is always the way *through*. Sooner or later, we've got to make a fight of it.

Our text refers to Israel's first battle. And the battle was not Israel's choosing. It was forced upon them just as the devil comes looking for us. This battle exemplifies every spiritual tussle that we engage in. We have to have moral and spiritual resources at our command if we hope to win. While Joshua fought down on the plain, Moses was up in the mountain holding on in prayer. Joshua and his men knew that Moses was up there praying for them, and the knowledge of that made all the difference.

Joshua was fighting and Moses was praying, and the praying was the hardest job. You that have had experience in both can judge. Have you ever tried to concentrate in prayer on one particular issue even for an hour without interruption, without allowing the mind to wander? Prayer isn't any child's play.

If we want to pray victoriously, either for ourselves or others, we must "get down to it." Moses had to sit down to it. It was a long drawn out struggle. It involved concentrated effort. Prayer is the supreme effort of the will. It means complete yielding to the will of God and nothing else. Like Moses surely felt many times that day, we want to stop praying and rush down to battle. *We want to do something practical.*

But the outcome of the battle was determined not by the fighters, but by the "prayers." This is called patience and endurance. Even Moses needed help to continue in prayer. Until we will begin to pray seriously, we will not have total victory.

Intense Earnestness

"Peter therefore was kept in prison: but prayer was made WITHOUT CEASING of the Church unto God for him." —Acts 12:5

The actual Greek word translated, "without ceasing", means literally, "stretched-out-edly." The translators thought of the prayer as stretching out a long time. But there is an even greater meaning intended.

Did you ever see a foot race? The runners are toeing the mark waiting for the starting gun to sound. At the critical moment, the gun cracks and they go spinning down the track with every muscle *stretched* toward the goal and prize. This is the picture of our text, the church stretched out in intense earnestness toward God. It is the same kind of praying Jesus did in the Garden as Luke records: "and being in an agony He prayed *more* earnestly." This prayer was intense.

This is the kind of prayer to which God pays attention, and answers. Isaiah prophesies: "Ye shall seek me and find me, *when ye shall search for me with all your heart."* Many times we do not remember the prayers we make from one day to the next and we hardly know whether God has answered. This is not praying with our whole heart.

In Tibet they have what are called prayer-wheels. They have a little round brass cup on top of a stick, and it revolves when the stick is whirled. The Tibetian writes out his prayers, drops them in the cup, and whirls the stick while saying the prayer. Many of our prayers are similar except the wheel is in our head instead of on the stick.

How different when the Spirit of God comes and earnestly carries our petition heavenward. Paul asked the Romans: "that ye strive together with one in prayers to God for me." He is asking that they agonize in prayer for him. How many of us have agonized in prayer for our pastor or leaders or family this week. Fervent prayer in the Holy Spirit changes things and most of all, the people who so pray!

Fervent Prayer

"...fervent in spirit; serving the Lord;"
—Romans 12:11

No greater minister ever came from the state of Connecticut than one, David Brainerd. This man, who died before he was thirty and gave his life for the American Indians, did his greatest work by prayer. The forest was his prayer-chamber. Dependent on the power of God, he reached a people whom he didn't even understand their language.

Once he preached through a drunken interpretor—a man so intoxicated that he could hardly stand. Yet scores were converted through the sermon. The only way to account for it is the tremendous power of God behind him through prayer.

The marvellous missionary revival of the nineteenth century is due more to Brainerd's prayers than to any other thing. His great compassion for souls inspired Carey to go to India, McCheyne to the Jews, and Henry Martin to Asia.

From his youth, Brainerd was moral and religious. He was disciplined in prayer and reading the Bible but none of his good duties brought salvation until at the age of twenty he yielded his life completely by faith to God—entirely by the righteousness of Christ. That which is gained with difficulty is held precious. The salvation he had received, he longed to bring to others. He recorded this in his diary: "I felt a power of intercession for immortal souls, for the advancement of God's kingdom. He enabled me so to agonize in prayer that I was quite wet with sweat..though the wind was cold."

Brainerd prayed for a double portion of the Spirit like Elisha had. So though sick with tuberculosis, David traveled through wilderness, wandered over mountains, and drudged swamps to preach and testify of the Gospel. Revival did not come until two years before his death. But in those days, men, women and children saw a zeal, a fire of life that caused distress for their souls and deliverance in Christ.

On his death bed he declared, "I longed to be as a flame of fire, continually glowing in the Divine service, and building up Christ's Kingdom, to my dying moment." This is "fervent in spirit" and it comes by prayer.

Don't Quit

"And he (Jesus) spake a parable unto them to this end, THAT MEN OUGHT ALWAYS TO PRAY, AND NOT TO FAINT." —Luke 18:1

The word "faint" in our text could well be interpreted—"and not become *depressed*." Depressed means to become dispirited, lose heart, pressed down, or dejected. Christ recognized this as a dangerous mental and spiritual condition. And He said the only antidote and remedy was "to always pray."

The greatest weapon the devil has invented to counteract our spirituality is spiritual depression. This is because depression is a form of quitting. The person who yields to depression has really *quit inside* already. In their heart they have let down; they have adopted an attitude of "What's the use?" Many have made shipwreck of their faith not through gross sin but allowing depression to dominate them. No wonder Jesus warned the disciples.

Depression is not only dangerous, it is evil. When we grope in a state of gloom and become dispensers of gloom, it adds up to nothing less than a spirit of ingratitude and impudence. When we rebel against the goodness of God, we are in reality exhibiting a rebellious mood against God. How the devil loves to have a bunch of "Christian sadsacks" in God's army. Nothing suits his purposes better.

Therefore, satan assults our minds continually to try to make us discouraged. He is a great "psychologist"; he seldom attacks directly but approaches individuals according to their sentimentality. Paul says that we are not to be ignorant or unaware of His devices. We must watch our feelings and moods. Satan waits to catch us in the right mood. Only faith will resist his darts: "this is the victory that overcometh...even our faith."

We all experience unhappiness, hurts and disappointments. When these happen, let us follow biblical procedure; submit them (and ourselves) to God in prayer, resist the devil and he will flee.

The Stubborn Prayer

*"He gave them their request; but sent leanness
into their soul."* —*Psalms 106:15*

A pastor friend told me of a strange experience. He was in a home where a poor mother was laboring under the grief of caring for an imbecile son who did not so much as recognize her in the slightest way. She told the pastor that years before when he was a little baby in his cradle, he was taken ill with scarlet fever. The physicians gave him up, declaring there was no hope. In her rebellion, she told God that she would never love Him again if He took her child from her. The little one recovered but never recognized his mother again. Over the years, her rebellion broke and she told the pastor, "How much wiser would have been the prayer of Thy will be done."

The Bible is filled with blessings and promises to the persistent in prayer, but not to the *arrogant*. There is a demanding type of prayer that will not take "no" for an answer, which may bring results—but results that lead to our own hurt. We may find ourselves with prayers answered that we may wish we had never prayed.

The nation of Israel had to learn this lesson several times. In the wilderness when they got tired of manna, they kept up a continual whine for "flesh meat" until God stuffed it out of their nostrils and ears.

The Psalmist said, "They waited not for His counsel but tempted Him in the desert." Our text says that God gave them their request, but gave leanness to their souls. They had to tell God what to do and what they needed. When they got it, they weren't satisfied.

The same thing happened in their cry for a king. Finally, God gave them a king and their kings burdened the nation with taxes and corrupted the nation with idoltry. As Hosea the prophet proclaimed, how much better off if they had made God their King. How often we, too, would ruin ourselves if God let us have what we so earnestly desire.

Jeremiah shows us the proper attitude in prayer when he says: "O Lord, I know the way of man is not in himself—it is not in man that walketh to direct his steps. O Lord, correct me, but with judgment not in thine anger, lest thou bring me to nothing."

Thanks A Lot!

"Father, I thank thee that Thou hast heard me."
—John 11:41

There are not a lot of Jesus' prayers recorded in the Gospels. And in nearly all that the Gospel writers have recorded, there is one common word: "Thanks." It seems to be Jesus' basis for prayer. Someone has purposed a simple formula for prayer—Thank-confess-ask. *Thank* Him for His answers and grace, *confess* our sins, and *ask* Him for help and things we need.

When we start with thanksgiving, it makes prayer a lot easier. Find yourself in an attitude of thankfulness and the whole world will appear brighter to you. You won't find it difficult then to confess your faults when you stand in the light of His thoughtfulness and perfection of purpose.

Jesus' thankfulness came out of a security in the perfect will of God. Life was not guess work for Him. He saw God's finger pointing the way and confessed, "I do nothing except I see the Father doing." Therefore, He could be thankful.

Look at Him feeding the five thousand. Folk had come a long way to hear Him preach. He felt their hunger and weariness. He seated them in companies and organized His disciples as waiters. Then He took a boy's lunch and "said grace." What a joyous scene. The little that Jesus had, He was thankful for. And people who find themselves happy with what they have usually get more.

At Lazarus' tomb, Jesus stood confident. How can there be joy in the midst of grief? Jesus would weep. His humanity would yield to the sorrow of the hour. But then Jesus turned and thanked God in a loud voice. Prayer was answered and then the rest of the gatherers joined in Jesus' joy.

It is good to be thankful when prayer is answered, but it is divine faith to thank Him at the start in all things: "In everything give thanks, for this is the will of God in Christ Jesus concerning you."

Our Prayer List

"After this manner therefore pray ye..."
—Matthew 6:9

Many believers have prayer lists for those they wish to remember in prayer. It is helpful remembrance both for prayer and recording God's answers to our prayers. While the Bible encourages us to pray for all men, there are five classes of people that should be added to any prayer list.

First, *the sick*. Jesus' personal exhortation for us to pray for the sick should be sufficient. But, moreover, it is an expression of our Christian love and compassion to our fellowman. It warrants us to bring all our weak and suffering ones to Him that they may be made whole. Christ Himself never refused the prayer addressed to Him by loving hearts for the healing of disease: "He healed them all."

Second, *the children*. Christ teaches us by direct example when He placed His hands on the children brought to Him and prayed. As little children, their characteristics are being largely decided. We must pray that they will grow inclined toward God and ready to do His will. Our children are most susceptible to Satan's deceit; we must pray for their protection.

Third, *our fellow laborers in church*. Jesus often prayed for His disciples. And He carried all Christian people on His heart. As God's representatives, all believers have significant responsibility in the world. We must pray for the pastor, the elders, and one another.

Fourth, *those that despitefully use us*. Jesus commanded us to do this even as He did it Himself on the cross: "Father, forgive them, they know not what they do." This is often not easy for us. But it is the way the fruits of the Holy Spirit can be exercised in our lives. We give no place to the devil when we surrender our animosities and place coals of love on those who do us wrongly.

Lastly, for *laborers for Christ's harvest*. When Jesus saw the needs of the multitudes, there was but one answer, more workers. The need exists today. Do we care enough to notice the needs of the multitudes and pray for them to be met? If we are fully committed, we may not be able to go but we can "pray." Intercession awaits us.

Praying For Others

"...and pray one for another, that ye may be healed."
—James 5:16

One of the greatest callings in the Christian life is prayer for others. No one knows or will ever know until eternity comes, the evils that have been averted from human lives by the prayers of others. If you really love people, you will pray for them.

Such love was in Paul's heart for the Philippian Church. Paul prayed four great petitions for these whom he loved that do well to be part of our prayers for others.

First, "That your love may abound yet more and more in knowledge and judgment." To Paul, a loving disposition was the supreme product of Christianity. Paul prays that this will be their goals and direction and it be developed in knowledge and judgment. Knowledge means acquaintance with the facts of a situation. Judgment means discernment of the proper methods in which love should express itself. Affections can cause people to do silly and unwise things without thinking. Christians ought to love intelligently and wisely.

Second, "That ye may approve all things that are excellent." Paul prays that they may discern that which has eternal value. Deception is on every hand—Eve, Esau, even wise Solomon were all fooled. The eyes of our understanding need to be opened.

Third, "That ye may be sincere and without offense till the day of Christ." The word "sincere" literally means "without wax." At that time, some vases had cracks in them which were concealed by wax. But a sincere vase had no faults of any kind needing to be covered. Paul prays that they be genuine, free from flaws, sound and whole in every respect—able to stand the strongest inspection—the revelation of the day of Christ.

Fourthly, "Filled with the fruits of righteousness which are by Jesus Christ, unto the glory and praise of God." Paul prays that they be "filled"—active, zealous for righteousness. This is the victorious and happy life of a Christian—trusting Christ to make life abundant, creative, and filled with good things. Can we believe the same blessings for our loved ones?

Does It Help To Pray For Loved Ones?

"...but prayer was made without ceasing of the church unto God for him." —Acts 12:5

As firmly as I believe anything today, I believe in the effectiveness of undying prayer for our loved ones. Here is but one example of hundreds I've encountered where the prayer of faith has brought salvation.

Scott Lawrence, the great Gospel hymn writer, of "He Loves Even Me", "Whispering Prayer" and others was for many years the king of New York's secular song writers. He loved the adulation and in his pride played the part to the hilt. Only one thing was he denied, the girl he loved—Victoria Barnes. It wasn't that she didn't love him, but she loved God even more.

In their relationship, Victoria prayed that Scott would turn to God, but he wouldn't see his need. He begged Vicky to marry him with the plea that she could change him for right. But Vicky stood in faith pointing out that only God can change a person. Until Scott would acknowledge that Jesus is Lord, the marriage would never work; there must be only one God in the home—not two.

In his pride, Scott left Vicky and she did the only thing she could—she prayed and prayed. As much as he tried, Scott could not walk out of either her heart or her prayers. As pride goeth before a fall, so it went with Scott. Alcohol and cocaine soon filled his life and his career disappeared into playing piano for whiskey and dope. As Scott disappeared, Vicky sent out a net of prayers even to rescue mission around the country.

That net drew Scott in one rainy night. Having spent a stretch in prison and now totally miserable of his own deeds, he huddled under two broken boxes in an alley, when he heard a woman's voice from the past: "We can have a beautiful life, Scott, but you must turn to God—God loves you and so do I." That voice brought him to his need and he ran to the nearest rescue mission and received Christ. When he was established in Christ, he visited Vicky, who was still praying. They had five wonderful years of marriage and ministry together before God took Scotty home.

The prayer of faith will find its mark for your loved ones too. Presented before God's throne, it is zeroed in to some "Scott Lawrence" in your home or family or circle of friends. No one can escape its target.

The Prayer For Healing

"For ye have need of patience, that, after ye have done the will of God, ye might receive the promise."   *—Hebrews 10:36*

One of the most trying experiences for members of any local church is to see people pray for healing time after time, without being healed. To pass it off, saying that God works in mysterious ways is not good enough. James says clearly: "The prayer of faith will save the sick." Why then are some not healed?

First, our text says we must "have patience" after we do the will of God. When we have asked for prayer, anointing with oil and the laying on of hands, we have done the will of God. But we have no right to tell God, "how, when, or where." Sometimes we hear so many testimonies of instant healings that we look to the experience more than to God. Often the person sharing the testimony does not include the waiting and trusting that went before. Trusting God is an important part of salvation; so often God allows us to learn of this before our healing is complete.

Then we learn that "God worketh in us to will and do of His good pleasure." Our healing is to accomplish His will in us and to glorify Him. In His love, God chastens and corrects us—sickness and healing are channels for that correction. Often healing can be accomplished speedier when we consider, "What is God's will in me?" and "What is God's pleasure in me?" It should never be "How quick can I get well?" but always "How quick can I set forth His glory in this temple of clay?" God is not running a clinic. He is running a church.

Finally, God in His eternal perspective does not count time as we. Jesus arrived to "heal" Lazarus four days after his burial. Daniel had to wait three weeks for an answer to prayer. Abraham waited fifty years. Sometimes God is more greatly glorified in our waiting. But like three Hebrew lads, may we say, "If it be so our God whom we serve is able to deliver us." God can and will heal.

Distress Of Nations

"and upon the earth DISTRESS of nations,
with perplexity..."   *—Luke 21:25*

Jesus, the greatest of all prophets, foretold that this sign—"Distress of Nations," would mark the end-time just before His Second—Coming. Can anyone deny this is the world's lot today? What nation if not at war is not in distress? Crime, hunger, economy, defense, racial tension, political unrest are common to all.

God places the responsibility of the condition of a nation on the shoulders of His people there. Christians know where distress comes from. And the Bible gives us a picture of how to deal with distress in a nation. It is found in the book of Esther. The "rotten" Prime Minister Haman had cooked up a devilish scheme to try to destroy the plan and purpose of God. Esther and her cousin, Mordecai, picture so well the people of God, valient and strong in battle and guided by the wisdom and counsel of the Holy Spirit.

We see how Queen Esther "wrestled" with the evil designs of Prince Haman. So must God's people "wrestle against the evil power and principalities" that work distress among the nations. Even though the "prince of evil," Haman, had sinister messengers on their way to every province of Persia to destroy God's people, yet *God intervened*. He dealt with the Emperor, himself in a sleepless night.

It will not take us any longer than Esther to win the battle against the Adversary today if we, like her, use the weapons which are not carnal but mighty through God to the tearing down of Haman's scaffolds.

First, Esther jeopardized her own life. Then Esther prayed and fasted, and encouraged others to do so. It was serious business; Esther didn't stop praying until she was sure that God would undertake. Then she went forward for the cause of righteousness. And peace was accomplished.

The "Distress of Nations" can only be solved this way.

Confusion

"The CITY OF CONFUSION is broken down: every house is shut up, that no man may come in. There is a cry for wine in the streets; all joy is darkened, the mirth of the land is gone. In the city is left desolation..."　　　　　—Isaiah 24:10-12

In a large city, a mother of three went to police for protection against her husband who threatened to kill her. They said it would cost her $75/a day. Two days later she and her children were brutally killed by her husband. This is desolation.

Reading our text, one wonders how Isaiah some three thousand years ago could see into New York City, Philadelphia, Mexico City: the big cities of today. But how accurate a picture.

Our cities are being broken down by bankruptcy and beaucratic confusion and corruption. The houses and businesses are shut up by the strangling and fettering of labor strikes. Whole sections of cities are headquarters for human debris, drunkenness, prostitution, criminals, and homosexuals. The spread of greed and crime puts all joy and things of value darkened under lock and key—fear reigns. This is the picture of desolation—and it is becoming the picture of many cities today.

Men have built this tower of Babal (confusion); now what can be done? Like Job said, "They were confounded because they had hoped." Men have built on wrong hopes and the result is disappointment and confusion. Can anything be done? God's word says, "God is not the author of confusion (tumult and unquietness), but of peace." So, men must first recognize their folly and repent, asking God's help.

Then God says if we return to Him, we'll not be confounded; "For the Lord God will help me; therefore shall I not be confounded." "They cried unto thee and were delivered: they trusted in thee and were not confounded." God will deliver our cities if we honor Him and pray!

Praying For Our Nation

*"Except the Lord build the house, they labour
in vain that built it: except the Lord keep the city,
the watchman waketh but in vain."* —Psalms 127:1

Heaven help us if we ever forget who built this great country of ours.
And it seems that many have. Somehow they get the idea that it was built
and kept by some kind of diplomatic wizardry. These diplomatic souls
believe that no one should ever have to be offended, so prayer must be
removed from school, from council meetings, from international affairs,
etc. And we must so subvert ourselves to cater to everybody, no matter
who or what they stand for.

How different from our nation's founding. Our forefathers had a
sense of the Almighty, like David: "I will fear no evil, for thou art with
me." When evil came, they boldly stood against it, throwing the tea over-
board, proclaiming liberty under God for all men.

Our community will be different; our nation will be different, when
we regain a sense of the Almighty. The Bible is full of promises: "Honor
Me and I will honor you." "Seek the kingdom of God and His
righteousness first and all these things shall be added." Any government's
declaration of their need of God and His guidance, help and favor, will
bring with it a reward that can be passed right on down to the lowliest
citizen of that community.

Men who acknowledge their dependence upon God and their responsibility toward God will be better lawmakers. A new sense of the power of
God will give us *men* in public office and not timid diplomats—men who
stand for righteousness and fear not evil.

Just as Israel prevailed when Aaron and Hur supported Moses' hands,
our leaders will prevail in righteousness only when God's people pray for
them and encourage them unto righteousness and rebuke if need be, any
approval of evil.

In God We Trust

*"There is no power but of God; the powers that
be are ordained of God."* —Romans 13:1

In regard to national allegiance and respect, our present generation
has recently struggled through one of the most trying periods in American
history. Yet we very well may be like the little fellow who was climbing on
the roof and before he got to the top he began to slip. As his descent
quickened and he came nearer to the edge, he thought he had better pray a
quick, short desperate prayer; so he cried, "Dear God, help me!" Just then
his trousers were caught by a nail and his downward progress stopped.
And the little fellow said, "Never mind God, I'm all right now." Our national attitude has just about reached that stage.

We have let a tiny minority of atheists take faith and religion out of
our schools and now we have groups advocating "freedom *from* religion."
And they have the audacity to use the constitution as their basis for trying
to remove Christian holidays from our calendar and the acknowledgement
of God from our courts and money. What could be further from the truth?
How many of our founders died to protect the freedoms of faith and the
creed of man's existence under a sovereign God?

Most alarming is that these groups represent such a minute percentage
of Americans. Yet they have succeeded in removing God's word from our
schools and in many area, the abolition of celebrating Jesus' birthday and
resurrection in our classrooms. What will be next? All it takes is for Christians to remain silent. How we need to understand the power of our text.
God ordains our leaders and He holds the power to renew our government
if we are but willing and desirous.

Can we see what our children are becoming? Will they have the inner
stamina and appreciation of their heritage to stand the next trial? We can
fortify the walls now with prayers and standing for righteousness.

JUNE:
Growing Through the Word of Truth

"Thy word is a lamp unto my feet, and a light unto my path." —*Psalms 119:105*

God's Word

"This book of the law shall not depart out of thy mouth; but thou shall meditate therein day and night, that thou mayest observe to do according to all that is written therein for then thou shall make thy way prosperous, and then thou shall have good success." —Joshua 1:8

This has been my favorite verse for so many years. What a wonderful promise it contains. The whole world is struggling, scheming and dreaming for a way to find success and prosperity. And God has promised it to every believer who will follow this one verse.

And oh, the unsearchable riches of God's word. I have read and studied it daily for over fifty years and it's still fresh and new and exciting every time I open God's word. And it works! From keeping a home to business and principles of finance , you will never go wrong if you daily read and heed God's Word.

Willard Cantelon
Elder Statesman of Christian Missions

Planted in Christ

"And he shall be like a tree planted by the rivers of water that bringeth forth his fruit in season; his leaf also shall not wither; and whatsoever he doeth shall prosper. The ungodly are not so; but are like the chaff which the wind drives away."
　　　　　　　　　　　　—Psalms 1:3, 4

Paul Finkenbinder
Missionary to Latin America

I have come to so appreciate and rest in the wisdom and ways of the Lord, and the promises of His Word. As I seek His face and find my way in Him, He plants my feet on solid ground. He gives me confidence and strength. I know that if I will be patient and steadfast, I will succeed in Him. I rest in that.

The ungodly have no such assurance. They may find gain, but it is temporary. Their lot is subject to the winds and storms of life. Fortuity holds no promise for them as it does for the believer.

For Good

"And we know that all things work together for good to them that love God, to them that are the called according to His purpose." —Romans 8:28

This verse is a continual blessing to me, comforting me in trials and asuring me of God's guidance. Whenever Jim and I are forced to make a decision (which is often) and we are not sure just which way is right, we claim this promise. It is comforting to know that *all* things will work for good, not just part.

God says here that if a Christian is seeking God, whatever happens is not by accident but is part of God's plan working together for good. Therefore, we can look for God and good in all things.

Tammy Faye Bakker
Singer, Co-host of PTL

The Bible

"All scripture is given by inspiration of God, and is profitable for doctrine, for reproof, for correction, for instruction in righteousness."
—II Timothy 3:17

The first book that ever came off a printing press was the Bible, and it has been the most widely distributed book in the world *every* year since. Last year more copies of the Bible were distributed than there are books contained in the whole Library of Congress.

The Bible is everybody's book. No other book has entered so widely, so steadily, so decisively into the thought and life of the world. It touches man in every area of life. For cleansing, for comfort, and for direction, It has no equal. It is the most hopeful book in the world. Man's barrages against it only further its popularity. The persecutions of the Nazis and now the Communists have only created a greater hunger for its reading.

From page to page, the Bible is full of the spirit of the morning. No literature matches it for pure "sunniness." It deals with every human problem and still snatches the crepe from the door of death. It looks for the latent good in bad men. It is Good News in the gutter. It peoples eternity with singing men and women. It faces the worst and believes the best.

The Bible is a book of practicality. It teaches how to think about life, feeds the heart with vision and ideals, and reveals the supernal pattern of manhood in Christ Jesus. It is a lantern for our feet in any situation. Its religious truths are essential to man's health in character, man's hope in service, and man's triumph in death. As simple as the alphabet and deep as eternity, it is on the side of humanity from beginning to end and has for every human woe a soothing balm and an answer for every human mistake.

Finally, the Bible is pure inspiration. It has brought out the greatness in simple men. It causes men to rise above circumstances, pride and chaos to conquer nations, evils, disease, and death. Its value cannot be measured, only experienced daily.

The Formation Of The Bible

"For the prophecy (of the scripture) came not in old time by the will of man: but holy men of God spake as they were moved by the Holy Ghost."
—II Peter 1:21

For many centuries, the Bible as the Old Testament was the sacred Book of only an insignificant number of people, belonging to a small and despised race dwelling between the River Jordan and the Mediterranean. Who would have thought that it would come to have more impact on the human race than all other volumes of books put together?

The strange thing that happened was that the smaller portion of the Bible, the New Testament, was added to the Old in the first century after Christ. And at once this book, like a swollen river outflowing its banks, spread beyond its historic bounds and limitations and flowed throughout the whole earth. For suddenly, the theme of the book came into focus. It is well said: the New Testament is Jesus Christ revealed and the Old Testament is Jesus Christ concealed.

Yet the unity of the Book can only be explained by its divine formation. The 66 books (Biblia) were written by more than 30 authors over a period of 1,600 years. Some were highly educated men like Moses and Paul, while others were herdsmen and fishermen. The books represent almost every form of writing and composition: history, predictions, biographies, odes, dramas, hymns, proverbs, and code of laws. And yet there is a miraculous unity in it, a divine harmony and order.

Its one grand theme is the redemption of man from the power of sin and death. The central figure is the *Redeemer*—the Lord Jesus Christ. To Him all parts of the Bible bear witness. The prophecies point to Him, and the events confirm the prophecies. The doctrines of the Bible reveal His nature, and the life of Christ fulfills the doctrines. The historical accounts reflect both the need of man for a Savior and the effectiveness of that redemption in converted souls.

The Bible, written in three different languages, was brought together in its present form over 1,800 years ago. It has more than stood the test of time—it has shaped our world!

The Authority Of God's Word

*"What things soever ye DESIRE when ye pray;
BELIEVE THAT YE RECEIVE them and ye SHALL
HAVE them."* —Mark 11:24

The evangelist asked the woman in the prayer line if she believed God would heal her. She responded, "Well, I hope so." Unfortunately, her hoping did not get her healed. Faith and belief are the only keys that unlock the doors to heaven's riches: "Faith is the evidence (title-deed) to things not seen."

Notice the tenses in our text. Existing belief (" have received"—past tense) is required to produce future results ("shall have"). Faith for provision and healing of the body is the same as faith for forgiveness. On the authority of God's word, you were forgiven before you felt forgiven. For example, if you are a beneficiary in a rich man's will, you are already wealthy the moment that rich man dies though you have not yet seen any of the money. Just so, everything bequeathed to us in our Lord's last will and testament (forgiveness, healing, riches, abundant life) is already ours by virtue of the death of Jesus. Faith is simply using what belongs to us.

What God has placed in our account to receive by faith is found in the Bible. Just as if a friend deposited a million dollars in the bank to your credit, you wouldn't examine your empty wallet to see how much money you have, but rather the passbook, so a Christian does not examine circumstances or feelings to evaluate his fortune, but rather the Bible. All things of God exist for us in the faith realm before they are manifested in the sense realm: "Cast not away therefore your confidence...that after ye have done the will of God, ye might receive the promise."

To walk in faith is to develop and attune the sixth sense of the faith realm—where we look to what Jesus promises and believe for the unseen and unfelt. Faith receives and praises God for the answer before the other five senses are yet witnesses.

The Bible Stands

"...Thy rod and thy staff they comfort me."
—*Psalms 23:4*

A Bible professor at an evangelical school was asked what he thought of the new "higher criticism" approach to the scriptures. He responded, "It is just that. All criticism, according to scripture, is sawing off the branch you are sitting upon. So higher criticism is just choosing a higher branch—you fall farther and harder."

History records sad endings for those who have chosen to reject and criticize the scriptures. On his deathbed, in misery, Darwin recanted all his theories of evolution and tried to repent. Thomas Huxley, who followed Darwin, found his victories in debates against defenders of the faith empty. Those scientists who found their heritage and faith in scripture, not only achieved great accomplishments for humanity but also found personal peace and happiness. The faith and zeal of God's able scientists like Galileo and Frances Bacon were instrumental in the Reformation.

For the investigative and mathematical mind, God has revealed Himself scientifically in scripture. One example is the numerical order of the Bible, the study of which is called Theomatics. A simple study of the Lord's prayer reveals it contains 77 words—a multiple of seven. Forty-two words begin with a vowel and 35 begin with a consonant—again both multiples of seven. The numeric value of the Greek words is a divisible by double seven and the prayer concludes with the word, "Amen" with numeric calue of 98—a double seven twice over. In the prayer there are *seven* separate and distinct petitions. And for good measure, there are 35 monosyllables in prayer...again, five times seven.

Is this a structural miracle? No, it simply means that this prayer and all scripture were put together by the Holy Spirit. And just as there is a word structure to the Bible that cannot be broken, God's word can structure our lives so we will stand and not fall.

The Influence Of The Bible

"Thy Word is a lamp unto my feet..."
—*Psalms 119:105*

In 1808, an American whaling ship landed at Pitcairn Island in the remote South Seas and found an ideal commonwealth presided over by one Alexander Smith—the sole survivor of the mutineers on the British ship, *Bounty*.

After these mutineers had set their captain and officers adrift in an open boat, they'd established themselves together with a number of native women on Pitcairn Island. Then, having destroyed their ship so as to leave no trace of their crime, they gave themselves over to every conceivable vice and abomination.

At length, Alexander Smith was the sole white survivor in the midst of a half-breed community as corrupt as Sodom and Gomorrah. But one day this sailor began to think about his own future and the future of those with whom he lived. Rummaging through a sailor's chest, he came upon a Bible. Henceforth, it became the island's textbook of instruction and standard for moral conduct.

In a few years, the Bible transformed this tropical Gomorrah into a community where there were no illiterates, thieves, liars, drunkards, profane swearers, adulterers or murderers, and in which there was no prison, no hospital, no insane asylum, because there was no need for them. The Bible found in the sailor's chest did the work, as it was used by the Holy Spirit of God to transform and regenerate human nature.

Today, in many circles, the accuracy and authenticity of the Scripture is still argued. But have we ever heard anyone say, "I tried the Bible, but it doesn't work"? The Bible is only empty to those who do not enter into its treasures of life and meaning for daily living.

Profitable

"All scripture is given by inspiration of God, AND IS PROFITABLE for doctrine, for reproof, for correction, for instruction in righteousness—that the man of God may be perfect, thoroughly FURNISHED unto all good works."
—II Timothy 3:16, 17

Madalyn Murray O'Hair and her little band of atheists succeeded in getting Bible reading taken out of our public schools. They said it might "contaminate" the minds of free thinking children today. And what has it produced? Thousands of young people who flitter from one pleasure to another with no purpose or direction.

The apostle Paul says all scripture is profitable—it furnishes a man with goodness. We have only to examine history for the Bible's fruit of revival and reformation to know that this is true. What man can read the Bible and not be troubled by his sins? Scripture vitalizes our conscience toward God. Reading the Bible will bring a spirit of repentance. Who can read it and not find a stirring in his soul to leave the gutters of sin or light a passion of righteousness in his heart?

The Bible is more than literature. It is inspiration. It contains a power to carry man forward against the sweeping winds of evil. It is all *profitable*. And yet it dares to deal with the most destructive and sensual sides of life. It is no fairy tale—it is a true account of the lives of real men and women, and it speaks to all of us, whoever we are, whatever our experience. No other book can speak so of crime, lust, evil, love and goodness and still be *all profitable*.

Our children are losing much if they don't receive the profit of God's word daily. The responsibility for their hearing it now rests solely on the home. We cannot afford to leave our children spiritually destitute.

The Sword Of The Spirit

"...the Word of God is quick and powerful,
and sharper than any two edged sword."
—Hebrews 4:12

John Osberg, a combat chaplain in the Korean War, was asked what the Bible meant to him there. He responded, "Let me begin with an admission. Many a night, as I lay trying to sleep in a fox-hole or ditch with enemy shells bursting all around me, I found myself terrified with the awful fear that grips the heart of nearly every soldier. Nights were often a nightmare and against such a background, I learned early the literal power of the Word of God. I would take a well-known passage of promise, like Romans 8:28, and just repeat it to myself over and over again, letting the deep message anoint my quaking spirit. It worked, not once, but time and time again.

"Men came in trucks to the front sometimes by the hundreds. There was no opportunity to hold services for these men who were new to the sights and sounds of mortal combat. New men were often simply brought to the front at night and told to dig in. What could a chaplain do for these young men? I found nearly all welcomed a New Testament. When I would return to see them, I'd be amazed at their knowledge of the scriptures. In dozens of instances, they were ready from their reading to accept Christ as their Savior. The only explanation come from the Book: 'The entrance of Thy Word giveth light.'

"Casualties were often heavy—row upon row of badly wounded men, waiting indeterminable minutes and hours for medical attention. What could a chaplain give to these? I found nothing better than some rich promise in God's Word, to be their staff and stay through the agony of coming days. For example, one night a close friend came through the aid station unconscious with a severe chest wound. In the few minutes before he was rushed off, I whispered in his ear the promise of Romans 8:39, which tells us that nothing can separate us from God's love. He recovered and later remembered nothing but the marvelous passage I had laid upon his mind. These precious words had given strength for recovery." The same Book men crave in battle can give us strength and peace for any daily crisis we may face today.

Threefold Cord

"A threefold cord is not quickly broken."
—Ecclesiastes 4:12

The triad is a great principle of Scripture. No matter where you turn, you find that the Holy Spirit expresses divine truth in the form of trinities.

God divides time into threes: past, present, and future; so also the universe: sky, earth, and sea; the three-fold temptation of man: lust of the eyes, lust of the flesh, and pride of life; the great enemies of man: world, flesh, and the devil; the office of Jesus: Prophet, Priest, and King; and the great Christian virtues: faith, hope, and love.

The image of the three-fold cord derives from God's own triune nature—the strongest and most secure bond in creation. From God's triune nature, God pronounces in Numbers 6:24-26, a triune blessing; in Isaiah 6:3, a three-fold sanctus; and in II Corinthians 13:14, a three-fold benediction. God has divided the Bible into a three-fold division— Genesis to Malachi: "Jesus is coming"; the Gospels: "Jesus has come"; and Acts to Revelation: "Jesus is coming again." There are three great events: creation, crucifixion, and coming again. There is the three-fold phase of Jesus' work: His atonement, His advocacy, and His advent. And finally, there is the three-fold promise of Christ: "I will build my church"; "I will send My Spirit"; and "I will come again."

The significance of these "triunes" is that in each, three are working and moving together to become one. So it must be in our relationship with God. The Bible in I Corinthians 10:32 tells us that the three-fold division of the human race—Jews, Gentiles, and the Church of God—will become one in Christ. Our three-fold nature: spirit, soul, and body is to become one in heaven. And finally, our three-fold nature: spirit, soul, and body is to become one in heaven. And finally, our three-fold obligation, to live, to labor, and to love, will become one in Him. This is God's desire: "That they may be as one, even as we are one."

What The Bible Doesn't Say

"The secret things belong unto the Lord our God: but those things which are revealed belong unto us and to our children for ever, that we may do all the words of this law." —Deuteronomy 29:29

Almost as significant as what the Bible says is what it doesn't say. How strange at first are the Bible's lack of curiosity about the future life and the silence of the Gospels about the childhood of Jesus.

The Bible is singularly silent too, about the crash and roar of great world events, saying nothing of the movements of empires and kingdoms, except as they touch upon the life and destiny of God's chosen people. Here, the Bible is as silent as the stars which look down upon a battlefield. On the other hand, there are certain kingdoms, the existence of which is known today only because of their mention in the Bible. Why?

A part of the answer is revealed in our text. Why does God choose to reveal anything to us? *"That we may do (obey) the words."* God's Word is not merely information or good literature, though it is both; it is food for life, light for our path, and stability in this world.

When Paul was in Athens, he found many who showed interest in the Bible just as a new thing to talk about. He left quickly. He warned Timothy that, to these, the Bible was a source for vain juggling and that he should shun them. He warned that in the last days, men would be ever learning but never coming to the knowledge of the truth. There are realms of deep understanding in God's Word, but God has made most of the truths of the Bible clear and simple that we may understand and obey. What He has omitted is left out for our good. But what is revealed is *ours* and is precious for life.

The Golden Rule

"Therefore all things whatsoever ye would that men should do to you, do ye even so to them: for this is the law and the prophets." —Matthew 7:12

Many philosophers and teachers have tried to summarize the precepts of life. One of the disciples of Confucius, for instance, tired of so many rules and maxims, said to his teacher. "Is there one word which may serve as a rule of practice for all one's life? Just one word? Confucius replied: "Is not reciprocity such a word? What you don't want done to yourself, don't do to others." Another of the ancients, Socrates, suggests: "What you are angry at when inflicted on you by others, this do not to others."

Aristotle was asked how we should behave toward our friends. He replied, "As we should wish them to behave toward us." The great Rabbi Hillel, when asked to summarize the whole law, said: "What is hateful to thee, do not to another. This is the heart, the rest is merely explanation." Seneca, the Roman teacher, said the best way to confer a benefit is "to give as we should wish to receive."

All these are worthy precepts, but Christ took this evident truth and made it a *rule* (The Golden Rule) of *positive action*. He extends it to include our dealings with all men...not just our friends or favorites.

Nearly everybody in America knows the Golden Rule as well as anything in the Bible, and many say it is their rule of conduct. But how many truly practice it? It is more than just "good manners"—it is having the same heart toward others as we do toward ourselves. This is not easy to live by. No wonder Chesterton said, "Christianity has not failed, but has been found difficult and laid to one side."

Jesus was not an idle dreamer. He could not ignore the hurts of one human being against another. He knew the way out of this jungle of greed, chaos, and inhumanity. Back of the Golden Rule is Christ! He has lived it, and His power can help us keep it.

Tell Me What To Do

"I will instruct thee and teach thee in the way which thou shalt go: I will guide thee with mine eye."
—*Psalms 32:8*

Ours is a day of professional counsel. It has become big business. Even our newspapers and magazines are full of it. There is advice to the lovelorn, advice to the investor, advice to the student, advice on medicine, motherhood, clothes, homes and about anything else you can name. To many, counselling is the new substitute for prayer and private devotion.

But none need stumble in the dark who trusts in God's direction. The agents of God's guidance are available to all who will use them: His Word, His Holy Spirit, His providences, His angels, signs, dreams, and a deep, unperturbed peace. What human sources could be better equipped?

No one or nothing will ever surpass the guidance and wisdom of God's book, the Bible. It is "a lamp unto my feet and a light unto my path..." It is a lamp, not a searchlight; so it requires daily reading. Whether you are the president of the country or the poorest citizen, God's word offers direction to you. Peter declares that the Bible is the supreme criteria "until the day dawn—until Christ's return." (II Peter 1:17-21)

All true guidance builds on the foundation of God's Word. The Holy Spirit quickens the Word and "guides you into all truth." The Holy Spirit can speak distinct words within or without one's own being. Acts 8:29 records, "Then the Spirit said," and Acts 16:6 says, "but the Spirit suffered them not." By God's Spirit, God can also grant His visions, signs, and dreams when supernatural guidance is needed. Close to Spirit guidance is the peace of God. Paul admonished the Colossians, "let the peace of God rule (or umpire) in your hearts." God's peace should rule or arbitrate the Christian's life. We don't dare violate it or do anything without it.

Besides these direct ways, God in His ability and inclination uses circumstances to prepare our individual ways. This is often mistakenly called "good luck." But the Christian knows that "all things work together for good" and the "steps of a good man are ordered by the Lord." Therefore, he expects God's guidance and can look even to events to direct him as he uses the key for receiving God's direction: "Seek and ye shall find."

Guidance

"Who is among you that feareth the Lord, that obeyeth the voice of His servant, that walketh in darkness, and hath no light? Let him trust in the name of the Lord, and stay upon His God."
—Isaiah 50:10

It seems we have developed an "instant" mentality in our country—from every kind of instant food to instant houses and instant service. The next thing I expect to be offered is "instant" education. Already, in our impatience and laziness, we are demanding instant "guidance". The occult practices of horoscopes, tarot cards and ouija boards thrive on this type of deceptive thinking. Americans spend millions and millions to go to psychiatrists to try to find some short cut out of their problems.

God's guidance may be slow but it is sure. Therefore, primary to God's guidance is faith. Nothing can be received without faith. And without it, we have no patience to trust the answer to come. The second step is to bring our problem out into the light to clearly see what we want. If you don't know what your problem is, then you don't know what help you need, if any. If you want a definite answer from God, you will have to present a definite problem to God. We should calmly try to reduce our need to a point where a decision can be made with God's help.

When this is done, it is time to pray and pray earnestly. Put your question squarely up to God for an answer. Then be still! Wait! Give God a chance to speak to you. God will use your mind like a screen to project His thought upon for you. At this time, you should lift your heart to God in quiet and happy thanksgiving.

If the answer comes then, follow it; if the answer is not yet come, walk confidently in faith, watching for it. Our heavenly Father is not limited in the means He uses, so we must be expectant. The answer may come from a friend, it may come from our own best judgment. Guidance will usually come out of faithful activity rather than inactivity; thus, we should not fear moving toward the answer. God will not be late, the answer will meet you in time.

Difficulty In Believing?

"A good conscience, which some having put away (thrust from them, R.V.) concerning the faith have been made shipwreck." —I Timothy 18:19

There are certain things in life one should never tamper with—things like your clock, your compass, the law and most importantly, your conscience. When you start tampering with your conscience, you may start calling good, bad and bad, good. That is where trouble starts and you lose your way. In our generation, our national conscience has been so tampered with as to provide gross license for abortion, marijuana, pornography, and homosexuality among other things. The result may be greater external "liberties" for some but at the supreme cost of their losing their way.

Conscience is delicate and our text suggests that rough handling will make shipwreck of one's faith. Paul says that when a Christian begins to tamper with his conscience, it will make God seem unreal. The things you used to believe without a doubt won't seem half so real. Heaven will begin to seem far away, prayer a waste of time and church attendance just a form. To have faith in God, we must have a "good conscience."

No one ever makes shipwreck of his faith because he is powerless to understand. The man who wants to do the right thing, who would rather die than knowingly do the wrong, and who cries out to God for help to do the right, will never miss the way! That is why even the child, the pagan, or the underprivileged can know if they don't argue with the inner voice of conscience. This is what Jesus meant when He said: "Blessed are the pure in heart, for they shall see God." He who wills in conscience *will see* God..

To be pure in heart is not to be perfect. It is rather to be sincere—to honestly obey the traffic lights that flash on and off inside our being. Do we want to find believing easier, and peace and contentment at night? The pure *see* their way. Let us then be careful with conscience.

The Inner Spirit

"My presence shall go with thee, and I will give thee rest." —Exodus 33:14

In His anguish of leading Israel through the wilderness, Moses cried out to God, "Show me the way". Here was a man with the same desire of many of us. He wanted to know the future. What was ahead? What would happen next? God's response to Moses? "My presence shall go with thee."

If there is a class of people to be pitied, it is those who are so troubled, anxious, and worried about the future that they visit clairvoyants, spiritualists, and fortune tellers in vain attempts to tear the veil of the future aside. What if it were granted to us to know the future as clearly as we know yesterday? Very likely, two things would happen. First, it would frighten us. We would hardly have courage to face it. Fortunately, life is so ordered that we must take things as they come—one day at a time. Second, we would certainly sit with folded hands awaiting the bit of fortune or misfortune we knew would be ours. Life would be like playing golf with a magnetized golf ball that was automatically pulled into the cup.

We should thank God that we don't know the future. It is enough to know that along one's pathway, whatever it may be, there stands a Presence—unseen but not unfelt. Our prayer is not "Show me my way?" for why should we place our trust in our own understanding? Our capacity is so limited. Trust rather than understanding will supply our need.

Rather than giving Moses his desire, God provided something infinitely better, "His Presence". No one can give a detailed description of God. Every person must know God for himself. There is such a difference between knowing about God and knowing God experimentally. It is easy to choose the better of the two.

We have all seen a little child walking, holding the hand of its father across a busy intersection. Though the traffic seems to bear down on them the child knows no danger. *Trust*—David learned this as he wrote, "Yea, though I walk through the valley of the shadow of death, I will fear no evil for *thou art with* me." The presence of God can make us walk with confidence and face every emergency in life courageously.

The Mystery Of The Kingdom

"He answered and said unto them, Because it is given unto you to know the mysteries of the kingdom of heaven, but to them it is not given."
—Matthew 13:11

Our Lord's statement in our text represents a turning point in His earthly ministry. Jesus has confirmed His messiahship with His mighty works but is rejected in the cities of Chorazin, Bethsaida, and Capernaum. Christ here is the rejected king. So from that moment He turns from the nation of Israel and offers not the kingdom but *rest* and *service* to those in the nation who are conscious of their need.

A rejected Christ and rejected kingdom necessitate a new program for Christ and the world. Jesus realized that the cross lay ahead of Him and a long intervening period before He should return to set up His earthly kingdom and rule upon earth. So the kingdom must come individually to the hearts of those who will respond and obey. The Lord teaches the disciples in parables which show clearly what God has been and is doing between the cross and the coming of Jesus. He prays and thanks the Father for He has "hid these things from the wise and prudent and hast revealed them unto babes."

This is the way for us, too, to understand the mysteries of God's kingdom—the parables and God's guidance in our lives. A babe is one who is dependent and rests upon his parents. When we become so dependent on God as to resist and reject the vain imaginations and fears of self and rest wholly on God, we will find a new clarity and understanding of God's word and will in our lives. "Blessed are the pure in heart, for they shall see God."

Does A Fleece Work?

"O Lord, I know that the way of man is not in himself: it is not in man that walketh to direct his steps." —Jeremiah 10:23

As many questions are asked about Divine Guidance as are asked about any subject of the Gospel. People ask, "Shall I put out a fleece?" They refer to a method Gideon adopted: "If the dew be on the fleece only, and it be dry upon all the earth beside, then shall I know..." (Judges 6:37). God honored Gideon's fleece but not as a test for divine guidance. Gideon already knew of the will of God. God had plainly said, "Go in this thy might, and thou shall save Israel from the hand of the Midianites."

Gideon's problem was fear and unbelief. His faith was weak, and he demanded a sign of supernatural intervention at the risk of divine displeasure. The fleece, therefore, was not a divinely ordained means of guidance, but a special accomodation to one man's weakness.

This need for special guidance is eliminated if we walk in obedience. Isaiah says, "Thine ears shall hear a word behind thee, saying, this is the way, walk ye in it, when ye turn to the right hand, and when ye turn to the left." The farther we are away from God, the louder God may have to speak to us. Saul of Tarsus learned this when the Lord said he was "kicking against the pricks." All of us have felt that divine pricking of conscience.

A key then to *receiving the will* of God is to be *in the* will of God. Without a perspective of where we are in God, we will never know His direction. People say "I'm not sure I have the ability to understand God's voice"—as if it were some special *gift*. We must cultivate our inner hearing. Jesus said, "Why do you not understand My speech? Even because you cannot hear My Word." We cannot be saturated with our own things and the things of this world and hope at the same time to be spiritually sensitive.

In Deuteronomy 28, Moses describes perfectly the self-led man looking for guidance: uneasy, restless, grieved of mind, fearful, uncertain, lacking assurance, discontented, and spiritually bound. Moses says this person is *out* of the will of God. The safest and best place in the world for you and me is right in the center of God's will. Let us today simply accept His Lordship and obey; He will clearly guide.

Choosing

*"All THINGS are LAWFUL for me—but all
things are NOT EXPEDIENT; all things are lawful
for me, but all things edify not."*
—I Corinthians 10:23

Not all things are a matter of right and wrong. In fact, for the Christian most decisions should involve a choice between that which is good and that which is best. There are some things a Christian may feel free to do because there is no divine command against them. Nevertheless, to do them would be undesirable for either his own spiritual welfare or the spiritual welfare of others.

The Corinthian assembly to which Paul wrote our text was comprised mostly of Gentiles, who had been raised as pagans, idol worshippers, and participants in pagan feasts where food was sacrificed to idols. Since their conversion to Christ, many had still been surrounded by pagan friends and neighbors who invited them, not to worship the idols, but to partake socially in the feast. This aroused a debate in the church: were they at liberty to accept such invitations? The question was finally put to Paul.

A portion of the church thought this was perfectly fine. They reasoned, an idol was nothing, only a piece of rock or stone. Paul quickly admitted that an idol was nothing but he warned that many young believers, still weak in conscience, wouldn't see that. So Paul cautioned the others not to make their liberty a stumbling block to the weak.

For this reason, Paul abstained from many personal liberties. To give himself completely to the work of Christ and the service of others, he abstained from marriage, from receiving a salary, and even much of normal human companionship. He illustrated his determination: "Know ye not that they which run in a race run all—but one receiveth the prize." It is one thing to be a Christian, it is another to win the prize. To gain the prize, one must often sacrifice certain personal liberties. But above all, says Paul, do all things to God's glory.

The Day Of Revelation

"For there is nothing covered that shall not be revealed; neither hid, that shall not be known. Therefore whatsoever ye have spoken in darkness shall be heard in the light; and that which ye have spoken in the ear in closets shall be proclaimed upon the housetops." —Luke 12:2 & 33

Today, these verses are finding individual and corporate fulfillment as never before. They are prophetic of God's work and instructive of His guidance. The light that came into the world by Jesus Christ and was rejected of men is being manifested and the darkness of men's hearts is now clearly seen.

Note the terminology: that "secrets would be revealed by way of housetops." What a curious but literal fulfillment of these words has occurred today. Television aerials on nearly every house in the country reach out to pull "secrets" into our homes. The events of Watergate and Nixon reveal that even the secrets whispered behind the fortressed walls of the White House will be revealed.

All oppression and injustice is based on hiding the truth. Our nation has hundreds of intelligence gathering and governing agencies to discern the truth. But they cannot hold a candle to God's C. I. A. (Central Intelligence Agency)—the Holy Spirit. It is the Spirit of God who reveals light and judgment on the world and leads believers into all truth.

These last days are days of revelation. Those that "hold the truth in unrighteousness" are being revealed. The barriers of understanding that have separated Christians of different denominations are being dissolved by the light of the Holy Spirit.

Rather than judge others or take vengeance, Christians should pray for the light of the Holy Spirit. The day "will reveal the truth."

By Things Seen

"For the INVISIBLE THINGS of Him from the creation of the world ARE CLEARLY SEEN, BEING UNDERSTOOD BY THE THINGS THAT ARE MADE, even His eternal power and Godhead; so that they are without excuse." —Romans 1:20

God has made the human mind a wonderful thing. It has the capacity to "see", discover, and understand. God has provided this faculty of genius that man might learn the ways of God. He says, "they are *clearly seen*."

God reveals His own intelligence in nature. The 3,000 polished lenses of a common blow-fly's eyes are a skilled piece of optics. And what company of craftsmen, having attained such a miracle of microscopic handicraft, could put it on an assembly-line and breed it by the thousands of millions? Somebody did and keeps on doing it.

God's sense of balance is observable everywhere. Academic men call it the Law of Averages, survival of the fittest, and cause and effect. There is a delicate balance in nature: any countryman knows that a massacre of owls and sparrows will end in a plague of field mice. There is Somebody upstairs who keeps things from getting topsy turvy despite the efforts of sin-crazed men to ruin this world of God's. If our government in Washington was allowed to run the earth on its own, we'd be out of business in no time.

Ordinary vital population statistics tell a wonderful story about God's concern for man. The percentage of boy baby births to girl births over the last twenty years has not varied more than four-tenths of one percent. Through war, sickness, and colossal changes, the proportions of boys and girls remains the same.

We may not be able to understand a power behind so vast a process: "No man hath seen God." But neither do we see or fully understand electricity. God Himself has said, "My thoughts are not your thoughts." We must view the Creator through human spectables, but as we see His works and concern in our lives, we can learn and acknowledge His Lordship. For in Him we live and move and have our being. It is just plain foolishness and open rebellion to deny God.

Authority

> *"Behold, I give unto you power to tread on serpents and scorpions, and over all the authority of the enemy: and nothing shall by any means hurt you."* —Luke 10:19

When God created man in His own image, He gave him mastery over all creation and all the forces of nature. Man was created a Prince and was born to rule. But man lost that mastery through disobedience. He lost title to the dominion, and instead of being *Master*, he became a *slave*. He transfered that mastery to the one to whom he yielded obedience; so Satan became "prince of this world."

Christ recovered that mastery for man through His obedience: "All things are delivered unto Me of my Father." Christ had to be obedient in all things, "even unto death; the death of the cross." Satan tried to make that obedience as hard as possible to try to divert Christ from His purpose. But victorious, Christ returned home to heaven with authority: "set him...far above all principality and power and might and dominion." "who... is on the right hand of God—angels and authorities and powers made subject unto Him." Why? He did this all for us.

If Jesus had acted on his own account, he surely would have ended the whole conflict with Satan then and not let it carry on for 2000 years. But he acted for us, and there is something for us to do in settling this conflict. Jesus says, "Take possession of what I redeemed, take what I have bought back for you." We must use the authority given us in Jesus' name. Satan is still a persistent fighter. He will not yield until he must. The Lord has given us the right to use Jesus' name—and we must insist on taking that right.

The vagabond Jews in Acts 19 learned that using Jesus' name was not a thing to be taken lightly. It is acting in the authority of what *Jesus has done*. That is faith—knowing that our Lord Jesus is Victor!

Smart Men Can Be Wrong

*"There is that speaketh like the piercings of a
sword: but the tongue of the wise is health."*
—Proverbs 12:18

In 1828 the school-board of Lancashire, Ohio passed the following resolution: "You are welcomed to use the school-room to debate all proper questions, but such things as railroads and telegraphs are impossible and rank infidelity."

None of us like to be wrong. In fact, heaven help the person who dares, if it not be our wife, the boss, or a "cop". But I've been wrong enough to suspect I'm probably not alone. In fact, history puts me in good company.

When Adam Thompson in 1892 filled the first bathtub in America, newspapers said this new-fangled idea would ruin democratic simplicity in the republic. Doctors said it would cause rheumatism and inflammation of the lungs. Cities banned the use of bathtubs in winter as dangerous to one's health.

Going along with the crowd doesn't always make one right. All the years that Noah was working in the shipyards the crowd thought he was wrong. When Gideon and his 300 guerrillas put the Midianites to flight, the crowd had already gone home, but Gideon won. When Elijah prayed down fire and put the prophets of Baal to shame, he was alone, but he won. They laughed at David when he carried stones to meet the mighty Goliath, but he won. When Jesus was crucified by the mob, He seemed to be going down with a losing cause, but *He Won*.

Being wrong about bathtubs and railroads is one thing, but being wrong about the Savior of mankind is quite another. Many who laugh and scorn at "new-fangled" ideas live to enjoy them. But when Judas Iscariot was wrong about Jesus and knew it, it tortured his soul, and he went and hanged himself. It hurts to acknowledge that you are wrong, but remember you have much company. It will only hurt more if you stay wrong and don't come to the truth for mercy and forgiveness.

Opinions And Conviction

"Let every man be fully persuaded in his own mind." —Romans 14:5

The great art of navigation depends upon the existence of certain definite points from which a skilled navigator can take a bearing. It may be a star, a lighthouse, a prominent headland; it doesn't matter which, as long as it is fixed. Granted the certitude of that point, the navigator can take a bearing and steer his course. The mariner could not take his bearing from a cloud; it moves and disappears. Navigation is possible only because of the existence of definite points and constant reference to these fixed marks.

We live in an age of the "open mind", especially in the areas of philosophy and religion. In politics, in sports, and in business, men have *convictions*, but in faith many hide behind *opinions*. As a result, they have no more direction in life than a mariner following a cloud. The newspapers of Billy Sunday's day were no more positive toward faith than they are to-day. But this comment in the New York Times speaks volumes about Billy's ministry: "It is refreshing to have a man come to town who really believes in something." This man doubted his doubts and believed his beliefs and changed America for God.

When a seaman takes a bearing and finds his position to be other than the one he had supposed, he does not doubt the star or the light. He doubts himself. We, too, are on a voyage in life and we, too, need definite points of reference. So when we encounter a howling tempest and find ourselves out of bearing, we do not doubt the lighthouse or star, but ourselves.

We must believe that "God *is* and that He is a rewarder of them that diligently seek *Him*." These must be convictions. There is plenty of room for opinion about the way we worship, the music we use, or our style of dress. But let us be fixed on the things that are fixed. Let us hold fast to the truth, or like the navigationless sailor, we may head in for a "dead reckoning."

Those Gray Hairs

"...gray hairs are here and there upon him, yet he knoweth not." —Hosea 7:9

Finding gray hairs has never been a joyful experience for anyone. There is a certain element of sadness in the discovery because it means that life is a thing of fixed limits; we're led to know in a pretty definite way that some time soon we will have lived our life.

The prophet in our text is speaking though of another tragedy: the aging of one who does not recognize it. He suggests that there can be a unconscious loss in life, that precious things can depart from us while we are busy here and there. Just as Solomon's temple was raised in silence, just as silently can a man's faith and his highest ideals decay and vanish. He may hear and see nothing, but what he once was ashamed of, he now shares. He has lost his fervent testimony in the midst of "good" activity.

Gray hair traditionally has been equated with wisdom. And the Bible says that experience is required for discernment between good and evil. What is our experience teaching us? Is it feeding or decaying our soul? The rich rancher in Christ's parable used his experience to lay up much goods for many years. But as his barns filled up, unknowingly, he had emptied and lost his own soul. This is where the tragedy lay.

It is hard for any of us to admit that we have gone back or slackened in our spiritual life. We would rather say we have become more *broad-minded*. It is popular in the world today to be more tolerant of all things. But we must watch that tolerance does not result in our *caring less* about that which is right.

Our life on earth is but a "vapor." We must with the Psalmist pray that the Lord will "teach us to number our days." And beware lest we lose the keen edge of conscience, the slackening of Christian service, and the nourishment of prayer and Bible reading. Each day counts for eternity.

Fear Not

"God hath not given us the spirit of fear..."
—*II Timothy 1:7*

There are 365 "Fear Nots" in the Bible—one for every day of the year. God intends us to live a life free from fear. In the words that Franklin D. Roosevelt made famous, "we have nothing to fear but fear itself." God's kingdom is positive! Jesus confirmed this when He said: "No man having put his hand to the plough and looking back is fit for the kingdom of God."

Pushing ahead into God's plan and kingdom requires all our faith and energy—the torment of fear will keep us from going forward. The devil, the author of fear and torment, will try everything to keep us from facing our fears and getting rid of them. Jesus is the light, and He desires to expose our fears that He may "destroy the works of the devil"—including fear.

The four lepers in the story of the Syrian oppression of Israel in II Kings are a beautiful example of facing fear and getting rid of it. They said, "Why do we sit here starving until we die? Let us go out to the enemies camp, the worst we can do is die." Crippled and handicapped as they were, they called the enemies' bluff—after they decided that death was better than the constant fear of death. They decided to get rid of their fears and wound up delivering the nation.

Fear is a work of death; it robs us of our power. It takes away our joy and eagerness to help and live for others. It destroys our testimony of what God has done for us. Why did the man with the one talent bury it? Because he was *afraid*. Fear will cause us to bury our talents and hold them back from God's service.

God hath not given us the Spirit of fear. Rather He says, "My peace I give unto you, Let not your heart be troubled, neither let it be afraid."

Heart Attacks

"Men's hearts failing them for fear..."
—*Luke 21:26*

In his discussion of end-time conditions in Luke 21, Jesus gives our text as a definite symptom of that time. And what is the greatest killer of adults in our country today? Heart attacks—hearts failing.

When we look in the Bible to see the history of Israel and God's people, we can almost see a pattern of human cycles. First, human beings progress from bondage to spiritual faith. Then spiritual faith inspires people to courage and courage leads to freedom. Freedom results in a measure of physical abundance and prosperity. But abundance leads to selfishness. Selfishness produces complacency, and complacency decays to the inevitable state of indifference. The next step down is fear, and fear leads right back to dependency, slavery, and bondage. This is the end of the line and the beginning again.

Not only did Israel find itself time and again in this cycle, other nations have as well, including our own. There is grave danger that our nation is on the downward side of the cycle. Complacency in government, education, and business is catching up with us. This is why men's hearts fail with fear. There is a growing dependecy upon the government, whether it be in the area of controls or of welfare. And what is the result? Bondage—greater taxes and governmental control in our lives.

History records that the cycle can be interrupted at any point by spiritual awakening and revival. This is the need today—that our courage and freedoms be restored.

The Courage Of A Coward

"He that doeth truth cometh to the light."
—John 3:21

People are different. To some, tradition, opinion, custom, society or precedent hold no more fear than a farmer's scarecrow with an empty broom-handle for a gun. To others these terrors of public opinion and criticism are real. To assert an unpopular view, to champion an unpopular cause, or to befriend a public enemy demands from them as much real courage as any martyr has taken to the stake.

The hero of our text, Nicodemus, was of the latter type. He is the gallant coward—a good man, believing in the right, but too fearful to stand for righteousness. As a ruler of the Jews and a member of that proud ecclesiastical court, the Sanhedrin, he came to Jesus at night in fear. His honesty is reflected in his questions, recorded in John 3. Their conversation is one of the high moments in scripture. As Nicodemus went to leave, Jesus tenderly but sternly told him, "He that doeth truth cometh to the light."

Nicodemus' courage was soon tested. When the Council plotted to arrest and kill Jesus, Nicodemus weakly suggested that their law did not condemn a man before he was heard in his own defense. His feeble effort was easily turned aside. But Nicodemus' moment of courage did come—at the cross. Priestly hate and popular fury had done their work, the disciples had fled, and the Lord of Life was dead. His body would have been flung into foul Gehenna but for Nicodemus and Joseph of Arimathea. They begged Pilate for the body of Jesus and provided Him with a proper burial.

We see here an evolution of love in the heart of Nicodemus. Finally, his love triumphed over his cowardly fears. Why did he wait until his Lord was dead? Alas, why do we all wait until, were it not for God's mercy, we should be doomed to a coward's fate? Jesus beckons us to the light. His love is stronger than human reputation or criticism, and with his love we can cast out these fears.

A Good Conscience

"There is yet one man—but I hate him."
—I Kings 22:8

Hugh Latimer, the great Reformer of the 16th Century, was preaching one day before Henry VIII and offended the king by some plain speaking in his sermon. The king ordered him to preach again the next Sunday and to make apology for the offense he had given.

So on the next Sunday, after giving out his text, Latimer began by addressing his own soul, "Dost thou know before whom thou art to speak? To the high and mighty monarch, the king's most excellent majesty, who can take away thy life if thou offendest. Therefore, take heed. But consider also from whence thou comest and upon whose message thou art sent? Even by the great and mighty God, who is all present and beholdest all thy ways, and who is able to cast thy soul into hell? Therefore take care to deliver thy message faithfully." He then repeated the sermon he had preached to the king the Sunday before.

That night the king summoned him and, in a stern voice, asked him how he could be so bold as to preach to the king. Latimer replied that he merely discharged his duty and obeyed his conscience, upon which the king arose and embraced him saying, "Blessed be God I have so honest a servant."

The Christian life gives man a place where he can stand. That place may become awfully lonely. Latimer may have been the first man to cross the king. In our text, Micaiah the prophet had to stand against 400 hundred false prophets in delivering the word of God to King Ahab. There are bodily dangers, and insults, and ridicule for standing by conscience, but there is inner freedom. When we reject the light of our conscience, we put our inner selves in prison by putting a disguise on ourselves and pretending to be what we really aren't.

The testimony of our heroes of faith are filled with obedience to good conscience. They stood and were tried and overcame.

JULY:
The Daily Walk of Faith

"Behold, his soul which is lifted up is not upright in him: but the just shall live by his faith." —Habakkuk 2:4

Releasing Your Faith

"Now faith is the substance of things hoped for, the evidence of things not seen."
—*Hebrews 11:1*

Ralph Wilkerson
Pastor

My Bible tells me that every person has been *given* a measure of faith. It is a gift. Yet I find many people praying for more without using what they have. The lack is not a lack of faith but lack of understanding how to use what they have.

The greatest thrill in my life is to see people release their faith. I have never read where the disciples prayed for faith but they often prayed for boldness. As they in boldness stepped out in faith, God moved to heal, deliver, anoint and provide the needs of the person. He can and will do the same for us as we release our faith.

Many Christians have not had their faith released because they are not in a place where God is moving. Attend a fellowship where God is moving and the Word of God is preached, (faith comes by hearing), and your faith is going to be released and increased.

The Power of Confession

"For verily I say unto you, That whosoever shall say unto this mountain, Be thou removed, and be thou cast into the sea; and shall not doubt in his heart, but shall believe that those things which he saith shall come to pass; he shall have whatsoever he saith." —Mark 11:23

The power of this promise is incredible. It is continually life changing to me. It means that we can move away mountains of problems, diseases, hurts, and unhappiness by the power of our confessions of faith.

Whenever a Christian really gets hold on this promise, it makes a new person out of them. They begin to confess the goodness of God and receive healing, confidence, assurance and the abundant life God has planned for us. This verse is not, however, a magic formula, but a deep truth that we should meditate on and let sink in our hearts and be established in our thoughts.

Vicki Jamison
Evangelist

Trusting God For All Things

"And we know that all things work together for good to them that love God, to them who are the called according to his purpose."

—*Romans 8:28*

Vestal Goodman
Music Artist

It may sound strange to say that this verse "works", but it does. It is a statement of faith and like salvation and other biblical promises it works only for those who believe it. I have lived by it and proved this glorious truth.

We as human beings prefer to see, but to trust is so wonderful. Even during a seizure of heart disease and open heart surgury, I have learned even more that Romans 8:28 works.

Only Believe!

"What things soever ye desire, when ye pray, believe that ye receive them, and you shall have them." —Mark 11:24

Archimedes, upon discovering the power of the lever, said, "If you find me a fulcrum to rest my lever upon, I can move the world." This New Testament text is the *fulcrum—faith is the lever*; and with it we can move two worlds at once, and hell as well. How do we exercise faith?

First, is there a difference between faith and believing? Yes, as much as between water at rest and water in motion. Believing is faith in motion. We can accept the fact that God is true, and the Bible a revelation from Him, and still not experience salvation. We must apply the truth. Believing, then, is putting confidence in God's testimony, and exercising what you know to be true.

Second, faith is God's gift, but believing requires our will. Faith is God's gift just the same as breathing, walking, hearing, and seeing are God's gifts. But just as God does not breathe, walk, hear, or see for us, neither does He believe for us. He has given man a capacity to believe the indisputable evidence of Jesus Christ and rests the responsibility to do so on us.

Third, faith becomes stronger as you exercise it and weaker as you neglect it. I don't believe any man is born with a greater tendency to believe than another. But the one who uses his gift will certainly get more. Use it, or eventually *you'll lose it.*

Faith is not limited. It says "all things are *possible.*" The law of the kingdom of God says, "Be it unto thee according to thy faith." As you exercise faith, you expand your "possibilities."

Growing in faith involves the four words of the above verse: desire, pray, believe, and receive. Choose, desire the goal; then pray and ask; expect and anticipate the answer now; and then take God at His word by receiving that good thing He has promised.

Faith

"LOOKING UNTO JESUS the author and finisher of our faith; who for the joy that was set before him endured the cross, despising the shame, and is set down at the right hand of the throne of God."
—Hebrews 12:2

Robert Louis Stevenson tells of an exciting experience that befell his grandfather while at sea. The ship on which he was a passenger was caught in a storm and being driven toward the rocky coast. When the storm was fiercest, he climbed up on the deck to face the worst. There he saw the pilot lashed to the wheel, steering the vessel with all his might away from the rocks into safer water. As he stood there watching, the pilot looked up and smiled. It was enough! The smiling face of the pilot was so reassuring that he went back to the cabin saying to himself, "We shall come through, for I saw the face of the pilot and he smiled!"

That is faith! We have a pilot who has conquered every storm, every evil, even death, in this old world, and He stands smiling, desiring to pilot any who will climb aboard His ship through the storms of life to eternal happiness. God's Word assures us that we, too, will be changed when we behold the face of the Lord. "But we all, with open face beholding, as a glass, the glory of the Lord, are changed into the same image from glory to glory..."

This is the key to faith—beholding our Lord and His will, fixing our attention on faith. An acrostic of the word faith may help us remember: Forsaking All, I Take Him. Faith is absolute trust in Jesus, God's only begotten Son.

Instead of looking at the problem and disappointment that makes us heart-sick, emotionally fatigued, worried, and emotionally upset, let us look to Jesus—the author and finisher of our faith. "It is the prayer of faith (looking to Jesus) that saves the sick." Let us stop the negative, destroying action that is decaying our minds, souls, and bodies. Let us fasten our eyes and thoughts on that which is fixed and unmovable—on someone we can trust and believe. God wants to help us—that is the whole meaning of the Bible. Have you had a stormy week? Look into "the face of the Pilot."

The Way Of Faith

"Make straight the WAY of the Lord."
—John 1:23

The great General William Booth, who founded the Salvation Army and brought revival to America in the last century, was once asked the secret of his faith. He replied: "I can give it in three letters, N-O-W." He believed what the Holy Ghost said: "Now, Today." He decided to seek God *now*. He sought God to believe *now*. He believed God to act *now*. And then he acted *now*. This is the way of faith. Bringing our faith into the *now* puts it in the perspective where it can operate. Here are some hints on how to have *now* faith.

First, *now* faith must have its *object*: "that your faith might be in God." God is always active—always ready and desirous to undergird and help us to do His will. Faith searches the scriptures for the goodness of God to receive and share. It is the *Scripture* which is the *foundation* of *now* faith. Faith does not rest on generalities but demands the written word of God. The devil knows if he can steal the "implanted Word," faith will collapse.

Second, *now* faith will pay its *price*: "Buy of Me gold *tried in the fire*." It will go through the trial of fire—not wait for the fire to go out or think of a way around. Just as our Lord went through the crucible of Calvary "for the joy set before Him," we must go through in faith that it be found "unto His praise and honor and glory."

Now faith knows its source: "Full of faith and of the *Holy Ghost*." Faith is not natural to fallen man but is the gift of God by the Holy Spirit, who gives us the "unction" to stand, seek, and go forward. *Now* faith knows its *sphere*: "With the *heart* man believeth..." God asks and tests: "Is your heart in it?" Our minds may theorize and analyze, but the heart feels the burden of sin and the load of anxious care.

Finally *now* faith says it is time: "While it is said, *Today*, if ye will hear His voice." Unbelief says tomorrow; faith says today. There is no need to wait. The fullness of life is *now*.

The Possibility Of Faith

"But He answered and said, It is written, Man shall not live by bread alone, but by every WORD that proceedeth out of the mouth of God."
—*Matthew 4:4*

In our present age of uncertainty and the unusual, the basis of all faith is not some magic formula or super hero but "Thus saith the Lord..." This has always been the way of faith: "Faith cometh by hearing, and hearing by the word of God." The primary revelation of God is that He is eternally the same today and forever. He is still speaking and His hands are still outstretched to heal and deliver. The divine heart which melted and broke at Calvary over lost humanity that was as sheep without a shepherd is no less sympathetic toward human need in these days of suffering.

Our Lord's earthly life was a constant challenge to the faith of men. Faith in Israel was buried over by the traditions of the law. So on the Sermon on the Mount, Jesus cried out: "O ye of little faith." Then He praised the Centurian, who as a Gentile through faith, put to shame those in Israel from whom much might have been expected. He told the Syrophenician woman, another Gentile, "O, woman, great is thy faith."

Today faith still struggles against the traditions of men. For generations men have groaned, endured and fought disease and satanic oppression on their own strength without calling out for God's delivering word. The heart of God longs for the response from men to seek and trust Him. He cries, "ask and ye shall receive"; "if ye canst believe, *all* things are possible." The Holy Spirit affirms the possibilities of faith: "Love believes all things"; "all things are yours"; "how shall He not with Him also freely give us all things?"

God enjoys and longs to bless His children of faith. The possibilities of faith include the answers and provision for your need today.

A Soldier's Faith

"If ye live after the flesh, ye shall die, but if ye through the Spirit do mortify the deeds of the body, ye shall live!"   —Romans 8:13

This was one of the favorite verses of one of America's great heroes of our preceding generation, General Douglas MacArthur. Now every part of the Bible was important to this military genius, who was also a man of great faith. In fact, he was known throughout the Pacific as a "God's Book" man. He lived by the Bible and constantly used it to illustrate his convictions in all areas of life. He was confident but tender in his faith.

This is illustrated in the story of the General's first assignment, when he was given a mythical harbor to defend in a military quiz. That harbor was isolated, stripped of all outside help (as was later actually the case on Bataan). The chief inquisitor asked, "Now Mr. MacArthur, in these circumstances, what would you do?" Young MacArthur responded quickly, "Sir, there are two things I'd do. First, I would get down on my knees and pray. And after that I'd go out and fight." Those two things are pretty much what has kept America going through the darkest hours—*Faith and Fortitude.* We need to be strong and of good courage.

The General once wrote, "It is my humble opinion that the religion which Christ came to establish is based upon sacrifice, and that men and women who follow in His train are called by it to the defense of certain priceless principles, even at the cost of their own lives."

But human strength and sacrifice were only a part of MacArthur. He had his own favorite translation of our text..."It must be of the Spirit if we are to save the flesh." He held no delusions about human need. At the height of his career soon after VJ day, he spoke of America's future..."Our need basically is theological and involves a spiritual revival and improvement of human character." "Ye must be born again."

Killed In Action

*"These all DIED IN FAITH, not having receiv-
ed the promises, but having seen them afar off, and
were persuaded of them and embraced them and
confessed that they were strangers and pilgrims on
the earth."*
                                        —Hebrews 11:13

By God's grace, it has been a number of years since we have had to
bury great numbers of American men killed in the tragedy of war. But
over the years I have officiated at the funeral services of several fine boys
whose epitaph read: "Killed In Action."

Regardless of our feelings about war, that is about the best epitaph
that any of us can have. Those two words, "in action", tell a big story.
There are so many folks who aren't in action at all. They are not fighting
for any cause but are lying down on the job, hoping somebody else will
fight their battles for them.

In the chapter of our text, we get a casuality list: "Gideon, Barak,
Samson, Jephtae, David, Samuel and of the prophets—who through faith
subdued kingdoms, wrought righteousness, obtained promises, stopped
the mouths of lions, quenched the violence of fire, escaped the edge of the
sword...waxed valiant in fight, turned to flight the armies of the
aliens...they were stoned, they were sawn asunder, were tempted, were
slain with the sword." Over the entire chapter, one could write: "Killed In
Action."

The apostle James tells us what has always caused wars: "Ye kill, and
desire to have, and cannot obtain." War is simply taking without asking;
its roots is the root of all sin—selfishness. And selfishness is waging a war
that goes on continually. What action are we taking against it? Today is
the day to fight the battle against selfishness.

It is no shame to go down fighting, but it's an eternal shame to be
quitter—a coward. Samson was "killed in action." Stephen was "killed in
action." Paul laid his head on Nero's block to be "killed in action." Esther
went into action saying, "if I perish, I perish." What will your and my
epitaph be?

Heroes Anyone?

"If thou has run with the footmen, and they have wearied thee, then how canst thou contend with horses? and in the land of peace...they wearied thee, then how wilt thou do in the swelling of Jordan?" —Jeremiah 12:5

Jeremiah was bewildered with life. His foes had him surrounded. His friends had deserted him. Wicked men prospered while the good suffered. It was more than he could bear. His spirit was crushed and he was ready for a nervous breakdown. How could he even pray, upset as he was?

His hot passion and feelings had gotten the best of him. But then a *calm settled over his spirit*. He listened and quieted his mind. After all, what had he really suffered but the ordinary ills of life? Others had suffered more than he. Our text is the conclusion this godly man came to after he got calm enough to think.

How many of us are like Jeremiah? Are we strong enough to face the tests of life? Do the little things still bowl us over? What would happen if we really had to face a big tragedy? How sure are our foundations for the storms of life?

Jesus noticed this problem when He went to Church one day. He saw two men: one had built on a rock, the other on the sand. When the test came (as it surely will), the first stood while the other was swept away. It is just plain silly to imagine that anyone is immune to trouble. Trouble can come from any place at any time.

There are few pillars which can prop our life and keep it from falling to pieces in the storm. But faith can. Faith is not tossed by storms. In fact, the storms of life are where faith shines. In the midst of the fiery furnace there walked in the fire with them a fourth—and the form of the fourth was like unto the Son of God. With faith one never walks a hard journey alone. There is a hero—the Lord Jesus Christ!

Three Great Elements Of Faith

"If ye know these things, happy are ye if ye do them."
—John 13:17

Our text speaks of the three elements of our faith—the *head*, the *heart* and the *hand*. The last mentioned is the demand of our day. The world wants to see our faith in action, a religion that works.

A Japanese student in Tokyo entered a Christian college purely for the sake of education, intending to retain his Buddhist faith. He and his fellow students rebelled against the poor accomodations, and this young man was one of a deputation of two sent to remonstrate the dean, Dr. Williams. The good man listened to their grievance and then said; "I cannot let you suffer this way, for I expect you one day to be the leader of Japan. I have a nice room with southern exposure; you must take that, and I will take your room." This loving faith won the young Japanese without further argument, reconciling him not merely to his room, but to Christ.

Christianity can be closely compared to the psychology of advertising. In advertising, the salesman must first give all the information; he flings out in broad headlines his startling facts. Next he aims to touch the emotions and to inspire the reader to desire and "need" his product. But with all this, he has still failed unless he has compelled the response of the will to go and purchase the product. Similarly Christian living involves belief, confidence and trust. Belief is the intellectual process; confidence is emotional and trust the volitional process.

Even as you cannot build a house without a foundation, you cannot build faith without knowledge of the truth. Knowledge is power: "A wise man is strong; yea, a man of knowledge increaseth strength." But transformation in Christ is more than information; it stirs the emotions. Tears and laughter and joy are essential. The faithful Christian will enjoy happiness not because he's always searching for it, but that in doing the will of God, this will be the result. Moreover, God will channel the emotions for power and unction to *do* His will. Many today waste their emotions on imaginary troubles on TV or in the movies, and ignore many real plights. While the path to perdition is paved with good resolutions, the path to heaven is paved with good performances.

Jesus has made faith practical. Our beliefs are best seen translated into life by doing and being.

Santification By Faith

"Reckon ye also yourselves to be dead indeed unto sin—but alive unto God through Jesus Christ our Lord."

—Romans 6:11

While I was at PTL, David Kelton one of the finest and hardest working staff members, told me this testimony: "For many years, my life was totally filled with drugs, alcohol, crime, jail, and misery. When I heard of Christ's forgiveness, I could hardly believe that I could become God's child. But Jim Bakker knew my past and still gave me a job. The first assignment he gave me was to be the usher to collect the offering. He was the first person who ever trusted and believed in me. When that happened, I began to respect myself and believe that God could make something out of me."

That word "reckon" meaning to regard or consider is so important for every Christian who would be a victorious one. Just as we are justified by faith, we are santified (set apart from sin) by faith. As with David, victory over sin is brought about more by trusting than trying. The freedom from guilt that David found when others trusted him became his best guarantee for his deliverance from sin's power.

God, too, knows all about our past. Yet, He still loves and trusts us. It is His goodness that leads us to repentance. When we realize God's trust and our place in Christ, we realize that satan is a defeated foe. He cannot condemn us anymore, and he cannot deceive us into trying to hide our sin from God; we realize He knows and still loves. So our lives can become real and honest and grateful. That makes us *alive!*

How To Increase Faith

"And the apostles said unto the Lord, Increase our faith."   *—Luke 17:5*

Just before His Passion, our Lord gathered His disciples and spoke to them about perfect love, bidding them to always forgive, no matter how much provoked and sinned against. Realizing how impossible was this task, the disciples knew the only way of obtaining such divine love was in believing rightly, so they cried, "Lord, increase our faith."

Their mistake was in misunderstanding the way faith comes. Their idea was that they possessed a certain amount and only needed an increased supply—like the man with some money would ask for more. Faith does not increase this way. Faith is like a seed! It contains the principle of faith within which will grow of itself, if we release it. Faith grows when we use what we have: "Unto everyone that hath shall be given, and he shall have abundance but from him that hath not shall be taken away even that which he hath."

Jesus told the disciples to *act*. As we *act* rather than *feel* forgiveness toward those who have wronged us, we prove that faith *does* cast out the evil, fruitless things from our hearts. Time and again, Jesus *spoke* the word of faith. There was no waiting or praying to the Father for the power. Nothing but the word of command and it was done. This is why Jesus says we will have that which we confess.

The spinster daughters of Zelophehad in Numbers 27 give us a good example. Fatherless and brotherless, they boldly went before Moses and said, "Give us therefore a possession among the brethren of our father." Moses took their cause to the Lord, and He honored it. He was pleased with their faith.

Let us not make the mistake of the slothful servant in not recognizing that the exchanger was at his very door, waiting to undertake and ensure a profit on his deposit. Let us act. "All things are possible to him that believeth."

Manifestation Of Faith

"...ASK WHAT I SHALL DO FOR THEE
before I be taken away from thee. And Elisha said, I
pray thee, let a double portion of thy spirit be upon
me." —II Kings 2:9

How much we miss because we do not fully understand how much an active faith is able to do for the soul. Faith is absolutely necessary to the life, the health, the growth of every believer.

In our text, we find Elijah stimulating Elisha's faith by asking him, "what he would desire of him." This is a vital ingredient of faith. It is clear and definite. True faith is never vague and can never be satisfied with generalities. Jesus said, "Ask, that your joy might be full." This is faith—knowing what we need and asking.

Faith is clear because it "cometh by hearing." Not hearing the voice of the preacher or the friend, but hearing the *voice* of God. God's voice is clear and sure. His voice is His Word clothed and illuminated by His Spirit. How quickly faith generates when the Holy Spirit makes His Word alive in our ears and hearts.

Faith is definite because it "worketh by love." There is a faith that works by fear; it is a faith that restrains. But the faith that is active, that accomplishes, is the faith that works by love. It is a deep persuasion within the soul, illuminating, purifying, invigorating, and inflaming the heart with light, love, and zeal for eternal things. You can be sure when it's done by love.

Faith is that which stirs up the gift of God within our soul. This is the unction of faith. John Wesley said, "Whenever I stepped out to a crowd of people, faith soared, and my mouth filled with argument." The gift of God is courage, power, love, and a sound mind; it is faith that stirs these up.

Finally, faith is activated as it bears witness to the truth, as it pleases God (God is victorious), and as it is released to grow. It is a common mistake to think that we will grow holy and become like Jesus by some unconscious process of development. The secret is in the growth of faith. It is running the race—pressing forward to win the prize!!

Enemies

"And they cried out again, Crucify him."
—Mark 15:13

Recently during a political campaign in our state, a newspaper editorial ran, "We like this candidate because of the enemies he has made." Every man who takes a positive stand for right is absolutely certain to arouse animosity, and sometimes the brightest star in the crown of a man's life is the fact he has dared to make enemies. Jesus had them, and He was the best man that ever lived.

This is not to say that we go looking to make enemies. The desire to get along with one another is commendable and biblically sound. But the desire to please people has its perils. There is always the danger that anxiety to please may be substituted for the obligation to serve. Our Christian faith has a two-fold purpose: (1) to further and enthrone the right and (2) to resist and dethrone the wrong. Could men like Moses, David, Paul, Luther, Knox, Wesley, Washington, Lincoln or King have achieved their purposes without having strong convictions and strong indignation about things?

There are many sincere people who find any kind of controversy and conflict distressing. We must be fair and make tolerances for them. But let us not make the mistake of thinking that this is a sign of spiritual maturity. It isn't! Jesus said; "I came not to bring peace but a sword." As long as there is evil in the world, there will be a need for fighting saints. There are forces of evil in the world today with which we can never compromise. In the midst of moral decay, Jude wrote "Contend for the faith." Let us not fear doing the same today.

The Breath In The Winds

"...Come from the four winds, O Breath, and breathe upon these slain, that they may live."
—Ezekial 37:9

This text comes from Ezekial's vision of dry bones. At first glimpse, it is an utterly discouraging situation. The condition of the nation is so hopeless and devoid or morality and faith in God, one would wonder if any power of regeneration could help. Ashes are everywhere. It is a picture of death and ruin.

The vision begins with Ezekial speaking: "Thus saith the Lord unto these bones." While God orginally organized carbonate, phosphate, and gelatin into bones, can even fleshless bones hear the Word of the Lord? What this prophet is saying is: *Behind all the desolation and wreckage is the living God.* That is what we today must know if we are to keep our souls alive! If a man is perfectly sure of God, everything else around him can be dead or dying, and that man will never be confounded. That is faith!

So God questions Ezekial's faith: "And he said unto me, Son of man, can these bones live?" To which the response: "Thou knowest." With man it is impossible, but to God *all* things are possible. As the breath of God moved on this valley of despair and disarray, a mysterious order began to happen: "And the bones came together, bone to His bone." It is the breath of God that makes all things that we can only see in part fit together into a clear pattern of *His Eternal Will.*

Every bone is in search of his fellow bone. There are mysterious go-ings on in the Universe that God would have me understand. The antenna of this human mind is just not sensitive enough to faithfully reproduce the whole picture. As Paul says: "Eye hath not seen, not ear heard, neither hath entered into the heart (mind) of man, the things which God hath prepared for them that love Him." My best and happiest moment is when the Spirit of God quickens me and I catch the fleeting flash of the glories of His eternal purpose. What has been dead and hopeless, all of a sudden begins to move and comes alive in hope and vision. What a *Life Giver* is our *God.* Where everything else ends, God begins!

Hindrances

"...That your prayers be not hindered."
—I Peter 3:7

When we talk about this thing called "faith", many people talk like either you've got it or you don't, there's not much you can do about it. I must admit I hear more of this talk from those who think they're among the group that don't have it. But the Bible doesn't speak in those terms; it says there is a fight to faith—it is a struggle and there are hindrances.

There is the hindrance of an *impure* conscience; "Holding the mystery of the faith in a pure conscious." Sin and deceit in our lives can make a shipwreck of our faith. The home of faith is purity and forgiveness.

There is the hindrance of *pride*: "How can ye believe, which receive honor one of another?" When men made other humans the source of their joy and satisfaction, they cut themselves off from the giver of faith which is God. The cure of this is honesty before God and looking to Him to meet our deep needs.

There is a hindrance of the *Adversary*: "When the tempter came to Him, he said, "IF" He tries to scare and frighten with his "buts"; he casts down and perplexes with his "ifs". His darts can be piercing but if we first receive the word of God in love, then Satan's darts have no sting.

Circumstances and those about us can hinder our faith. IF we listen to the voice of friends over God, like Abraham to Sarah, we may miss God. Our own failures can cause us to stumble. But if we like Peter keep faith, failures need not be cause for remorse but become stepping stones to victory. The lack of faith of others about us can hinder. The unbelief of the 10 spies was contagious. That is why we need to be a part of a healthy church to grow in faith.

Perhaps the greatest hindrance is our own heart of *unbelief*: "Take heed, lest there be in any of you an evil heart of unbelief." While faith is a divine principle of life implanted in the soul by God, unbelief is an evil principle of resistance to God implanted by the devil. We must resist this attack of the enemy and guard our hearts with the truth.

Limiting God

"They...limited the Holy One of Israel."
—*Psalms 78:41*

There are some scary statements in the Bible—like, "Will a man rob God?" Our text is another. But it raises a question we all should face: Are we limiting God? What restrictions have we set up against Him?

First, are we limiting God to the big moments in our life? Every one of us who believe have moments when God is so real to us and we bask in His presence. But what about the moments when we are low and confused? Are we to believe He is any less near us in the valley than on the mountain-top? He has promised: "I will never leave you nor forsake you." He is just as much in the little things and difficult things as the great things.

Then, we can limit God in regard to the human instruments He uses. When we do this, we sit in judgment and conclude that God couldn't possibly use this one or that one. We make our selections and set our qualifications. Who are we to say what God can use and can't use? We have a sovereign God. So often his choice is mysterious: He wants a nation which will bless the world, and He chooses a company of slaves in Egypt; He needs a birthplace for the Savior of mankind, and He chooses a stable in tiny Bethlehem. It isn't what we would expect.

We can in this way limit God in prayer. We make up our mind what kind of an answer we want. We put on conditions: that if God does this, I will do this. Is not God bigger than our thoughts? He is able to do abundantly above what we can ask or think.

Finally, we are tempted to limit God sometimes in regard to the way in which He speaks to us. We say: "If God spoke to men in such and such a way, He *must* speak in the same way to me." God is always speaking! His Holy Spirit is our guide and interpreter. God wants to fill us with His Spirit and let His Spirit guide us into all truth!

When we believe, God is only limited to His nature, love and truth.

The God Of Miracles

'Ye men of Israel, hear these words; Jesus of Nazareth, a man APPROVED of God among you by MIRACLES and WONDERS and SIGNS, which God did by Him in the midst of you, as ye yourselves also."
— Acts 2:22

People today want to see what they are getting. They want the facts before their eyes. We now have truth in lending facts, product content facts, nutrition facts, service estimate facts, consumer facts, and on and on. In religion, too, people want to see the facts of faith. Either Christianity is a miracle or it is nothing.

Jesus intended that the Christian faith be both miraculous and demonstrative. The things which Jesus did on earth, like the resurrection of Lazarus, healing the blind, restoring the maniac, could not have been done through human power, and required supernatural power. Moreover, he performed these miracles, not in secret, but before fault-finders, enemies, and friends alike. His works were such that those about could not deny the facts. And He freely welcomed examination of His miracles. Peter recorded: "We have not followed cunningly devised fables, but were eyewitnesses of His majesty" and John said: "We have seen with our eyes,...and our hands have handled, of the Word of Life."

There were some who failed to see the mighty works of Jesus—the disinterested and unbelieving: "He could not do many works there because of their unbelief." Multitudes were not healed, because they had not faith in Him as the Son of God. Jesus ministered by: "according to your faith be it unto you." Faith is the main ingredient in receiving the blessings and miracles of God.

Jesus sent out His followers with the same Divine miracle-working power that worked in Him. The authority of their Gospel was to be substantiated with "power to heal the sick and to cast out devils". The writer of Hebrews confirms that they did just that: "God also bearing them witness, both with signs and wonders and with divers miracles and gifts of the Holy Ghost, according to his own will." God's ministers enjoy the same privilege and power today. We can and will work the works of God if we will believe.

Witness

"Wherefore seeing we also are compassed about with so great a cloud of witnesses, let us lay aside every weight, and the sin which doth so easily beset us, and let us run with patience the race that is set before us." —Hebrews 12:1

The record of men and women changed by faith in Christ and strengthened to overcome the severest of difficulties has never ended. The cloud continues to grow.

Helen Keller was blind and deaf from her infancy. By slow steps she painfully learned to appreciate a world more fortunate people take for granted. By faith she became one of the wisest and most useful women of her day, raising high the standard of love and confidence for all with similar handicaps. Her strength: "Faith. It is the dynamic power that breaks the chain of routine. Faith reinvigorates the will, enriches the affections, and awakens a sense of creativeness. Active faith knows no fear. It is a safeguard against synicism and despair. It is a safeguard against cynicism and despair. True faith is not a fruit of security. It is the ability to blend mortal frugality with the inner strength of the spirit. *It does not shift with the changing shades of one's thought."*

Herbert Hoover rose from an orphan boy to become President of the United States, carrying our nation through four of the most trying years of its history. His strength: "My Christian faith. I believe not only that faith will be victorious, but that it is vital to mankind that it shall be. Our discoveries in science have proved that from the galaxies in the heavens to the constitution of the atom, the universe is controlled by inflexible law. It took a Supreme God to create these laws. Man is differentiated from the beasts by a spirit from which springs conscience and spiritual yearnings. It is impossible to believe that there is not here a divine touch and purpose from the Creator of the Universe. I believe we can express these things only in religious faith.

"By faith, the founding Fathers of America enunciated the most fundamental view of human progress since the Sermon on the Mount—when they stated that men received from the Creator certain unalienable rights, which should be protected from encroachment of others by law and justice. *Always growing societies record their faith in God—decaying societies lack faith and deny God."* May we continue in this spirit.

Mountain Moving Faith

"...Arise, Take up thy bed and walk."
—Mark 2:9

At thirty-nine, Franklin D. Roosevelt dived in the icy waters of Eastern Canada and came up paralyzed by the cruel blow of polio. He had just suffered defeat in his race for Vice-President of the United States. Doctors and friends believed he was through—his life would have to be along the sidelines. But Roosevelt himself had not given up. He simply did not accept invalidism and became President for four terms.

Men do not arrive because their paths have been smoothed for them. They arrive because of determined faith. Defeat or victory is mainly an inside job. We all start with obstacles, with some handicap or other. Nothing is ready-made!

Let's look at some of history's greats. First, Julius Caesar, Alexander, Socrates, Moliere, Richlelieu, Napoleon—it is probable that all of them were epileptics. When Catherine the Great of Russia was a child, her body was so twisted and deformed that for years she had to wear a brace day and night. She was 26 years old before the bones of her skull grew together.

We think of some of the world's great authors. Robert Louis Stevenson's life was a continuous succession of colds, congestions, hemorrhages and fainting spells. Lord Byron and Sir Walter Scott limped through life on club feet. Milton and Homer were blind. Schuller was another epileptic, and Heine wrote from a bed blind and half paralyzed.

Handicaps are the common heritage of humanity. That's what makes men "overcomers" and champions. And the experts don't always get it right. Louis Pasteur hardly passed chemistry. Louisa Alcott was told she could never write. Caruso's music teacher told him "You can't sing." The newspaper editor told Disney that his drawings showed no real talent. Edison, as a boy, was told he was too stupid to learn anything. The list goes on and on. The conclusion: "Don't sit around and mourn your fate. Take inventory, count your blessings instead of your problems. Look up!"

Faith For Healing

"And the Lord will take away from thee all sickness—and will put none of the evil diseases of Egypt, which thou knowest, upon thee..."
—Deuteronomy 7:15

Anyone who has been severely ill will agree that sickness is a bondage whether it be in the body or the soul. That sickness is not in the eternal plan of God should be clear from its nature. Jesus came to liberate; sickness oppresses.

Who do we associate with bondage? Satan, of course. "Whosoever commits sin is a servant to sin." Satan would drag us down under his power and if not by spiritual bondage then with physical bondage. He works to cloud the mind, paralyze faith, quench hope, and tear down the life process. Doctors give scientific names to this servitude but it only disguises the attacker.

Jesus' mission to mankind was to liberate: "The Lord hath sent me to proclaim release to the captives, to set at liberty them that are bruised." Even as Christ, the *Liberator*, is a person, so Satan, the *prison keeper*, is a person. And only Christ can bind "the strong man." Christ's atonement on the cross was made to free us from sin—not only from its power in our soul but its penalties inflicted to our bodies.

Jesus bore sin's penalties: "Surely He hath borne our griefs, and carried our sorrows." The word *"griefs"* is often translated sickness and diseases in the Old Testament. The word *"sorrows"* is elsewhere rendered "physical pain." He bore these that we might be free of them. "With His stripes, we were healed."

The Syro-Phoenician Woman

"And she said, Truth, Lord: yet the dogs eat of the crumbs which fall from their master's table."
—*Matthew 15:27*

The story of the healing of the daughter of the Syro-Phoenician woman is a clear picture of how divine healing is given by faith. This woman was a Gentile, and certainly she had very little knowledge of God. Very likely she had never heard a promise or passage of Scripture in all her life. Everything seemed against her—she didn't belong to God's people but simply came with a need.

When she came to Jesus, He seemed against her, too. To her pitiful cry, He didn't answer. And to the disciples' appeal to send her away, he questioned her right to receive His Divine mercy. At His feet, he then seems to insult her—calling her a dog—the type in the East of that which is unclean and unfit for fellowship. Yet in the face of all this her faith only grew stronger, until at last she drew out of His very refusal the argument for her blessing. This is the nature of true faith—*difficulties cannot injure it..*

True faith rests on the hard rock of truth. Testing and difficulties only shake out the doubt until it is settled in the truth. God knows there is no comfort in doubt or unbelief—only misery and darkness. In this woman's testing, Jesus brought her to the truth of her own unworthiness and sinful self. But He never tempted her to question the goodness and mercy of God. Satan does that but not God.

Her realization of her unworthiness gave her the true basis for receiving faith and her request—faith is a gift. She asked for a crumb, even as a dog would receive. Jesus not only granted her request but blessed her: "Great Is Thy Faith."

When your faith is tested, realize God is settling it on solid ground. His goodness will prevail.

Faith For Strength And Long Life

"That thou mayest love the Lord thy God and that thou mayest obey His voice, and that thou mayest cleave unto Him: FOR HE IS THY LIFE, AND THE LENGTH OF THY DAYS..."
—*Deuteronomy 30:20*

If we were to go down the list of heroes in the Bible, we would find that every one of them was strengthened by God—not just spiritually but physically. Their obedience to God brought new strength and physical vitality.

Abraham's obedience rejuvenated his life so much that he fathered many children during his second century on earth. Moses' physical life was touched by God: "Moses was 120 years old when he died, his eyes were not dim, nor his natural force abated." King David's dying testimony was "Thou has girded me with strength." Solomon, his son, writes often in Proverbs of promises of strength: "He increaseth strength." The prophets, Daniel and Nehemiah, testified and prophesied of divine strength.

The New Testament writers confirmed this witness. Luke, the physician, records Jesus' promises of strength and "power over all the enemy." Paul commanded the Ephesians to "be strong in the Lord", prayed for "the power of Christ", and testified that he was "strengthened with all might."

Even as God promised long life for obedience to parents (Ephesians 6:2), that same divine strength is ours when we transfer our obedience to the heavenly father. Godly living means healthy living. Too long, Christianity has been associated with sick rooms, hospitals, and the needy. It may start there, but the heart of Christianity is health, strength, and vitality. John's prayer is for us all: "I pray that you may prosper and be in health, even as your soul prospers."

Faith For Dying

"For we know that if our earthly house of this tabernacle were dissolved, we have a building of God, a house not made with hands, eternal, in the heavens." —II Corinthians 5:1

Faith in dying is perhaps the supreme test. How does what we believe hold up in the hour of death? Is it a comfort or a mockery? Few of us will ever be faced with martyrdom, or dying for our faith. But each of us faces uncertain death at any moment. What will we hold to in that hour?

St. Paul gives his testimony for the record in our text. Years earlier Moses declared the eternal God was his refuge and underneath were the everlasting arms. David declared his foot would not be moved by His keeper. Isaiah stated, "When thou passest through the waters, I will be with thee." Jeremiah's faith was strong when he wrote, "I have loved thee with an everlasting love." Solomon, the wise man, saw: "Or ever the silver cord be loosed, or the golden bowl be broken, or the pitcher be broken at the foundation or the wheel broken at the cistern—then shall the dust return as it was—and the spirit shall return to God who gave it." But the Bible's view was never any higher than Christ's declaration to Martha: "I am the resurrection, and the life: he that believes in Me, though he were dead yet shall he live. And whosoever liveth and believeth in Me shall never die."

The comfort and hope of the scriptures have strengthened men all through history. A modern summary of the biblical view declares: "Much of our horror of death comes from the feeling that it is the enemy of work and play. Sleep makes it possible for us to work the next day. Death makes it possible to live on. It has therefore a real contribution to make to life in the large, being the gateway through which we slip from the lower life into the higher, from the briefer into that which is eternal."

That perspective is only possible for those who do love life. And Jesus is the life, here and beyond.

Thirty Minutes

"...What is your life?..."

—*James 4:14*

With the soon coming of Jesus Christ, our lives could be caught up by either death or the rapture at any moment. God says that we should be ready to meet Him at any time, but what would we do if we as believers had thirty minutes to sum up the affairs of our life. In our last thirty minutes, we would see things in their preciousness, beauty, and privilege as never before.

First, we should realize the tremendous value of time. Certainly, we would reflect upon our moments of life up until now. For the believer, eternity has begun, and time is its reflection. The difference in men is very largely the difference in their use of time. Recently, astronomers in England and France spent thousands of dollars and weeks of time trying to find just one sixteenth of a second. This was the slightest discrepancy between the sun's time as recorded at Greenwich and at Paris. Nonsense you say? Not really, in that Greenwich time determines longitude and thus the boundaries of many lands. Similarly, do not the noiseless fragments of time determine the spiritual boundaries of our lives?

Then, we should have a quickened sense of the beauty of this world, not only the outer beauty of the sky and mountains, flowers, birds, and trees, but the deeper beauty of purpose, coordination, and unity. This sense of beauty gives us appreciation and hope.

Then, we would like to try to do some of those things we have left undone—whether to encourage a loved one, comfort the broken hearted, warn the lost, or help bear the load of the overburdened. We would appreciate those we love and desire their best care. Human reputation loses sight of its importance as we prepare for eternity. A cup of cold water given means more.

We might think of our preparation for heaven. As we look into the Bible for a moment to read Psalms 23 or John 14, we find comfort and hope. We communicate with the Spirit within, and are assured that He will guide. Our brother James warns, "Life is brief like the vanishing vapor", but it is sacred and of infinite value, because it is the good gift of a good God.

What Is Death?

*"...In the day thou eatest thereof thou shalt
surely die."*   —Genesis 2:17

Our common meaning of death is the death of the body. It is the
biggest thing we're conscious of, the thing we feel most. We see the
body we loved so much lying lifeless, and then the utter absence of the
loved one. The spirit that looked out from the eyes, spoke out from the
mouth, and reached out from the hands is gone.

The common meaning is correct as far as it goes. But there is more.
The Bible gives us a fuller picture. Practically, it begins with a defini-
tion of death—in picture form. God is showing Adam around the
garden, making him feel at home. He stops under a tree and warns, "in
the day you eat thereof, you will die." It is the tree of choice. God is
pleading for man to use his power of choice rightly. By using his power
of choice rightly and constantly, he will become like God. But to
choose wrongly and disobediently will be death: "in dying, thou shall
die."

We see death's picture in Adam's and Eve's sin. They are separated
from what they had been before. Things are not between them as they
had been. They try to hide from God, thinking that because they cannot see Him, He cannot see them. There is no difference in God—it is in
their spirits that the separation occures. Thus, the process of their sin
brought death even before they died, as we see in the story of Cain.
Bodily death to Adam didn't come until 900 years later.

The real meaning of death is a separation in spirit from God. It has
a beginning, a process, and a final result. It affects man's spirit toward
God at once; by and by it comes to affect his body. Death is unnatural;
it is not in God's plan. He never planned a separation from man. Life is
full contact with God, and death is a break in the contact. The present
stage occurs in one's spirit or attitude toward God. The final and lesser
stage is death to the body.

The atonement of Jesus delivered man from death. In the cross he
put "death" (separation from God) to death. He voluntarily took upon
Himself the death that belonged to us. Then He brought up life—His
own, a new sort of deathless life that could never know any taint of
death. Jesus was and is victorious over death. He now reigns for all who
will choose life and be delivered from death's bonds.

Death—Friend Or Foe? (I)

"It is appointed unto man once to die..."
—Hebrews 9:27

There are two words that mark the boundaries of our earthly existence, and those are—*Birth* and *Death*. Both are common experiences to all men and all earthly living things. No matter how hard we try, we cannot run away from death. There are more than 3 billion people in the world today, and every time your heart beats, fifty of them die.

Despite the commonness of death, man has never become accustomed to it. Death has always seemed an intruder. We think of it as an uninvited, rude, persistent guest.

Some people have tried to familiarize themselves with death so that when it came, it would not seem so sudden and strange. The ancient Egyptians tried this by putting a skeleton in a seat as a guest to represent death at every feast. But there is no evidence that it ever made the real visitor any less feared or more welcome. The cardinal principle of the ancient Stoics was to be unmoved by either pain or pleasure, joy or sorrow—hence to face death with unmoved minds and unfeeling hearts. But Stoicism never banished the fear of death. And it never put hope in the human heart.

A certain King of France forbade anyone ever to mention death in his presence. This may have saved his majesty a few hours of worry now and then but it didn't stop the unwelcomed visitor from coming to his door. Much like that king, our Christian Scientist friends say, "There is no death: It is a delusion—the result of a disordered mind." But when the pulse stops on your father, mother or brother, and you put the body in the cemetery, where is your illusion? You may refuse to call it death, but that does not alter the facts.

So what is death? Death is but the culmination of the process of alternation and decay in man's body that has been going on since sin's advent into the world. Death in the human body is inevitable. But to think, as some do, that that is where the story of death and of life stops is tragedic. Nothing could be farther from the truth. Life does not die and that's our thought for tommorow.

Death—Friend or Foe? (II)

"...I go unto my Father."

—*John 14:12*

We have talked about man's fear and revulsion to death—and its inevitable meeting with us all. At first glance, even Jesus seems to have recoiled from death. He prayed to be delivered from it. In the face of it, He felt forsaken. However, he was meeting more than death. He was facing sin, the cause of death. And He was facing the *judgment* (the accusation of Satan on mankind) of which physical death is but a part.

Jesus seldom used the ugly, terrible word—*Death*. He loved rather to call this experience, *sleep* or *rest*. He knew what He was to do with death—*rob it of its sting and its terror.* In the crucifixion and resurrection, Jesus did not want us to be afraid of death. He shows that while death is still a very real thing, it destroys only the temporary house in which we live, leaving untouched the life: the mind and the soul. Death now no more touches or affects the real man, any more than a sword can cut a sunbeam.

Death, the last great enemy, becomes a great friend. In Heaven we shall know nothing of death. It is a friend because by it the soul may wing its way home. Jesus said: "I go to my Father." His Father's house had been His eternal home. The death of God's children is for them also a home-going. Christ says this to His disciples, "That where I am there ye may be also." Jesus, then, has changed the whole view of death for us.

Here it may still be somewhat dark; there it is all bright. Here it may be "goodnight"; there it will be "good morning." It is the gateway to better things for which we have longed and dreamed. *It is the gateway to perfection:* "when He shall appear, we shall be like Him." But let us remember that his promise is not without condition. It is for those who follow Christ. Our victory is through Christ: in Him, death can be a friend.

A Time To Die

"A time to die...He hath made everything beautiful in its time." —Ecclesiastes 3:2, 11

"A Time To Die." How can that be beautiful? When one thinks of the sorrow of bereavement, the aching loneliness it brings, it is hard to think of it as beautiful. Yet our life and the world of nature and society would be much poorer without the inevitable fact of death. How?

First, the fact of death adds a new intensity of life. It's like a football game—you've got just so much time to score. Travellers going on a short vacation are eager and anticipative. The briefness of their stay makes them eager to see everything. Likewise, death has put a passion into humanity to redeem the time. Because our life on earth is short and uncertain, it makes each day precious.

Second, death lends value to the common things of life. In war when death is near, young men realize the values of Mom and home. The rose, the beautiful flower, is held dear because tomorrow it will fade. We often take for granted good health until it's gone; the same can be said about the goodness of parents. The shadow of death subdues us. It brings a tenderness that otherwise would be missed.

Third, the fact of death touches with tenderness all social relationships. Surely, the world would be a harsher, colder place without death. Would we so value our human friendships? Would we nurture the godly traits of compassion and pity if humans were not fragile? I think not.

Finally, death enables us to understand. It purifies the vision so often blinded by the dust of life. Someone has said, "Our own are never ours until we have lost them." It is expedient for us that they should go away, as in loftier senses it was so for Jesus. We understand and appreciate them as never before. Here, we seldom have the right perspective. Just as dark night reveals the stars, we waken to many a thing that was there all the time, that we missed until death came along. Yes, death can become a blessing, if it teaches us "to number our days."

Stung

"The sting of death is sin; and the strength of sin is the law."　　　　*—I Corinthians 15:56*

History records the Romans once arrested an entire church of fifty-odd people with the pastor, whose name was Linneaus. They were all locked up in one small cell for four long, bitter, agonizing months. On some sort of Roman holiday, as the last attraction in the terrible Colosseum, the entire church was brought in. They came out with their clothes torn, bodies diseased, vermin-infested. They had not had food or water. They got down on their knees in the arena, and Linneaus stood in their midst, threw back his head, and lifted up his voice in prayer to God. The crowd listened quietly to hear what he might say. Instead of praying for freedom or God to strike down their enemies, the pastor prayed that God might give them grace to die in such a manner that their very deaths might be a testimony unto salvation to their tormentors.

To them death had no sting. Today, to be "stung" means to be taken in—to be victimized or made a fool of! *Sin* is a sting.

First, sin is the sting of making the *wrong choice*. We are beings of choice; we choose every day. It's bad enough to make a wrong choice in marriage, business, religion, and locality. But to make the wrong choice for eternity is tragic. People make that choice daily.

Then, sin is the sting of *neglected opportunity*. "Therefore to him that knoweth to do good and doeth it not, to him it is sin." The agony of regret: "I could have had a home, a marriage, or gone to school, or into business; but didn't." We could have spent time in prayer, in God's word, and given for souls. There is never a convenient time. We succeed only when we say with Christ, "I must".

Finally, sin is the sting of *failing to put God first*. "For whatsoever is not of faith is sin." The little "foxes" are those things that draw us away from God. These we must avoid. Whatever does not engender faith or tries to make us anything less than we are—children of God—will cause regret when we stand before God at His throne.

AUGUST:
Building Christian Character

"As ye have therefore received Christ Jesus the Lord, so walk ye in him: Rooted and built up in him, and stablished in the faith, as ye have been taught, abounding therein with thanksgiving." —Colossians 2:6, 7

Christian Courage

"I can do all things through Christ which strengtheneth me." —Philippians 4:13

Norma Zimmer
Singer

In my youth, I had the worst inferiority complex imaginable. When I went to church I always wanted to sing in the choir but I felt I wasn't good enough to sing with them. But God changed my heart and gave me a peace and confidence in life.

He taught me that I can "cast my burden upon the Lord and He shall sustain me" (Psalms 55:22). These promises have brought me through valleys that otherwise would have been unbearable.

Philosophy of a King's Kid

"Rejoice evermore. Pray without ceasing. In EVERY THING give thanks: for this is the will of God in Christ Jesus concerning you."
—I Thessalonians 5:16-18

These verses have become my lifestyle for the last twenty years and have given me high victory. They are directives from the Father for all King's Kids to enjoy Heaven's Best while tripping on planet earth. And it really works.

Harold Hill
Author, Speaker

When we really *know* that our Heavenly Father plans every event of life before it ever reaches us, ("we *know* that *all things* work together for good for them that love God"), then we can really *be* thankful and not complain about anything ever. That truth thrills my soul.

When we find it hard to be thankful, we just pray and lean not on our own understanding but trust in Him. It's God's promise and it works every time.

Broken Ground

*"And we know that all things work together
for good to them that love God" —Romans 8:28*

Dale Evans Rogers
Movie Actress

This verse is so precious because I had to claim it so many times in my life. It's so sufficient even when we suffer.

I've wondered why Christians have to suffer, and I've found that the Bible says that the rain will fall on the just and the unjust alike, the justified and the unjustified. The difference is that when the rain falls on the unjust, it is falling on hard, parched ground. When it falls on Christians though, it is falling on broken ground so it softens more and enriches and the flowers grow. Beautiful things grow when the rain falls. If I didn't believe Romans 8:28, I never would have made it.

The Same Words From Three Sources

"He hath said in his heart, I shall not be moved."   —*Psalms 10:6*
"And in my prosperity I said, I shall never be moved."
—*Psalms 30:6*
"Because He is at my right hand, I shall not be moved."
—*Psalms 16:8*

These voices from three different kinds of men come from the Psalms. All are confident. The first is the voice of a wicked man, filled with insane presumption and defiance. The next speaker is a good man who's been lulled into false security by easy times. Finally a humble, believing soul speaks, expressing a sweet trust in God. The same word but what a difference *in meaning*.

First, the wicked man displays his mad arrogance of godless confidence. And we are no stranger to that today. This man builds his whole life on a false foundation and the Bible says in the same Psalm (10) that he is a fool. In these days, it hardly seems possible that any intelligent man would say, based on his own ability, "I will never be moved—adversity can't get to me." Disease, accident, or failure can hit the strongest at any moment. Any life that builds it foundation on self will surely fall in the stormy trials of life.

The second man, a good man led astray by his prosperity, thinks too that he is protected. It is easy to get the false notion that good times are here to stay. Just when we let our guard down, a host of enemies creep up on us. God, in His mercy, lets us have a jolt, disciplines us, to bring us back to reality—and our needed trust in Him. Jesus cautions us to beware when all men thing well of us; and humble ourselves when we stand, lest we fall.

The third man's words are the same but his qualifying phrase makes all the difference: "Because He is at my right hand." This is *faith* and a long way from presumption or indifference. This man has put his hand in the hand of God. He has taken God as his ally and companion. He won't move without God's Presence. His confidence is not in himself or in good times but in God. He has a right to say: *"I Shall Not Be Moved."* Today, if God is at our right hand and His presence abides in us, we can say the same.

When? For Whom?

"And we know that all things work together for good to them that love God, to them who are called according to his purpose." —Romans 8:28

This text deals with one of the oldest problems in the world: the why of pain and suffering. This question has many sides, and many theories have been advanced. All contain a measure of truth, but the answer is found in God.

One view holds that all suffering comes from God. This view accepts God as the Creator of all things but does not agree with the biblical command to wrestle with the devil against evil. Another similar view holds that all things that happen are foreordained, and we are simply as clay in the Potter's hands. This view pictures God as the Supreme Will but makes a mockery of Jesus' commands: "Come Unto Me" and "Go, make disciples of all nations."

Another view sees all suffering as the result of sin. This view recognizes trouble as caused by wrong living and transgression of God's moral laws. The wages of sin is death. But it doesn't account for Job's experience or, as Jesus pointed out, the death of innocent people as well as guilty in accidents, earthquakes, natural catastrophes, etc.

A final view holds that all suffering is an illusion. But though much illness is certainly psychosomatic, death and torment are real, beyond the limitations of human thought and will.

Over all, we see the common strain that though forces of evil exist, no foe can harm us permanently from without if our inner life is right with God. The condition of our text says, "to them that love God." Those that love God are promised the working out of good even in the unhappiest of life's circumstances and conditions. The cross, emblem of God's love, is perhaps the key to understanding this verse. It was out of seeming total defeat and darkness that the supreme victory was won. The Son of God's perfection came by way of suffering. Even Jesus did not know that complete vindication of the love of God until He had passed into resurrection life.

Only eternity will fully reveal the answer to all life's riddles. In the meantime, we must *trust*.

Those Certain Moments

"And I knew such a man, (whether in the body, or out of the body, I cannot tell: God knoweth;) How that he was caught up into paradise..." —II Corinthians 12:3, 4

Dr, Harry Fosdick, the great Bible teacher, tells the story of his childhood: "When I was fretting or in a bad temper, my father would say to me, 'Where's Harry?' And I would respond, 'Why, here he is.' And then he would say to me. 'No! You are not Harry. Harry is lost. Go find him. I want Harry!' So, catching his meaning, I would wander off through the house getting myself under control until, returning, I could face him again saying, 'I've found him. Here he is."

There are times when even the best of us need to go off and find ourselves. The apostle Paul found himself in that position in the twelfth chapter of Second Corinthians. Faced with "jealousy, temper, rivalry, slanders, gossiping, arrogance, and disorder", Paul is in a down hour. What does he do? He looks to the best moments of his life—recalling 14 years back when he rose to the third heaven and God was so real to his soul and revelation was so clear. Instead of moping in misery, Paul looked to the best in his life for inspiration and interpretation of life. This is the secret for building a strong character.

In these perilous last days, the question is not whether or not difficult times will come; the question is whether or not we will be at their mercy. Can we still trust and base our lives upon our hours of vision, happiness, and revelation when troubles come and sweep over our soul? When troubles to blow Paul away, he dropped anchor—the anchor of faith based upon his tried hours of light and blessings. We each need that anchor of faith in Him.

Faith-Building Patience

"For ye have need of patience, that, after ye have done the will of God, ye might receive the promise." —Hebrews 10:36

For most people, patience is an intangible, passive virtue. They do not see it as an active moral force. But it is! I see this best illustrated by, of all things, the scientific law of recoil.

This law says that if I exert energy to push away an obstacle, I experience not only an outgoing force toward the object but also a return force exerted by the resistance offered. When I exercise enough force to move the desk in front of me, I easily recognize the force on the desk but seldom the reactive force of the desk toward me. But it is there and expresses itself in the heat which my exertion has generated and in the muscular fiber that it stores up in me.

Similarly, "the trying (resistance) of our faith worketh patience." says James. Patience is the building of our reflex moral force. Stored up in us, we can draw upon it each day to meet and overcome life's difficulties.

The Australian black-butt tree is grown in fat and luscious forest soil. It receives abundant rainfall and grows so close together that it is sheltered from wind and storm. Never having a hindrance, it reaches tremendous bulk. The value of this epicurean product of ease and plenty? Worthless! It has neither resisting power, structural strength, or heat value. Conversely, the English Oak has a battle from its birth—beaten by many a blast, it develops great strength. The result—it has a hundred times more breaking strength and ten times more heat value.

So it is with man. With the trials of life, God moves through our soul a steady stream of moral force that is more than enough to melt the adversary!

Jacob

*"Fear not, thou worm Jacob...I will help thee,
saith the Lord..."* —Isaiah 41:14

The life of Jacob was a *paradox* full of contradictions and violent alternations. At first glimpse, he was about the meanest, smallest kind of man you ever saw. Yet favored of God, he enjoyed wonderful visions and experiences of communion with Him. On the one hand we find him practicing deceit and meanness; on the other, you have him wrestling with angels and camping with God's host about him. At once a crafty, mean, over-reaching schemer; he became a prince of prayer, loftily ambitious and loved of God.

There are many Jacobs in this world today. At work or on the ball field, you'd think they belonged to the devil's own bodyguard, but at church you'd count them as the most spiritual and earnest of men. What do we do with them? Count them as redeemed or pass them off as hypocrites? God gave Jim Bakker some great advice about this: "You love them and I'll judge them."

Jacob's sins were quite conspicuous on the outside, but God looked beneath. All of us have many great sins, but though they might not be noticed by others, they cannot be hid from God. Underneath, Jacob manifested the one thing of all things that pleases God: faith. His soul was filled with the sublimest hopes of the nation which was to spring from him. Esau his brother, who was far more righteous outwardly, cared nothing for God's promise. Surely, Jacob was one of the world's strong men—whatever he did, he did with all his heart. *Heaven* and *Hell* were contending within him.

Jacob chose badly many times and reaped what he sowed. But his pivotal hour came when he met God face to face at Peniel. Here he saw his sin in its true light, and helpless and penitent, he cried out to God. He found calling on God far better than his own craftiness. He was no longer strong in his own character but stong in God. Thank God for the Jacobs, Peters and Davids of the Bible. They give us a picture of hope for any sin-sick soul and a warning not to judge our brother in need.

Tempted

*"For we have not a high priest which cannot be
touched with the feeling of our infirmities; but was
in all points tempted like as we are, yet without sin."*
—Hebrews 4:15

Temptation is an everyday experience common to us all. The poet has rightly said:

To every man there opens
a way, and ways, and a way;
And the high soul climbs the high way
and the low soul gropes the low;
And in between on misty flats
the rest drift to and fro.
But to every man there opens
a high way and a low,
And every man decides
the way his soul shall go.

Even the Son of Man was not exempted from the responsibility of choosing whether he was going to travel the *High Way* or the *Low*. In the wilderness he had to choose: Was He going to perform the great task of human redemption for which He was sent into the world, or was He going to seek comfort and wealth and all that goes with it.

The temptations the devil brought to Jesus are common to our lives. First, Satan tempted Him to turn stones into bread. Whose needs were to be put first? We, in the midst of a luxurious and often greedy world, must decide the same. The second temptation was close to the first—to accumulate things in this life. Wealth and material things are equated with power in this world. For wealth means power to manipulate and control; but for the believer having material wealth is the power to give and serve. We decide.

The third temptation was to perform an entirely useless action for the sake of display. Which of us doesn't want respect? We crave attention and admiration. Nearly all our advertising is aimed at this appeal—instant respect without moral responsibility. The devil knows our weak points. We will be tempted today—but through Christ we can win! He did!

Run With Patience

"...Let us run with patience the race that is set before us."   —Hebrews 12:1

"Are you a grumbler?" If so, you're not alone. Everyday living demands quite a supply of patience, and some of us fall short. Yet, impatience is a serious matter: our grumbling and lack of patience reveals in us a lack of trust in and fidelity to Jesus Christ.

Many have walked this path before. When the Lord revealed to Joseph in a dream that he was going to be a ruler, it didn't mean that God would do it the next day. When Samuel anointed David to be king of Israel, it was no sign of God's displeasure that David went back to tend sheep and was pursued by enemies for years. Yet many who feel a call from God rush off to failure instead of patiently preparing for this life-work.

As He did with Joseph and David, God has good reasons for requiring patience of His children. First, He lets us know who is in control. God is our Lord and not the butler. Those gifts and callings upon our lives are for His glory, not ours. So many of us get impatient with God for not doing the things we want Him to do as quickly as we want them done. We might ask ourselves why we want them so fast. David learned: "I waited patiently for the Lord and He inclined unto me and heard my cry."

Second, patience implants God's nature in us towards others. If we would but remember how slow we were to yield to God and how patient God was in bringing His light and truth to our own hearts, I'm sure we'd be more patient with others. And the Bible commands us, "Be patient toward *all* men." That is a tall order and gets down to the nitty-gritty of life—the irratating boss, the nagging wife, the carelessness of our children, the mistakes of others. But know God has set these before us to give us opportunity to develop and demonstrate the Spirit of Jesus Christ.

Standing By Or Standing Fast

"Watch ye, STAND FAST in the faith, quit you like men, be strong." —I Corinthians 16:13

We are either "standing by" or "standing fast." Now in television, "stand-bys" are sometimes essential when problems come up. But in our faith, we do not need "stand-bys". The fact is that we have too many of them. What we need is more real performers.

It seems that every church has two types of persons. While some are always busy with more than they can handle, others are always waiting for something to turn up—waiting for the "right" opportunity to serve but never seeming to find it. Often these folks are well-equipped to serve: they have the training and talent, and they know the Bible. But something special has to happen before they can do anything for Christ!

These "stand-bys" become nothing more than by-standers. They are members in good standing but haven't gotten out into the ballgame. When they continue to sit on the sidelines, they lose faith: "How shall we escape if we *neglect* so great salvation." If we do not have an active faith, pretty soon we have none at all. We live in a troubled world. And if we do not exert an influence, we will absorb the one we're supposed to be fighting. When we don't give out into the world, something of the world will be coming in. It has been said, "Backsliding is not a state, it is an active malignancy."

Standing fast is rather an affirmation. It is taking a stand for Christ in this world. It is active and requires being alert, brave and invincible. When we suffer for our belief in Christ, Paul says we are not to be passive about it. "Nay, in all these things we are more than conquerors through Him that loved us." This is standing fast. Like the trees in the desert, we stand fast because our roots go deep—deep enough to recognize that having a source for our life is dependent on standing fast to the belief that: "faith is the victory that overcomes the world." When we are standing fast, we will stand for the truth, stand against the enemies of the faith, and above all stand for Jesus. You cannot "stand-by" and "stand fast," too!

Weights And Besetting Sins

"Wherefore seeing we also are compassed about with so great a cloud of witnesses, let us lay aside every weight, and the sin which doth so easily beset us, and let us run with patience the race that is set before us." —Hebrews 12:1

There is a custom in many sports of introducing the former champions in the audience before any championship race or bout. Here in Hebrews God calls the roll of champions. They're at the race, and we hear their comments. Abraham says, "You can do it—you can win." Enoch says, "I learned to walk on and on!" After God names the champions, He says, "Now, you are in the race." You have to be a Christian to enter and Christ is our manager.

There is one great helper in this race, our Lord Jesus. The former champ can only encourage and say it can be done. But if we take our eyes off of Jesus, we're lost, for He is the "author and finisher" of our faith.

In this race there are two great besetting hindrances: *weights* and *sins*. Many people carry weights or faults that are not actually sins but keep them from victorious living. It may be a habit of not looking up and frowning. Learn to smile! If you have an unpleasantness about your voice, take lessons to get rid of it. It is not a sin to be ignorant, but it *is* a sin to stay ignorant and it's not a sin to be lazy but it *is* a sin to give up to laziness. God says to lay aside these faults—get into action, correct them and move ahead!

Then there is besetting sin. We all have a weak place. That is where Satan attacks. We need to stop, acknowledge it and confess it and then lay it aside. Don't keep your eyes on it.

The race is at hand. We run with patience, and that's difficult. Learn to pace yourself, to be led by the Spirit. There are results like character that you can't get in a moment. You've got to stick at it. "The righteous shall *hold on* his way."

The champions are applauding us. They had their problems as well. But look unto Jesus, get rid of your faults, lay aside the besetting sin, and be patient. It is a long race but you can do it!

In The Stocks

"Who having received such a charge, thrust them into the inner prison, and made their feet fast IN THE STOCKS." —Acts 16:24

Nearly every person has his feet fast in some kind of "stocks." They may be ill health, financial embarrassment, faulty and insufficient education, or something in our character. There are always some restricting circumstances crippling our action—some handicaps.

Because of this we are tempted to be unnerved. We forget that our competitors have disadvantages too. Altogether, the influence upon men's spirits of the consciousness of weakness or poor equipment for any work is enormous. It tends to break the spirit and that leads to failure.

But are our stocks bigger than we? They need not be our masters. Men have succeeded in spite of the stocks that have held their feet in cruel and painful misery. History says that perfect equipment does not win in battle; it is the spirit behind the equipment. How do we overcome the stocks?

First, we find contentment in them. Paul and Silas had been beaten with stripes. With swollen ankles and bleeding backs it's not easy to be cheerful; yet they sang praises. It is much easier to bewail our misfortunes than to make the best of them, but there is no victory there.

Then, these stocks can act as a stimulus and inspiration. Paul and Silas' song in prison produced more power than their sermon that day in Philippi. Our song might not produce a divine earthquake, but obstacles only prove as an incentive when we have a "winning spirit."

Finally, we must act to the very limit of our freedom. Paul and Silas couldn't do much for Jesus in prison, but they did what they could. We can "bloom where we are planted." When we do all we can, He comes with His power to help. For, God has chosen the "weak things" of this world to confound the mighty.

Strength For These Times

"...What went ye out into the wilderness to see? A reed shaken with the wind?"—Matthew 11:7

The answer to this question Jesus put to the crowd was obvious. It had not been a "wild-shaken reed" of a man who'd attracted them to the wilderness, but rather "a pillar" of a man who stood firm against every wind that blew. Anyone who had heard John the Baptist knew him to be a man of courage and conviction.

Thank God for men like that today! It was men like this who built our great nation. And today we need them more than ever. John Wesley was not "a reed shaken by the wind." He was only a little man, never weighing more than 120 pounds. But the founder of Methodism stood in the power of God against all the winds of England's corrupt moral life and the scorn of a bitter, dead state church. His inner strength in God bore fruit. At 83 years of age, Wesley wrote, "I am a wonder to myself. It is now twelve years since I have felt any sensation of weariness. (Though he rose regularly at 4 a.m.) I am never tired...such is the goodness of God...with either writing, preaching or traveling."

John Knox, the great pioneer of Presbyterianism, had "iron enter into his soul" while chained to the benches and oars on one of France's big galley ships. Then he shook Scotland for God and defied all the thundering threats of Bloody Mary. Likewise was John Bunyan another man of strength and courage who faced the need of his times with stout heart. His preaching made sinners tremble as he spoke to them of certain punishment if they failed to repent. He stood against many threats of death.

There seem to be few men of this type today. More are of the type "that wavereth like a wave of the sea driven with the wind." These follow the popular mood and never find strength to stand. These last days, when Satan is about as a roaring lion, demand strong men. We must not quit or let men shift our faith in God and righteousness. "Having done all, stand..."!

Keep Alive Inside

"Restore unto me the joy of thy salvation; and uphold me with thy free spirit." —Psalm 51:12

The Man Who Played God is the story of a great musician who thrilled vast audiences. He gives a concert that displays the glory of his genius. Then, in his dressing room, he plays for the king who has come to honor him. In the midst of the program, a bomb aimed at the ruler explodes in the room. The musician suffers a concussion that renders him deaf. All the glorious faith in beauty and in man that has inspired him goes out; he revolts at the cruelty of fate that has robbed him of his greatest gift. He retreats to his apartment, refusing to see or talk with anyone. As he paces his room, he takes out opera glasses, a sad reminder of his former life, and bitterly watches the parade of humanity in Central Park.

Then one day he sees a boy and girl, and with his glasses, he reads their lips. He learns of their love, thwarted by the boy's serious illness. He sees the girl say the physician has prescribed a cure that will cost a large sum and watches them pray that the money will come—and a thought strikes him. By a servant he sends the sum and word that God has sent it. This seems to him a jest at God, but after a while he reflects that perhaps the joke is on him.

Thus by doing for others, by showing his sympathy for them, he finds interest in life. He begins to live again.

Some of us, too, need to find faith again. We need to become warm and vibrant again. The television, the newspapers, the competitiveness of work, can easily make us hard. We lose faith. But for every hurt, every crime, every broken home and wrongful deed, there are flowers, and kindness, and love and faithfulness. That is why Paul says, "Think on these things." When your faith is at the end of your rope, tie a knot in it and hang on. There is a brighter day coming.

Fight Another Round

"Let us not be WEARY in well doing: for in due season we shall reap, if we faint not."
—Galatians 6:9

The Greek word for "weary" is used in four other places in the New Testament. In each it is translated "Faint", and is used with the message "don't be a quitter." Our text could therefore, be translated, "Let us not be faint-hearted and discouraged in well doing—for *in due season* we shall reap if we do not tire and give out—and fall by the wayside."

Many Christians miss great blessings because they don't hold fast until the due season. God promises there will be a harvest time: "We shall reap." But just as for the farmer, so for us, there must be ploughing, harrowing, planting and cultivating first.

Any worthwhile Christian endeavor requires some preparatory work. Adoniram Johnson labored for 6 years in India before he cut a single sheaf. The great missionary Carey toiled seven years before his heart was gladdened by one convert. Tyler in South Africa saw 12 summers pass before he saw the first Zulu accept Christ. James Gilmour, almost gave up after 7 years with no converts in Mongolia, but he stuck to his post and after 8 more years finally saw one convert and then tribal revival.

These were all pioneers of faith, but every Christian can be a pioneer according to the gift of faith—adding new creativity and content to his work. This is the key to conquering weariness. Routine rusts the body and soul, but creativitiy invigorates. For example, walk for an hour and you'll feel refreshed, but stand still for the same time and you'll be exhausted.

Routine also takes our minds off the goal. This is dangerous. When we seek new creativity for our labors each day, we find our soul pressing toward life's goal and reward. "Jesus, for the joy that was set before Him, *endured...*"

The Courage Of Christ

"He steadfastly set His face to go to Jerusalem."
—Luke 9:51

Who do we think of when we think of people of great courage? Some would say their favorite war hero, or the astronauts, or men of great conviction like Martin Luther King, or those who overcame great handicaps like Helen Keller or Joni. But there is one that outshines them all: Jesus of Nazareth.

Living a life of moral purity in the midst of sinners, He met with increasing opposition and persecution. Yet he never showed any signs of fear or weakness. Single-handedly, he drove the money changers out of the Temple. He boldly told the truth: "Ye are of your father, the devil." When King Herod was seeking to kill him, he never cowered, but replied undauntedly, "Go ye and tell that fox!" and went on about His Father's will.

Jesus knew all that was awaiting Him. He clearly told His disciples about the rejection He would suffer, the torture of His death, and the details of His crucifixion. He knew that Satan would mobilize every power in the kingdom of darkness against him: the treachery and desertion of friends, the malice and conspiracy of church officials, the base ingratitude of the multitude. Yet in courageous faith, Jesus strode down this road. There was no quivering or whimpering.

How is such sublime courage and heroism possible? There is just one answer: He did it because He loved us. And with His courage, He nailed to the Cross our sins of cowardice. That faith can give us courage today. There are still the work of Satan and the enemies of Christ to face. It takes courage and boldness to confess Christ before man...to uncompromisingly support the truth. It takes courage to live godly in an ungodly world. It takes courage for our Christian youth to say "no" to the world's allurements and enticements. We will never be victorious without courage. Jesus didn't take it for granted, he communed constantly with His Father for the strength and courage He needed. This is how we receive, too—with prayerful faith and practice.

More Than Conquerors

"In all these things we are MORE THAN CONQUERORS through him that loved us."
—Romans 8:37

This world has seen a lot of conquerors. History is built around their rise and fall. Greece and Macedonia give us the name of Alexander. This conqueror built a war-machine that became the scourge of the world from the Near East to India. Along came Rome with its Caesars who built their roads and marched their armies to victories that were to dictate the peace of that time for many a generation.

Spain, with its Cortez, Pizzaro, and Columbus, boasted its conquerors and its galleons and warships bearing gold and precious jewels. The pride of England has been the pride of conquerors. From its Wellingtons and Nelsons, from Richard the Lion-Hearted to Winston Churchill, they have fought with bulldog tenacity. France, too, has had its glory under little but mighty Napolean, who beat his drums from Sweden to Egypt.

Every nation has had its share including our own. We take pride in Washington, Jefferson, Lincoln, Roosevelt, to name a few. And the Bible is full of heroes: Moses and Joshua, Gideon and Esther, David and Jesus. Besides national heroes, we have heroes in science like Newton, Bacon, and Galileo; in medicine like Pasteur; art and sculpture have their Michael Angelos; literature has its greats in every language; and sports build their halls of fame to honor their heroes.

The apostle Paul had the stuff of a champion. He was always in there to win. He didn't run for second or third but for first—no matter the cost. But Paul wasn't satisfied with being a conqueror in this world, for the Christian finds a conquest beyond. Alexander and Napoleon could conquer the world but not themselves. No man is really free who cannot command himself.

Thank God for the conquest of worry, fear, jealousy, lust, anger, and malice. The battle for conquest of self is the biggest battle in the world. But we have the victory "through Him that loved us." He won the victory over all the things of self that enslave us. And in Him we share that victory.

Satan Falling From Heaven

"...I beheld Satan as lightning fall from heaven."
—Luke 10:18

Jesus made this statement after the 70 had returned from their first missionary journey. These were not ordained ministers who had been especially set apart; their appointment was temporary and informal and their mission local. They were in effect the first Christian lay workers. Christ had sent them out two by two in every place where He Himself was about to go in order to prepare the way.

Their mission was a complete success. They returned to Christ elated in His name. They had not only healed the sick in body but restored the sick in mind. "Lord, even the devils are subject unto us in Thy Name." Then comes the great response of our text. Jesus takes what they have done as being part of the accomplishment of His own task—prophetic of the future. Their healing of the sick and joyous challenge and victory over the power of evil was pledged in earnest of His own complete and final victory over all the "hell" that is in the world. They could only "see" the results of their local mission; but He could "see" His victory over the devil, over disease, over death and evil of every kind.

Christ, in that little provincial spot could see Victory and in Him, we, too, can see Victory. We are in the midst of conflict, but we must not lose sight of what our efforts and sacrifices of love are attaining.

Edward Jenner and Louis Pasteur, upon making successful discoveries, must have let their minds run forward to anticipate the future blessings of health and have declared "I beheld the Satan of disease fall...". In seeing our nation founded in unity and faith, Washington surely thought, "I have seen the spirit of disunion and division fall." After the Englishman, Wilburforce, fought a lifelong battle to end slavery there, he could see "the Satan of greed and cruelty fall."

It is a wonderful thing to "see" the victory of what is right and God-appointed, to have the witness within yourself. It enables the weakest faith and faintest hope to find support and confidence. Christ is still in our conflict to the end. "The battle is the Lord's".

Reconciliation

"Where there is neither Greek nor Jew, circumcision nor uncircumcision, Barbarian, Scythian, bond nor free: but Christ is all, and in all."
—*Colossians 3:11*

The Bible is a book of human relationships. At the heart of every page is the message of reconciliation. The life of Jesus was a life of reconciliation. And in Christ, we have the ministry of reconciliation.

Our text tells us about racial reconciliation (neither Jew nor Greek), religious reconciliation (neither circumcision nor uncircumcision), social reconciliation (neither Barbarian nor Scythican), and economic reconciliation (where Christ is all in all).

Personal relationships and Christian community must always be built on individual reconciliation and concern. It starts in the heart. The issue is not the color, religion, culture or social or economic position—you will find bad apples in every barrel, and good ones, too. Men of several races crucified Jesus; the religious condemned Him and the pagan did the dirty work; the poor and commoners mobbed Him while the rich and social leaders snubbed Him and "washed their hands." At the cross, every human being stands guilty. And the cross of Jesus Christ stands for all as a means of reconciliation—He did it for all of us.

The cross of Calvary isn't the exclusive possession of the American people. It belongs to the whole world. That's why every real Christian is a missionary. He wants the other fellow to have and enjoy what he has and enjoys. In Christ, there are no aliens or uncultured or unfit. How easy it is to be a snob. But God's Word says, "God *resisteth* the proud."

One of our greatest diplomats, John Foster Dulles, summarizes the issue: "The most significant demonstration that can be made is at the religious level. The overriding and everpresent reason for giving freedom to the individual is that all men are created as the children of God, in His image. The human personality is thus sacred."

A New Mouth

"A good man out of the good treasure of his heart bringeth forth that which is good; and an evil man out of the evil treasure of his heart bringeth forth that which is evil: FOR OUT OF THE ABUN-DANCE OF THE HEART HIS MOUTH SPEAKETH." —Luke 6:45

Today, with modern medical equipment, doctors give us blood cultures, x-rays and all kinds of tests. But when I was growing up, we only had the family doctor. No matter what was wrong, the first thing he would ask you to do when he came to examine you was to open your mouth and stick out your tongue. That tongue seems to tell the whole story. I believe God meant to tell us something in that.

There is all the difference in the world between the mouth of a real born-again child of God and the mouth of an unconverted man or woman. When we find Christ as our personal Savior, our language habits naturally begin to change. There is an inner cleansing of foulness, evil and hate. And when the inner man get clean, the tongue gets clean, too. There is a good feeling and joy in being clean. The Proverbs say: "a man hath joy by the answer of his mouth." How sad it is to hear much of the language of this world. The language of the gutter is on our movie screens and in our schools and in our business places, where it was never tolerated before. When you hear this talk, you cannot help but come away wanting to take a bath to feel clean again. How we need the rain of the Holy Spirit to cleanse the mouths in our land.

It is not just what comes out of his mouth that distinguishes a Christian. A believer will want to put good things in the mouth that which glorifies the Lord. No discussion is needed to elaborate on harm of alchohol, tobacco, drugs, even over-eating. The Holy Spirit gives us a new taste—a taste of good things, the good things of God's word. A new heart, a new nature, a new desire, a new mouth, a new language—these are the inheritance of every believer by the Spirit.

"Killjoy Was Here"

"But let it (the adorning) be the hidden man of the heart, in that which is not corruptible, even the ornament of a meek and quiet spirit, which is in the sight of God of great price." —I Peter 3:4

Killjoy may be a term of another generation, but the meaning is not hard to figure out. I think they call it today a "wet blanket." In any case, have you ever considered what makes people attractive, or unattractive? Certainly, it is not just physical assets. Pretty people are not always the most popular.

The scriptures do not describe Jesus as physically beautiful. Yet he was deeply loved by men, women, and children, because of His love for all men. The Master's beauty was in His sympathy, understanding and helpfulness. The secret that He left us is this: *Beauty is something that begins inside and works outward* and not vice versa.

When we think of selfishness, meanness, brutality, or hatred, we think of ugliness. When we think of love, generosity, kindness, and understanding, we think of beauty. It is really what we think of a human being that causes him or her to be ugly or beautiful in our eyes. In this way, Jesus gave us the standards for beauty by his own example.

Where the law asked an eye for an eye cold justice, Jesus brought warmth and mercy. Men hard as nails were captivated by Him and surrendered unconditionally to Him. People knew instinctively that Jesus loved them and that His love was genuine and unselfish.

That kind of beauty is contagious. Where selfishness and meanness dry up and cower, love creates vitality and energy. It makes the eyes sparkle with life and good humor. The world loves a lover. It can't help itself.

Jesus' beauty still transforms—it can take "the killjoy" and make it "the joyful." It is not for sale; it is found wherever His name is lifted up and His presence felt. Beauty is the product of the new creation.

The Shadow Of Self

"Therefore now, O Lord, take, I beseech thee,
my life from me: for it is better for me to die than to
live."
—Jonah 4:3

This may surprise you, but this was the best prayer that Jonah ever uttered. His greatest need was to die out to Jonah. Until the prayer, Jonah's life was a supreme example of the odiousness and foolishness of the spirit of selfishness, especially for one who professed to work for God and the souls of men.

Jonah was one of the first of Israel's prophets whose writings have come down in Scripture. Living during the reign of Jeroboam II, he had a very successful ministry among his own people. His ministry furnished the impetus that lifted Israel out of depression to the highest point of power in all her history. If his career had ended here, he would have been recorded as being one of the most successful prophets in history.

But God gave Jonah a new commission: to go to Nineveh of the Assyrians. Because of his strong nationalistic feelings, the call was unexpected and unwelcomed. His whole self-will rose up in rebellion and determined not to go. But Jonah learned you can't hide from God, and the messengers of judgment (storm) and mercy brought Jonah to a place of obedience.

Preaching in Ninevah, Jonah temporarily seemed like a crucified man. As long as his work succeeded and the people listened and repented, he was satisfied. But when God met the repentance of the Ninevites, old "Jonah" rose in fury because his reputation was tarnished.

As much as for Ninevah, this mission was to test Jonah. To serve God when it doesn't suit, to obey when it doesn't please, to serve out of a love for God and the souls of men are tests for anyone who desires to be used of God. Jonah and every servant of God must die to selfish desire before being truly used of God. God loves to make us partakers with him in the fruits of our work, but we must seek His glory and not our own.

Bells And Pomegranates

"A golden bell and a pomegranate, upon the hem of the robe round about. And it shall be upon Aaron to minister: and his sound shall be heard when he goeth in unto the holy place before the Lord, and when he cometh out, that he die not."
—*Exodus 28:34, 35*

This is one of the clearest pictures of New Testament salvation given in symbolic form in the Old Testament. There are two outward signs to genuine salvation: *what you say* and *what you are*; or in Biblical language: *confession* and *fruit*. These are the twin results of divine grace at work in the human heart and the two things that make up our testimony before the world.

The writer of Hebrews teaches us that in this Old Testament picture is a true sketch of a present day believer-priest. Upon this robe of righteousness (which I present to God and this world) are to hang the bell of confession and the pomegranate of fruit in alternate succession. The symbols are carefully chosen of God. What sound more sure and sweet than that of a golden bell? What seed more fruitful than the pomegranate?

The bell and the fruit are in alternation. There is not all fruit or all sound, but they are equal. The confession must be equal to the daily walk; and the life lived equal to the confession. Notice, the sound of the bell comes first—then next the fruit. The ringing witness of the cleansing Spirit, too, precedes the bearing of fruit in our lives. The witness is vital: "bells shall be heard, that he die not." A dumb, speechless Christian is a dead Christian. Whether it be a church or an individual, the life and vitality begin to drain when testimony and praise of the works of Jesus cease.

The writer of Hebrews in Chapter 10 builds on this picture, commanding us to boldly "draw near" the holy place, holding fast *the profession* of our faith without wavering (that's the bell) and considering one another to *provoke unto love and good works* (that's the pomegranate). It's the same combination of confession and fruit. This is our challenge in life—to ring a bell for eternity and share our seed that men may bless His name.

Spots And Wrinkles

"That He might present it to Himself a glorious church, not having spot, or wrinkle, or any such thing..." —*Ephesians 5:27*

Every day we face the common household problem of "spots and wrinkles." My cleaning bill amounts to quite an item; I am concerned with my "outward man." And then there are the women-folk who fight wrinkles on their faces. Americans spend more yearly for beauty culture than all but a few nations spend on their total food budget. Is it any wonder that our God has been willing to make a huge investment in the culture and beautifying of the "inner man"?

God has had His hands full with spots. Even our Bible leaders had their share, marring and hindering their usefulness as God's children. Abraham's spot was deception. In plain English, he was a liar; he lied to his wife and about his wife many times. And his sin passed down to others. His son Issac was a liar and Issac's son, Jacob, was one of the best ever. It was a bad spot in the family's character, and it took God a long time to rub it out.

Moses' spot was a "hair trigger temper." His sister, Miriam, had a vicious tongue. David had a great spot—not taking his eyes off other men's wives. Then Jonah, another preacher, had a bad spot—turning away when things didn't go to suit him. Yet God loved and used all these, and He is patiently working in our lives to cleanse us from all such spots that mar our character.

He's working on our wrinkles. "Spots" indicate impurities which ought not to be there while wrinkles indicate the absense or the lack of virtues and graces which ought to be there. Many "good" people try to be content with a negative religion, following the rules, but they miss a lot of positive things they need to make a well-rounded, filled-out Christian character. God wants our lives to be positive—to bear fruit, to attract a lost and needy world to Christ.

Whatever our"spots or wrinkles," God is there patiently working to cleanse and fill, that our lives might be to His Glory.

Have You Become Violent?

"And from the days of John the Baptist until now the kingdom of heaven suffereth violence, and the violent take it by force." —Matthew 11:12

There is just one kind of violence that the Lord approves of. It is a violence of conviction, or moral living, and determination to set forth Christ in a way that will create a spiritual force in the community which no evil power can withstand.

John the Baptist had this kind of violence in his soul. He was the God-ordained forerunner of Christ's first coming. He appeared to make this special announcement and presentation of Christ to the world. And Jesus said that he wasn't any spineless "reed" shaken by the wind or stylish "clotheshorse" indulging himself in the soft and easygoing manner of his times. Rather he was a *Messenger* hurrying with Heaven's message—a man with one intense motive in life and that was to hasten the coming of Christ!

Today, Jesus is about to come back again. And God is now looking for clean-cut, earnest, outspoken messengers who will be so all-out for God that through the "spiritual violence" and intensity of their testimony for God, a moral and revival force may be engendered for good and lead to an awakening in the world that will prepare all believers for the Second Coming of Christ.

This world has been under the rulership of the Prince of the Air, but it is being overcome by the kingdom of Heaven through spiritual force—the energy that is the result of vision and earnestness and dedication to the entire will of God such as John the Baptist made to the cause of Christ. Soft clothing and instability will never move people to conviction. We must be earnest, getting off the fence and believe as never before. There must be a force of faith operating in our life and home, church, and business.

Let us get violent, not against our fellow Christian, but against sin and degeneracy, and become violent for God and His righteousness.

Dare To Be A Daniel

"But Daniel purposed in his heart that he would not defile himself with the portion of the king's meat, nor with the wine which he drank..."
—Daniel 1:8

If ever a guy was on the spot, this young man Daniel was. He was a thousand miles from home and only seventeen years old—a captive among captive people. Daniel was being given a course for a place of leadership in the Babylonian government. If he made good, not only would he be out of slavery for the rest of his life, but he would be financially secure in a place of prestige and honor.

But this young man had convictions. He loved God and had been taught from childhood not to eat meats offered to idols or defile himself with strong drink. But the Babylonians believed a person would not be healthy without these meats and drink, so the king prescribed this diet for the Hebrew students.

Daniel had to choose. Most likely, refusing to eat would end all his chances in school. Convictions can be the most expensive and inconvenient things in human life. But how they are needed! They are the foundation stone of character. Daniel had the same pressure as you or I to compromise. No doubt, Satan was saying; "Don't be a fool and throw away this opportunity of a lifetime." But "Daniel purposed in his heart that he would not defile himself." Life, to him, wasn't worth living if he couldn't live it cleanly.

I imagine he heard the voice: "this is the way everybody does it." We have all heard that—to which the wise man wrote: "The fear of man bringeth a snare." Fear of man caused Peter to curse, Pilate to condemn, and many a Christian to fall. "All that live godly in Christ Jesus shall suffer persecution." It does take courage.

How all of Daniel's pride must have fought it: going against the social custom, endangering his reputation with the king, risking all the monetary rewards. Yet when Daniel swallowed his pride to stick with his convictions, God honored him. He delivered him from his enemies and honored him with position, prosperity, and long life. God will not let us down either if we have courage to break with the crowd and refuse to compromise with evil. He is our shield and buckler.

Trust

",,,but I will trust in Thee."

—Psalm 55:23

We all hear sermons about trust from our pulpits, and the natural tendency is for us to react, thinking: "It is fine for you to talk about trust in your secure little nitch, but you don't know my situation." Let us then consider the kind of man who wrote our text. Was he happy? Were things going well? What were his circumstances?

The opening cry of this Psalm is: "Hide not Thy face from my supplication." It was the prayer of a man unanswered. There was no response to his uplifted crying. What is our response when we hit a dark tunnel and pray and pray and pray? Will we say: "But I will trust?" This Psalmist did. He refused to regard silence as indifference, knowing that a thousand years are as a day to our Lord. He will answer!

The Psalmist continues in confession of his fear: "The terrors of death are fallen upon me. Fearfulness and trembling are come upon me..." If David wrote this, as is likely, he was one of the bravest of men. Yet this man was scared. There are times when circumstances loom as a giant over us and make us want to run. The Psalmist stood and dealt with this fear with the words: "But I will trust."

This was also a man imprisoned: "O that I had wings like a dove, for then would I fly away and be at rest." There was no dungeon or steel bars; he was just down in the dumps, fed up with his problems, and tired. Do we find ourselves stuck in a trying position, caught in the monotony of routine, feeling like the walls are closing in? The rest is where David found it—under the shadow of His wings: "But I will trust."

Finally, here was a man deceived. His hurt came not from an enemy but a friend: "but it was thou, a man mine equal, my guide and mine acquaintance." Have you ever been let down by a pal, a close friend? These are the darkest hours of life. Not the walls closing in, but the roof caving in. Yet the Psalmist in the midst of the ruins of that friendship, deserted, let-down by one who was a brother, says: "but I will trust in Thee."

No, these were not words written in a comfortable little nook; they were the experience of a man in the grip of despair—who nonetheless even in his suffering reached the height of saving trust.

Singing In The Fire

"Wherein ye greatly rejoice, though now for a season, if need be, ye are in heaviness through manifold temptations." —I Peter 1:6

Sometimes we think it strange when God's people suffer affliction. The question is often asked, "Why is the Christian life drenched with so much blood and blistered with so many tears?" Peter answers that only as faith is tested through manifold trials can it be "formed to the praise and honor and glory of Jesus Christ at His appearing." These early Christians were buffeted for doing well: reviled, persecuted, exposed to mockery and reproached for the name of Christ. And Peter says that the same afflictions were the lot of their brethren throughout the world.

For us, too? The Bible says, "it is given unto us not only to believe in Christ but to suffer for His name." The best of Christians may be in great heaviness through manifold trials. Why? God tries them for their own good. The Word says Jesus "was made perfect through suffering." And a servant is not greater than His Master!

The word "trial" signifies an experiment—a testing to prove a value or strength. Peter knew what he was talking about. Jesus had allowed Peter to experience the trial of his faith...Christ had prayed for him. He prayed Peter's faith would not fail and it didn't. So years later Peter could comfort other Christians.

We are told that the finest China in the world, *Dresden China*, is burned three times or more. Why does it go through that intense fire? It is necessary so that the gold and crimson are brought out more beautifully and then fastened there to stay. The trial of our faith is not just once, but often if need be, that the beautiful colors of Christian nobility might work so in us as to bring honor and glory to Christ. Trials are for but a season, that one day you will be receiving "the end of your faith—even the salvation of your souls."

Thanksgiving For Inner Strength

"For this thing I besought the Lord thrice, that it might depart from me. And He said unto me, My grace is sufficient for thee..."—II Corinthians 12:8, 9

Have you every wondered why life is difficult? Why is the coal and oil and uranium we need so badly for energy buried deep beneath the earth's surface? The soil that we need for food cannot be taken captive without a fight against rocks, weeds, erosion, etc. The lumber we need for our houses resists with its toughness; the precious and beautiful minerals drive men deep below the ground and hide in hard ore; even the rivers we use for power and transportation resist the harnessing and bridging. Why all the strange difficulties?

When we look at the climates of the world, we find differences in the races of men. Where the climate is severe without being fierce and over-powering, you will find the most capable races. The stronger men do not come from the softer climates. And God wants strong men—strong in Him!

In our text, the apostle Paul had experienced a buffeting of Satan, a physical problem ("thorn in the flesh") that was making life difficult. Three times he prayed for the Lord to take it away. But instead of changing Paul's thorn, God changed Paul's spirit. God said, "It shall remain but you will be strengthened for I will pour *My Help* in upon your life." And out of that experience Paul learned of a new strength and power for his soul.

Many of us recount God's benefits to us more for outer things than for inner strength. We thank God more at the table than at the altar. Paul thanked God for things like pureness, longsuffering, the word of truth, the armour of righteousness, the power of God, unfeigned love, chastening, and kindness. These are the things that give victory and peace in the storms of life. For us, too, God will not always remove our difficulties—but He will make us equal to them!

Calamities

"And it came to pass, after a while, that the brook dried up, because there had been no rain in the land...I have commanded a widow woman there to sustain thee." —I Kings 17:7, 9

There is no one, it seems, who is immune to the calamities of life. In fact, they appear to have a place in God's divine providence for man. They can startle us and make us think. In the midst of them, people begin to ask questions about God. Some go further and not only think about God, but about themselves and their destiny.

The context of our scripture is God's provision for His servant, Elijah, during a famine in Israel. In His loving care, God had hidden Elijah from the wrath of Ahab and provided food and drink. But the brook dried up—what about the care of God now? Elijah was to learn something new.

Living by the Brook Cherith, he had received the natural supplies of the earth and learned that all of nature was God's servant. Now he was to live by an empty barrel and an exhausted cruse. His eyes were to be opened further to the ingenuity of God's love, quickening his faith into a deeper level of dependence. God is going to use a starving woman's faith and love—a humbling experience for this prophet. But "where two of you shall agree", there is the provision of God. Strange companions, but the faith and love for God of these two made a circle through which God could work.

When the "brook dries up" in our lives, it may be for the same reason. Many times the things that draw humans together, whether at work, or in marriage or friendship, are superficial. After a while, God allows those things "to dry up". The solution is a spiritual one! God wants to bring us into a deeper level of living and a finer spring of love. It takes a new resource in God, a new venture in prayer.

The entire Christian life is a miracle or it is nothing. The superficial will pass, but the new creation is ever renewed and renewing itself in God—"a root out of dry ground" like the desert plants. Their secret of having no visible resource, is that their roots go down 20 or 30 feet or more, tapping some perennial spring hidden in the crevices of the strata. No blight or drought above can reach their foundations. This is God's work in our lives: "let your roots go deep in Him," "hid with Christ in God."

SEPTEMBER:
Holiness and the Fruit
of the Spirit

"But the fruit of the Spirit is love, joy, peace, longsuffering, gentleness, goodness, faith, meekness, temperance: against such there is no law." —Galatians 5:22, 23

The Simple Gospel

"For God so loved the world that He gave His only begotten Son, that whosoever believeth in Him, should not perish but have everlasting life."
—John 3:16

James Blackwood
Music Artist

This is the simple, clear message of the Gospel. We put it in words and add a melody and sing about it. We see it pictured in a thousand ways in the Bible. We see it depicted in nature. All of life is sparked by God's love.

My favorite chapter in the Bible is I Corinthians 13. It tells me how to love and reminds me of the purpose and motivation that should be a part of everything I do. Singing never loses its meaning and vitality when I remember and sing about God's love.

Let Us Love

"A new commandment I give unto you, That ye love one another; as I have loved you, that ye also love one another." —John 13:34

Love is the greatest power in the world and the wonderful thing is that it is one thing that everybody needs and wants. It is the universal representation of God; no matter where you go or who you speak to, you can be God's servant if you love.

When we love we do so much. Not only does Jesus command us to love, but He says that if we love, we will keep His commandments. Therefore, we can please God just by loving.

Dr. James Johnson
Former Under Secretary of Navy

People tell me that it is hard to love, I agree. But I can speak from experience of some of the roughest storms of life, it is harder on us if we do not love. Love sets us free. God helps us to love; He tells us "we can do all things through Christ who strengthens me." Therefore, I can love.

The Power of Praise

"In every thing give thanks: for this is the will of God in Christ Jesus concerning you."
—*I Thessalonians 5:18*

Merlin Carothers
Author, Pastor

I am continually amazed at how well life works when we simply live it according to God's word. The simple truth of this verse to thank God in all things transformed my life and gave me power to face seemingly impossible situations and emerge through them victoriously.

I am just as amazed at how well this verse works in other's lives. The testimony given in the book, *Prison To Praise* has been used to transform ten of thousands from defeated Christians to victorious believers, simply by beginning to give thanks in all things. This tells me that victory in life comes by obedience rather than feelings. When I obey God, regardless of my feelings, God will bless and deliver me out of my troubles.

What Is Spirituality?

"...ye which are spiritual..."
—*Galatians 6:1*

What is spirituality? This is a term used today in many forms—even in reference to unbelievers. What makes a man spiritual? Let us look in the scriptures and examine some of the characters who are spoken of as outstanding instances of spirituality.

If we were to ask a member of the Israelite tribe of Dan who was the most spiritual man of his tribe, he would say Samson. This unlikely character, with a coarse sense of humor, a sensual nature, and a fitful patriotism, had the Spirit of the Lord come upon him on four different occasions. He offered God his strength and found his way among the heroes of the faith in Hebrews 11.

Bezaleel, the craftsman and designer of articles for the Tabernacle in the wilderness, was "filled with the Spirit of God." This man was a layman and had nothing to do with prayers or offerings. His spirituality was shown in his eye for *beauty* and his skill to create it. Banished from the art center of the world (Egypt) and disciplined from making any graven images, he still consecrated his artistic taste and skill to the service of the Lord.

In the early church, we see Stephen as "a man full of the Spirit." Chosen to serve under the Apostles as a deacon, Stephen fitted their need for men of *tact* and *reputation for fairness*. Thrust into attention by the persecution of the Jews, Stephen offered his intellect to God's service ("they were not able to withstand the wisdom and Spirit by which he spoke") and died a martyr's death.

Finally, we see Barnabas, "a good man and full of the Holy Spirit." He was a Gentile, but a good-hearted man who with his graciousness and hospitality eased the way for the Gentiles to become a part of the church.

What did each of these men have in common? Consecration. Each took his talents and dedicated it to the cause of God as he understood it. Their talents weren't spiritual in themselves—but it was what they did and allowed God to do in them that made them spiritual. Life is not to be divided into secular and sacred. All life may be "spiritualized" by those who dedicate it to holy purposes.

The Grace of Appreciation

"She hath done what she could..."
—*Mark 14:8*

Someone recently said, "You can reduce life down to pure mathematical terms—the *minus* and the *plus*. The *minus* people leave us poorer and the *plus* people leave us richer." That view is rather simplistic but it speaks to a subject that cannot be overrated: *appreciation*.

Have you ever noticed what are the things that make or break your day? How often it is the little things—a heart-felt "thank-you", a big smile, the door opened, the word of encouragement. Hard, different things? No, rather just doing what could be done.

What insight in the words of Jesus, "she hath done what she could." He could see the great value in things ordinary people were doing. When the woman broke the alabaster box, He alone appreciated it. When the widow cast her mite into the treasury, He saw in a flash the splendour of her giving. Men of his day appreciated a cup of wine—He a cup of water. How wonderful was His appreciation of the human heart.

He could look at a harlot and see a potential worshipper, at a despised tax-gatherer and see a faithful disciple and writer of the Gospel. Nothing was so common to be without beauty. To Jesus the lily was more wonderful than Solomon. He had good words for the sparrrows, and individual love and kindness to the children.

Jesus' secret? Love—you've got to love to have appreciation. Love opens our eyes to see beauty and goodness. If you were to buy a little jewel box, you would surely require it to be perfect. But let your son make one for you and it can have a hundred faults and rough spots, yet you appreciate it because it is the workmanship of the little chap you love.

Everybody is important and has an important job to do. How needed are our simple words of encouragement and appreciation!

What Is Goodness?

"For He satisfieth the longing soul and filleth the hungry soul with GOODNESS." —Psalm 107:9

Even Jesus refrained from accepting the title, "good." But goodness is one of the most important characteristics of the born-again Christian. Goodness is the fruit of the Holy Spirit. It transforms the believer and makes him recognizable as a follower of Christ.

Goodness is a many sided fruit. One side is *truth* and honesty. When you love Jesus you love truth. Paul writes that one way to "be renewed in the spirit of your mind" is to "put away lying."

Another side of *purity*. All creation groans to see the full redemption and return of Christ. God created the world in goodness and purity but man's evil has brought corruption to all. Through Christ we can again be "partakers of the divine nature (goodness), having escaped the corruption that is in the world through lust." A good test of our goodness is what we choose for our amusement and recreation.

Then goodness is real *life*. For the world the goodness of Madison Avenue may be having a new fangled popcorn-popper. God's goodness avoids the shallowness and goes to the depth of the heart. It means love: thinking for others. It means a happy home life. At work, goodness is a genuine respect for our daily job. A Christian will take his job as his pulpit.

Finally, goodness is our expression to others in the world. It is our consecration, written across our checkbook. It is our desire to share our faith with others, and it means standing up against evil, being concerned about the welfare of our fellow man.

In a day when all respect is questioned and in a country which has lost most of its heroes, our neighbor in the world wants to see real "goodness" in Christians. What do they see in us?

Faithfulness

"...it is REQUIRED in stewards, that a man be found faithful."   —I Corinthians 4:2

Faithfulness is a required course of study in the school of the Spirit. Some courses offered are electives, but this one is required for all—though some would say that they have already mastered it.

There is a worldly faithfulness that is not of God. A tombstone inscription illustrates this: "He was born a man; he died a grocer." The ghost in Dickens' *Christmas Carol* could hardly convince Scrooge that thrift and success in business were not the end in faithful living. Rather, true faithfulness is walking in sincere stewardship before God and our fellowmen.

A little child had seen a poor man on the street in evident need. "Oh, Mamma," she said, "let's help him!" But the mother rushed her on, saying it was none of their business. So that night after she had said her prayers, she added, "O God, bless the poor man on the corner." And then remembering her mother's words, she continued: "But then, it isn't any of our business is it, Lord?"

Faithfulness is everybody's business. God has created everything according to the principle of stewardship—the soil, the animals, the family, etc. God so loved the world that *He Gave*. In this way, life is a trust. Man with his free will can violate the "law of stewardship." But if he does, he will face it in eternity—"to whomsoever much is given, of him shall much be required."

The heavenly accounting will not just include our possessions, but our very lives. God has made us for Himself, and when we take our lives out of His hands for selfish pursuits, we are robbing God. Paul understood his stewardship obligation when he said: "whether we live therefore or die, we are the Lord's."

Whether we have received one talent or ten—we must use it.

Regularity

"...the same commit thou to FAITHFUL men..." —II Timothy 2:2

It is almost trite to say that life is made up of things which are regular and things which are irregular. But regularity in our lives is as important as it is in our bodies.

Try as we will we cannot make all things regular. We cannot arrange a time table for the weather. The farmer cannot schedule the harvest, and the merchant cannot schedule the flow of customers. In fact, some forms of irregularity add spice to our lives, for they lead to surprise. But generally irregularity leads to disorder, and regularity leads to order. If we are to produce something definite through our Christian testimony, we must give attention to building up regular habits.

There can be regularity in our rising in the morning. A good start is important not just in a foot race, but in a successful day. God's mercy (and direction) is new every morning and a short "briefing" with God's Word and prayer for direction and guidance can be the most valuable time spent in our day.

Then there can be the regularity of the family altar. In the busy world, it is difficult to bring the whole family together for morning and evening prayer. But family worship when regularly adhered to does more to keep unpleasantness and sin out of the home than anything else. It is the great cure of the disease and failure in the home.

Finally, there should be regularity in church attendance and giving. Going to church is so much more than hearing a sermon; it is entering into living, deep commitments with brothers and sisters in Christ. These cannot be maintained and developed without regular participation.

If we build regularity in these areas, we will find new strength in our Christian character and security in the ways of God.

Thanksgiving

*"I THANK MY GOD upon every remem-
brance of you."* —*Philippians 1:3*

This sentence was a trademark of the great Apostle Paul. It appears in every epistle except one. Sometimes it was accompanied by assurance of prayers, sometimes by a list of virtues of those named and sometimes by a hint of that inner compulsion. But in each, it expressed Paul's deep thankfulness for his human associations.

Paul didn't try to hide his thanks in private; he spoke out so that all might hear. And in his thanks, he addressed men and God at the same time, hinting that these friends were gifts of God. In prison Paul's thanksgivings to men were limited to letters, but traditionally thanksgiving centered around the "breaking of bread"—sharing meals together.

The table has always been the world's great medium of sociability. We become really known to each other in the breaking of bread. How picturesque the King James language in Revelation 3:20 which reads "I will come in and sup (fellowship) with you." God so valued fellowship with man that He sent His only Son to die a cruel death to restore that fellowship.

We, too, value our human relationships—probably more than we know. Be away from your friends for a while and see how much you miss them. The ultimate in penal punishment today is solitary confinement-separation from human relationships. How often do we say thanks for those human friendships, not just to God but to men? We know that God desires our thanksgiving; are not men made "in His image"? We all appreciate commendation and gratitude. We even struggle to win medals and trophies. Could it be that if we gave men more thanksgiving there would be less struggle? When we thank God at the table today, let us also thank our fellow friends—gifts of God.

Kindness

"And let fall also some of the handfuls of purpose for her, and leave them, that she may glean them, and rebuke her not." —Ruth 2:16

Our text comes from the story of Ruth where Boaz invited Ruth to glean in his fields and commanded his harvesters to purposely leave grain for her. My mother used to describe this kind of thing as being "accidental on purpose" and it is the heart of kindness.

Ruth had come down in the world. Once she had been well off—but now for the sake of her dead love, she had taken Naomi's poverty voluntarily upon her— and she must swallow her pride and go out to glean with the other poor folk. Now, the rich Boaz could have easily come and brought her a bag of corn and said, "Here, we feel sorry for you." She might have received it, but would have suffered inside. The good-hearted Boaz was thinking of Ruth's feelings when he helped her.

The way this Bible story shows how a farmer took special pains to save the poor woman's pride, makes us feel that kindness is something very important as far as God is concerned. We all know that unkindness hurts. But kindness can hurt, too, when done in the wrong way. The example of Boaz is the height of kindness in thinking of a way to help Ruth in a way most agreeable to Ruth.

For most of us, it does not take much to make us happy. Happiness is more that which happens to us than which is given to us—a beam of sunlight falling on our face, a smile from someone, some little token of a friend's good will, the impression our neighbor conveys that he is glad to see us.

This is being kind; it isn't a great task. But it takes attention and concern. Many think that kindness is a special gift for someone else. Really, we lack kindness because we forget; we don't pay attention; and we don't realize that when we've forgotten that, we've forgotten everything.

Gentleness

"...the fruit of the Spirit...is gentleness."
—*Galatians 5:22*

A prominent businessman spoke of his secret of success. He said, "The surest way to be successful is to apply the 'gentle touch' in everything you do."

It is true, we'll never find the answer if we are "pressing" or "striving" continually on edge. The golfer who makes the longest drive down the fairway swings his club with amazing ease—the expert typist types with ease. And the person who lives happily lives with ease. He gets things done by going about them quietly and calmly. This is the fruit of gentleness.

We remember the story of the contest between the wind and the sun to see who was stronger. Just as in removing the man's coat, the sun's warmth was more effective than the wind's blast, so was the Son of God in doing His Father's work. Jesus was never hurried, never anxious; He never wasted time or energy, and yet He did the biggest job this world has ever seen in just three years. Jesus' calmness was based on faith. It stemmed from something inside.

We, too, can live without pressure. As the song says, "God Is Still On The Throne." Over and over the gospel message says, "Let go and let God." This is the way of the Spirit. "The way of the transgressor is hard," but Jesus' "yoke is easy and His burden is light." The Spirit works readily and mightily on our behalf when we learn to yield ourselves to His disposal. The Psalmist voiced this as: "Thy gentleness hath made me great." God is our power, our strength, and God is Love.

As our lives move into His channel, with confidence, there comes a gentleness that agrees with God: "Let there be..." "Let."

Health Through Joy And Gratitude

"For we are unto God a sweet savour of Christ..."   *—II Corinthians 2:15*

Down at the bottom line, God appears desirous to risk everything on our willingness to recognize His gift and *thank Him* for the love that gave it. It is this sense of seeing that everything is a gift that is the heart of our Christian faith. The Giver remains out of sight—His hand unseen—yet He yearns for response and gratitude.

The greatest inspirations of life have sprung from hearts of gratitude! The majestic songs, "Messiah", "Creation", "Marseillaise", "The Star Spangled Banner", all sprang from hearts overwhelmed by a sense of appreciation. Many times ruin, suffering, and poverty spread around as these singers sang their song. Having nothing, they were aflame with gratitude.

During World War I, when Belgium had been invaded by the Germans and its cities ruined, the Kaiser said to King Albert, "Now you see what your oppsition has brought upon you. What have you gained? What have you left?" Albert turned to him and said, "I have my soul."

In our material-oriented world, Jesus still speaks, "If you should gain the whole world and lose your soul—what profit have you?" We have got to live with ourselves. We can be stripped of all outward possessions and still be happy if like Albert, "we have our souls." Our joy and happiness depend largely on our appreciation of God, for it is He that feeds our souls.

Gratitude is having the eyes to see God's goodness for our souls, and the perfume out of which the fragrance of joy arises. If we would be truly happy, we must be grateful. For if we lose our sense of appreciation, we lose our zest for life. Gladness comes from gratitude.

Happy People Are Healthy

"Beloved, I wish above all things that thou mayest prosper and be in health, even as thy soul prospereth." —III John 2

Over and over in God's word, there is intimate connection between happiness and good health. Joy and happiness form a tonic—a genuine stimulant. Joy is a producer of vitality every bit as much as gloom and depression have a tendency to exhaust and depress the nervous system.

The great old expression of good cheer, "hail," is the same root word as "heal" and "health"—suggesting again the affinity of happiness and health. One of the greatest blessings of the present renewal movement in denominational churches (Pentecostal as well) is the great manifestation of praise and "hallelujahs" in church services. People used to think that singing and cheering could only happen at a ball game. Now, people are going away from church feeling refreshed and relaxed, which is exactly what the Bible says should happen when we gather in the Spirit: "this is the rest...and this is the refreshing."

We learn in Hebrews that the sacrifice of praise is the most acceptable offering we can lay at the Master's feet. When we look at David's life, we can see that one reason why God called him a man after His own heart is that he was so full of praise and thankfulness. And when we see that God promised the Israelites in the wilderness perfect health if they would obey him, it is not strange that God rewards those of thankful spirits with good health.

Many of us do not come to God in thanksgiving because we have failed or sinned, and we fear He is not pleased. We misunderstand what pleases God. His Word says God is pleased when we come to Him in faith. And what better evidence of faith than joy and thanksgiving. So let us draw near in thanksgiving, even if just to thank Him for forgiveness because we have failed.

Peacemakers

"Blessed are the PEACEMAKERS: for they shall be called the children of God." —Matthew 5:9

Abraham Lincoln, President during America's bloodiest war, is perhaps the greatest illustration of a peacemaker in modern history. He could endure snobbishness, forget insults, and make his opponents so vividly aware of his appreciation of their honest purposes that he could often persuade them (almost against their will) to unite with him in some needed measure. Such men are the true creative spirits of humanity—using sure and kindly diplomacy to persuade men who cannot agree on all things to unite at least on some measure that is for the common good. These are powerful men! They have a right to be called "sons of God!"

Christian peace is active. It does not mean an absence of struggle or fighting. That may be peace in its own way, but it is the peace of the tomb. No, Christian peace is a movement. It cooperates in good work and is eager for friendly intercourse. It feels the need of a brother's counsel and wisdom. Peace does not slip up in the dark and overpower us; it is, according to the Psalmist, something we seek and pursue.

How does trouble begin? The cause of the quarrel is rarely the root. It springs out of some previous and hidden attitude of the mind. It begins when we judge our brother. We take an unfavorable view before we know all the facts: "Judge not." If we give men a square deal in the long run they will give it back and there will be peace. But for many, it takes more than simple justice. *We must have mercy.*

Those who take the first steps in showing mercy are following Jesus. No wonder Jesus says, they shall be called the "sons of God".

Grace

"The grace of our Lord Jesus Christ be with you all."
—Romans 16:24

Our religious crowd talks a lot about this word, grace. We speak of "the throne of grace," "falling from grace," "in the state of grace." But what do we mean? Once Joan of Arc, the heroine of France, when her persecutors tried to trap her by asking whether she considered herself to be in a state of grace, replied; "If I am, I bless God's mercy; and if I am not, I pray that He may bring me into it." Grace is exhibited in that very answer, for it is modesty, humility and lack of self-consciousness which are the very essence of grace.

The word, *grace* as it appears in the New Testament is the Greek word, *Charis*. It was taken from secular literature by the writers and vivified and deepened. Its original reference was quite external, meaning *a pleasure—giving beauty*. Popular among the Greeks to whom outward beauty was religion, it spoke of symmetery, proportion and beautiful coordination.

Certainly, much of that same meaning is ascribed to our Lord by Luke who wrote; "Jesus increased in wisdom and statue and *in grace with God and man*." The deeper content of the word may be rendered "gracious"—meaning to be kind, especially to those who don't deserve it. We see its meaning in the picture of the "gracious hostess," kindly interesting herself in what interests others and caring for their needs. It is seen in the familiar connotation of "graciousness": well bred, gentle and noble.

But it is best seen in our Saviour. We see Him with the despised Samaritan woman at the well. What a gentleman! Instead of rebuking her or getting up and leaving, He shares with her some of the greatest nuggets of life. It was to her that He first proclaimed His Messiahship. Unexpected kindness, that is grace: "If thine enemy hunger, feed him; if he thirst, give him drink." Undeserved love: "while we were yet sinners, Christ died for us." That is grace *indeed*.

Our Greatest Cause For Thanksgiving

"...GIVE THANKS at the REMEMBRANCE of
His holiness."   *—Psalms 30:4*

All of us can find some reason for thankfulness in the material side of our lives. Some of us have fared better than others. But we have a roof over our heads, clothes on our backs and food in our stomachs. We can say the same about our physical well being. Some of us are not as healthy as others. But we are alive and useful—for this we are grateful.

Our text relates remembrance to thanksgiving. Thanking is simply remembering, seasoned with justice and reverence. How often we forget so easily. It is good to look backward and see what God has done! When we do, I dare say without exception, we can all say that God has not left us or forsaken us.

Our remembrance leads us to God and His holiness. Let's take the case of two men. One walks out to a day when the earth seems wrapped in gloom and darkness. Frost has pinched off every blossom and leaf. The air swirls about as a deadly foe. He is disappointed, his hopes are faded and his success turned to failure. The only relief for the man in his adversity is God. The other man opens to a world of beauty. The suns blossoms all about. The air springs with health and vitality. He is happy; his hopes are blooming. This man needs God as much as the other. The one needs Him as a refuge in his trouble—the other needs Him as an expression for His gratitude. Therefore, proper remembrance will lead us to thanksgiving to God in all things—the refuge in the storm and the giver of all sunshine.

God is equal to every occasion and worthy of our thanks. God is with good men in their adversity as well as in their prosperity. Thje story of Job teaches us that truth. For troubles that have arisen from causes beyond our control we may trust with thanksgiving in the holiness of God. For blessings abundant for all His goodness, we give thanks and rightfully so.

Pity!

"Straightway one of them ran, and took a sponge, and filled it with vinegar, and put it on a reed, and gave Him a drink." —Matthew 27:48

The hours of noon-tide darkness were drawing to a close when, for the fifth time on the Cross, Christ's lips, drawn with burning thirst, parted with the words, "I thirst". Many stood by the cross, but one whose ear had been quickened with growing pity heard the low-uttered word of pain and ministered to our Lord's need. A small incident, moistening the lips of a dying man, but it marked the dawn of a new era—of Christ-honoring pity. It also illustrates four distinctive characteristics of pity.

First, she is bright-eyed. No Lazarus can lie at the gate in hunger and pain. She sees him afar off and runs to meet him. The faint murmur, "I thirst," rouses her to action. Others may be deaf to the appeal. But pity is quick of ear and bright of eye for action. Whether it was the cry of "no wine" at the wedding, the mourning of "if thou hadst been here", or the plea of the blind beggar "if thou wilt", our Lord moved to action with bright eyes of pity.

Second, pity is quick-footed. That unknown minister of Christ's need *ran.* He did not wait for another or stay in the grandstand 'til the "show" was over. He saw the need and moved to help, nimble but not hurried so as to stumble.

Third, pity is quick-witted. She is quick at inventing or finding a way to administer help. The thirst must be quenched—but how? There is the sour wine, but it's beyond his grasp; but here is a sponge, yonder a pole, and where there's a will there *is* a way. Pity uses all of its human resources, not just emotion, but its keen mind and disciplined body.

Lastly, pity is indifferent to obstacles. To her a discovered need is a proof of an existing relief. She heeds not the cry of the crowd: "Let us see whether Eli will come to save Him." No *Laissez-faire* doctrine for her; she will find a way to meet the need, and she does not tire easily.

Pity beckons us today. Our means of helping are usually very near at hand—if we will but look and then put them to use. Let us not despise the privilege of something even less than a cup of cold water, even moistening the lips of some sufferer.

Laughter

"Then was our mouth filled with laughter, and our tongue with singing:....the Lord hath done great things for us; whereof we are glad."
—*Psalm 126: 2, 3*

From across the ocean in England comes a story about a precious saint named Nannie. Nannie was a homely lass born to bring up other people's children and never to have any of her own. She joined the household staff of a wealthy family to take care of their little boy.

The family soon learned of Nannie's incorrigible habit of believing in God's goodness no matter what. They thought she went too far when she went about gaily singing her hymns after the wind blew the roof off the house and the rain ruined the best carpets. Nevertheless, her persevering good humor won the affection of the little boy almost to the jealousy of his mother. It happened that another little one was expected, and Nannie assured her mistress she could care for both. Sadly, this was not necessary as only a month before the new baby arrived, the little boy fell ill of scarlet fever and died. The great house became a place of gloom and tears.

At breakfast, a week after the funeral, one of the parents barked at Nannie: "What are you grinning at? Your behavior is out of place." Instead of shrinking, Nannie walked over and placed her hands on the angry master's shoulders and said, "There is a new little soul coming to this house. Why should he or she come into gloom like this? Your baby should be welcomed with happiness and I'm going to smile for him or her." Through Nannie's cheerfulness, the family took courage and their new son became one of the happiest fellows imaginable.

God is not the God of gloom—He is the God of cheer. One of Jesus' favorite expressions was : "Be of good cheer." He was an optimist. He believed in men when no one else believed in them. He cried with them and laughed with them. He knew that holy laughter can liberate the Spirit and uplift and cleanse. God wants His people to be a happy people.

Worry

"Take therefore no thought for the morrow..."
—Matthew 6:34

One of the great psychologists of all time, Professor William James said, "The sovereign cure for worry is religious faith." Faith and worry are opposites—one will kill the other, and vice versa. The Greatest said, "Take no thought for tomorrow."

Worry is one of the biggest killers in our land, especially among the middle aged, who "fear forty and gray hairs, cancer and death, and beyond all that, the chance of something after death." The upsurge of interest in the subject of life after life is likely based on worry as much as on curiosity. As the opposite of faith, the consequences of worry are inefficiency—a paralysis of one's best efforts and an undermining of one's health.

The basis for most of our worry is self. Self is looming too largely in one's thoughts. Get rid of selfishness and most worries will go, too. That is why faith is the cure. Faith takes the center out of self and puts it squarely and rightly with God.

The message of Jesus tells us why we needn't worry. Your Father knoweth. Your Father loveth. Your Father cares and wills for you only the best.

We need to respond to God by (1) bringing worry to God and leaving it there; (2) going out and doing the thing you know to be right; (3) forgetting the impact on self but thinking what this will do for Christ and how God will help. Christ, not worry, will soon be enshrined in the heart.

Anger

*"Be ye angry, and sin not: let not the sun go
down upon your wrath."* —*Ephesians 4:26*

Recently some doctors put a tube down through the nostrils of a man
into his stomach. They tested the contents of his stomach, according to the
states of his mind. When he was in good humor, digestion went on nor-
mally; but after they had purposely made him angry, digestion completely
stopped. Only when they brought him back into good humor would digestion start again. Their conclusion: "You ought to be of good mind when
you eat—otherwise, lay off eating."

A doctor could not find any physical basis for the constant vomiting
of one of his patients. His only clue was a casual remark that her mother-
in-law was coming to visit. Taking that clue, he contacted the husband,
suggesting that he have her postponing her visit. When this happened, the
vomiting stopped. Resentment had upset her digestion.

Doctors tell us that stomach ulcers are often caused by anger and
resentment, and they will return even after being removed by operation—the edge of the wounds become reulcerated if resentments aren't
eliminated. A doctor at the Mayo Clinic testified that he could see a
stomach ulcer healing before his very eyes on the X-ray pictures when a patient surrendered her resentments.

A rattlesnake, when cornered, can become so angry that it will bite
itself. This is exactly what harboring hate and resentment against others is:
a biting of oneself. We may think we are harming others for their wrongs,
but the deepest harm is to ourselves—our bodies and souls.

There is a good sense of anger. It is an instinct of self-protection and
for the protection of others. It causes us to stand up and fight against harmful enemies of the human personality. We are angry with evil, and
therefore we stiffen ourselves against it and oppose it. But the weapon we
use against evil is not anger. It is merely the motivating force. The Lord's
anger is for but a moment. When we let our anger go uncontrolled and
unharnessed, we let a raging tiger loose. Leave vengeance to God.

Losing Temper

"Be not hasty in thy spirit to be angry: for anger resteth in the bosom of fools."
—*Ecclesiastes 7:9*

The story goes, there were two Irishmen who were on bad terms with each other. The friends of Flaherty claimed that he had been insulted and urged him to vindicate his honor. But Flaherty would have none of it, observing prudently, "Look at the size of him. The man's a giant." Flaherty saw the value of counting to ten, which was what Solomon was getting at when he said, "a living dog is better than a dead lion."

This is certainly one good reason for not flying off the handle and letting our temper have the best of us. Another was given by the army chaplain who preached to the men of the folly of yielding to a hasty temper. After the sermon, one of the officers who recognized his problem but not to the point of change told the chaplain, "I have a hair-trigger temper and I can't help it; when I let go, there's nothing I can do about it." Without response, the next Sunday the chaplain spoke on self-deception and vain excuses, pointing out that even the one with hair-trigger temper, in the presence of royalty or commander not only could, but would control himself. And concluded the spiritual lesson, "there is one more important than earthly royalty or commander in our presence—The Lord Jesus Christ, who is King of Kings." Jesus does sees us. "The love of God constrains us."

The Bible gives us two great examples of victory in this area. The brother disciples, James and John, were rightly nicknamed ,"the sons of thunder." Early in their discipleship, they were desirous to call down fire from heaven on the Samaritans. But these got their temper under control. Love constrained them. James was the first martyr and John has become known as the "disciple of love." They learned that love was to be the greater weapon.

Filth

"What is man, that he should be clean? And he which is born of a woman, that he should be righteous? How much more abominable and FILTHY is man, which drinketh iniquity like water?"

—Job 15:14, 16

Sewage is getting to be one of the greatest problems in our country. The construction of new homes, apartments, etc. is probably curtailed more by a lack of sewage treatment facilities than by any other thing. Every year billions of dollars are spent in ridding our homes of garbage and sewage.

Yet there is another kind of sewage that is an even greater problem today—moral sewage. It is more dangerous than an epidemic of cholera or typhoid, and unless we move to stop it, it can swallow up our nation. Filthy words are now so common that schools are putting them in textbooks for our children. Statistics tell us that despite our laws, more than ⅔ of all pornographic literature filters down into the hands of children. And little is said in protest.

But the Bible has much to say about moral filth. Jeremiah warned the people of his day that God's wrath was upon them because of their lewdness and filthiness. Paul clearly tells the Ephesians: "no unclean person, nor covetous man—hath any inheritance in the kingdom of Christ". Rather he says a Christian should put off all these: "anger, wrath, malice, blasphemy—filthy communication out of your mouth." St. James adds a big amen. "Wherefore lay apart all filthiness and superfluity of naughtiness, and receive with meekness the engrafted Word of God."

Men have literally let their minds become a cesspool of rot these days. As Jude wrote to Christians in an evil society to "contend for the faith," we too can pray and content for righteousness in our home and school and newstands and community.

Laziness

"The sluggard will not plow by season of the cold; therefore shall he beg in harvest, and have nothing." —*Proverbs 20:4*

Amanda Smith, the great black woman whom God raised up and used in such a wonderful way, tells a story about herself. One day when she was just a poor washwoman and maid, she found she couldn't hear in one of her ears. So she asked the Lord to heal her but she got worse and worse. Finally, she went to the doctor and said, "Doctor, I asked the Lord and He didn't do anything for me, so you look in that ear and find the trouble." The doctor examined the ear, cleaned out the wax and Amanda could hear as well as ever. Old Amanda said, "The trouble was, I wanted the Lord to wash my ears for me."

Laziness is not a popular subject, especially to Christians. But there are a lot of folks in the family who are just like Old Amanda or that fellow in Proverbs who wakes up in the morning and says, "there is a lion in the street." He won't get up. The very thing that should make him get up, keeps him in bed. If there is a lion in the street, he should do something about it, but no, he lies back down and lets the lion prowl and eventually harm somebody while he waits for trouble to come and go.

All the worthwhile things in life are difficult. You show me the kind of difficulty you will work through, and I'll tell you what you are—what kind of character you have. Work never hurt anyone. In fact, it is part of our redemption: "Faith without works is dead." It is the evidence and outworking of our salvation.

Christ said, "My Father works, and I work also." Work wins! Maybe you wonder why God has not moved in an area of your life. Have you faced the difficulty and done that which you know to do? Work together with God. *Work Wins!*

Devolution

"I went by the fields of the slothful..."
—*Proverbs 24:30*

In its youth, the barnacle, that unpopular creature that attaches itself to ships, is a free-swimming animal. But, by and by, it fixes its head to a piece of wood and takes a lazy life. Its organs of touch, sight, and locomotion wither away. Its legs serve merely to carry food to its mouth. It's a pretty sad sight—especially for one that in its youth was lively, independent, and free-swimming. Those who talk so much about evolution should study the life of the barnacle.

The same thing holds true in the life story of nations, communities, and individual men and women—those whose life history after youth is one of retrogression, descent and loss. They are caught in the spirit of this world, the suction that unresisted will pull everything down. Facing and working through struggles and difficulties gives a person inner strngth. But too many become like the barnacle. As they grow older and "fatter", they are content with the fortune and name they have made for themselves. We see them, like the barnacle, sitting on their duff kicking food into their mouths.

There is a need for constant effort and will if we are to rise about the world's suction. We grow and prosper spiritually as we grow and prosper physically—by making use of the powers we possess. The spiritual life we obtain from God through the New Birth has to be cultivated and put to use in order to maintain itself. One of the most serious questions a man can ask himself is: "What am I doing for my soul?"

There are no short cuts, no lazy ways in the spiritual life. Nothing is gained without effort and investment: of our time in prayer, our regularity in fellowship, our concern for our neighbor. It is so easy to slide! Jesus said we must go by the way of the straight and narrow. So let us learn this little lesson from nature.

Fault-Finding

"...I do remember my faults this day."
—Genesis 41:9

It's usually easy to get a fault-finding party together. In fact, most people need no special inducement to this favorite pastime. It is easy work requiring no talent, brains, or character. But to look for one's own faults is a different thing. This requires determination, accuracy and honesty. There must be accuracy in naming the faults and no yielding to the temptation of shifting the blame.

The context of our text is where the butler, restored to his position for over two years, stands before Pharaoh. When he left his cell, he promised to speak a good word for Joseph. But he forgot. Two years later, the Pharaoh had a dream, and the butler remembers and openly confesses; "I do remember my faults". That's what everyone of us ought to do. It's good to take inventory, and Christians are no exception when it comes to forgetting—especially the same things!

As I look at my life, I see many and some may relate to you: (1) Allowing earthly duties to crowd out God—being too busy. (2) Giving place to unkind thoughts. (3) Talking too quickly. (4) Failing to use God's promises. (5) Failing to ask or even let God help me. (6) Finding fault in others. (7) Nursing a grudge. (8) Neglecting God's means of grace. (9) Becoming self-satisfied and not pushing forward in righteousness. These are just some I see in me.

Now the question becomes: What shall we do about our faults? First, the Bible says to *confess them* all to God and to others if they are hurt by them. The second step is to quit them—not by ourselves but with God's help. And finally, recognizing our weak points we should apply the healing power of God and prayer to those areas, knowing that beside you is the compassionate Christ who assured the stumbling disciples: "I have prayed for thee".

Being 'Cussed'

"...let him alone, and let him curse..."
—II Samuel 16:11

The character of whom our text is speaking is a fellow named Shimei. Not quite the kind of person you'd want as a friend, he belongs in the "rogues gallery." He appeared on the scene in one of the most tragic hours of the life of David.

King David had a handsome play-boy son named Absalom. He had personality plus, with beautiful, wavy locks that were his pride and joy. He was the epitome of style and current fads and manners. And he used all that charm and personality to wean away the hearts of the people from his father and steal the throne. It was the saddest chapter in David's life: here the mighty king who slew Goliath and built the nation, had to flee for his life to avoid civil war.

As David flew the capital for safety, he encountered "Shimei, a man of the family of Saul, who cursed David and threw stones at him and his friends." As a relative of the late King Saul, Shimei was probably bitter. But there was more. He was the type of individual who can't bear to see anyone else prosper...who hates and writhes against anyone in authority. This likely was boiling in him for a long time, but he was too frightened for his own hide to do anything before. Now was his chance, a true example of the coward who hits a man when he's down.

Have you met such a one? If not, you probably will. What do you do? Do what David did. If David listened to his fellows, he would have cut off the dog's head. But David wisely ignored the curse and went on. To notice every snarling gesture was beneath the dignity of a king. And in Christ that we are. Follow David: "Let Him Alone." Forgive and forget, and go on your way, minding your own business.

Hastiness

"...an evil beast hath devoured him; Joseph is without doubt rent in pieces." —Genesis 37:33

It is plain human nature to jump to conclusions: to quickly add up the answers and forget to add God into them. This was Jacob's problem. Unfortunately, as a youth, his mother taught him to deceive his father Issac. In deceiving others, he opened his heart to being deceived himself.

How often the facts are the opposite of our fears! The Bible story of our text teaches us this lesson. Jacob's beloved son Joseph is away on a journey, and a blood-stained coat is brought to the father. Jacob concludes Joseph has fallen prey to some wild beast. Like many, Jacob feared the worst. He looked at what Satan could do instead of what God could do. How often we do the same when we board an airplane or hear a "rumor."

We must not be too hasty in reaching conclusions. Joseph wasn't dead no matter how badly torn and stained the coat was. Most of our fears never come to pass, but they might as well for what they produce in our hearts in the meantime. Joseph was on his way to Egypt and fame, preparing to become the very instrument of life and provision for the father who had given him up for dead. How many years Jacob was to waste with his head down in sorrow because he looked at the circumstances and not up to God.

How apt are Jesus' words of encouragement to us to not worry—sufficient are the troubles we experience without adding those which we don't. Jesus tells us to start looking for blessings: "Seek and ye shall find." God was kinder to Joseph than he imagined. His own sin had blinded him from God's goodness.

Let us confess and plunge our sins in Jesus' blood, so we can look up for the bright and hopeful side of everything.

Hypocrites

"For there must be also heresies among you, that they which are approved may be made manifest among you." —I Corinthians 11:19

Many people in the world say they want no part of the church or Christianity because of what they call hypocrites. But the fact is that hypocrites are the best recommendation genuine Christianity can possibly have. Did you ever see a counterfeit penny? No? Why? Because it isn't worth counterfeiting. A five dollar bill is counterfeited because it is worthwhile. Have you ever seen a counterfeit infidel? No, because infidelity and unbelief and sin aren't worth copying. Rather, there are counterfeit Christians because there's a value in genuine Christianity that makes it worthwhile for selfish reasons to imitate.

The church does have its share of hypocrites, and it is largely because we don't make salvation a clear cut break from the world. Most hypocrites are those who are still riding the fence. They have not come all the way in from the world. But what other men are has nothing to do with what you ought to do. God never commanded you to follow another man. He says to all of us alike, rich or poor, learned or ignorant, good or bad, "come unto Me and I will give you life and him that cometh to Me I will in no wise cast out."

There are no works, no ethical code, no personal followings of another that can purchase the salvation of our souls. Therefore, since no other person's action other than the gift of God in Christ can determine the eternal state of our souls, no hypocrite or hero can stand between us and God. Let us not judge but rather rejoice that God has offered us, has made us to be part of something that is the greatest thing, the most imitated thing in the world. We have the real thing in Christ!

A Good Loser

"I know both how to be abased, and I know how to abound..." —*Philippians 4:12*

St. Paul had experience with both prosperity and adversity. He had grown up in a prosperous home, and his Roman citizenship speaks of his social position. His education was among he best of his day. Yet he penned the words of our text while in a Roman dungeon. During the years that had passed since Paul had seen the blinding light and heard the divine voice, his life had been anything but one of ease. Paul summarized his autobiography in II Corinthians 10, and the list of physical and mental perils and adversities are more than most whole families would experience.

Yet Paul was triumphant. I have met many today, who like Paul, have squarely met some of the harshest adversities of life: the diseased, those who have met tragedy, suffering, emotional and mental grief. I think of Merle Womack, Joni and others. There is something in the infirmity that is absolutely radiant. There is triumph in their character and poise in the thing that has downed and abased them. They do something for everyone around them. There is no smell of death and defeat, only life.

The other side is abounding. Now not everybody knows how to abound. The wise man said, "The prosperity of fools shall destroy." For some, wealth reeks of death because it is ill-gotten at the hurt of others. For others, luxury has been granted with little effort. And the soft luxurious life causes the fiber of the soul to deteriorate. But a few, with the gain of prosperity, still maintain the vigor of usefulness and service to society that they started out with. This is knowing "how to abound".

Whether we abound or are abased, win or lose, we can radiate life, because He lives!

Whole-Heartedness

"...in every work that he began...he did it with all his heart, and prospered." —II Chronicles 31:21

Some time ago two men were talking about another in the same business who had failed. They were discussing the causes of his failure. The one said, "He seemed intelligent enough and had material advantages." The other replied, "I don't wonder that he failed—he didn't put anything into the business—he didn't even put himself into it."

This man is typical of many today, but he wasn't the kind of man Hezekiah was. Hezekiah was one of the best kings ever to sit on the throne of Judah. God prospered all his works. His secret? He did everything whole-heartedly. He made no concessions. When it came to idolatry, it all had to go. We know little of his intelligence, but we know he always gave everything he had. And his life stands out bright and clear as that of a whole-hearted man.

Without belittling brains or education, statistics would surely bear out that for every time men fall through lack of brains, twenty times they fail through lack of heart. Hezekiah wrought with all his heart and he prospered. The same promise and reward are available to us if we, too, give our whole heart to life.

St. Paul gives a hearty amen to this teaching when he writes, "Whatsoever you do, do it heartily as to the Lord." Paul's P.S. adds emphasis because Christ was our example. He never shirked the hard or unpleasant tasks but said, "My heart is to do the will of Him that sent me." He never complained or looked for the easy way—all the way to the cross. He did it with his whole heart "for the joy that was set before Him." And He prospered with Heaven's reward.

Therefore, a reward and crown awaits us if we dig in and serve the Lord with zeal and a whole heart.

OCTOBER:
Christil in the Home, Church and Government

"...that thou mayest know how thou oughtest to behave thyself in the house of God, which is the church of the living God, the pillar and ground of the truth."
—I Timothy 3:15

As One

"As the trumpeters and singers were as one, to make one sound to be heard in praising and thanking the Lord; and when they lifted up their voice with...instruments of music, and praised the Lord... that then the house was filled with a cloud...".
—II Chronicles 5:13

I believe this verse gives us the key to ministering the Gospel in music. It makes such a difference when we minister as one; it is the difference between performing and ministering.

Every concert or service before we minister we pray that God will make us as one not just as a group, but with Him and with the people. When we do the anointing (the cloud) of the Lord comes in and fills the place and we find our music free and genuine praise. That's what we want to be minsiters of His love and praise.

Reba Rambo
Music Artist

A Divine Calling

"Before I formed thee in the belly I knew thee; and before thou camest forth out of the womb I sanctified thee, and I ordained thee a prophet unto the nations." —JERIMIAH 1:5

Ron Hembree
Author, Pastor

I believe that just like Jeremiah, each of us have a divine destiny and calling from birth. Even in the womb, God can see our human potential and gifts us with personality, intelligence and unction to fulfill that calling.

With our free will, we can choose to accept or refuse that calling. If we refuse what God has for us, our full potential will never be actualized.

As a minister and pastor, I believe a major part of my life is to counsel, teach and encourage people to move into what God has called them and help them avoid Satan's distractions and pitfalls.

The Christian Home

"That ye study to be quiet, and to do your own business, and to work with your hands, as we commanded you. That ye may walk honestly toward them that are without, and that ye may have lack of nothing." —I Thessalonians 4:11, 12

These verses give us a simple formula for abundant and fruitful Christian living. The kind of life it suggests is so different from the world view. I believe Paul is encouraging us in so many words to mind our own business, letting God lead us and not be dependent on the world.

The world is an arena of strife and the devil would try to get us caught up in it: "so that your minds should be corrupted from the simplicity that is in Christ." I believe our philosophy as Christians in our homes should be to strive to keep our lives in simple faith, nondependent on the world.

Graham & Treena Kerr
TV-hosts, Author

The Family Altar

"For I know him, that he will command his children and his household after him, and they shall keep the way of the Lord, to do justice and judgment; that the Lord may bring upon Abraham that which He hath spoken of him." —Genesis 18:19

Abraham, the man with whom God chose to establish His covenant with man, was a parent whom God could trust to teach and guide his children. This is the importance that God places on parents teaching their children: the Hebrew word for "parent" also means "teacher."

The state of affairs today is that many parents are not in command of their households. They have delegated their role as "teacher" and left the job to the school teacher, Sunday School teacher, TV, or luck. Tens of thousands of these parents now visit their "children" on weekends at prisons. How much better if they had invested 10 minutes a day in the home to establish a family altar. Ten minutes a day will mean over 60 hours of Christian education a year, and just these few hours will mean the difference in a child's destination and a parent's sorrow or joy. Parental guidance and instruction is not an option in scripture: "Father, provoke not your children to wrath but bring them up in the nurture and admonition of the Lord."

Moses in the law admonished the parents of Israel to "teach diligently thy children...when thou liest down, and when thou risest up." Sounds like a fulltime job doesn't it? This is the emphasis God placed on the family unit, and as long as Israel obeyed this commandment, she prospered. The strict adherence of many Jews to this principle through the centuries has preserved their race long after many others have disappeared.

The family altar is God's one and only guarantee for keeping the home together in these days.

Christ In The Home

"...the house of the righteous shall stand."
—Proverbs 12:7

The great evangelist Billy Sunday loved to speak on the home. He would say: "The greatest altar in our land stands not in some magnificent cathedral—it stands in the home of average Mr. and Mrs. American Citizen."

Paul spoke of this kind of altar in his letter to the Romans: "greet the church that is in their house." This indicates that the strength of the early Christians was in their home life.

The "Church" in our house is still of prime importance. Too often, what is left to the institutional church must be accomplished in the home. Which is more effective: to hear beautiful statements of the power and possibilities of love in Sunday School Class or to see love in action by personal example and sacrifice in the home? A boy may sit in Sunday School and hear how much faith means in a man's life, but if he does not see it in action at home, will he not question this truth? How much more strengthening when the family gathers after a meal, reads God's Word, and prays together about their needs and desires. One of the Old Testament Prophets asked this question, "What have they seen in thine house?" The lives we effect most are our children's; they can always sense the reality of religion. If we live it, they will know it and receive it. If we don't, they will see it's only a show.

The promise of salvation to the Philippian jailor in Acts 16 was not just to him, but also to his house. Our living altar in the home can bring salvation to all that dwell there.

Marriage And Divorce

"What therefore God hath joined together, let
not man put asunder."   —Mark 10:9

The foundation of any community or nation rests upon the strength of the home. The home, and with the home the institution of marriage is the central and fundamental fact in our social structure. Whatever assails the home attacks the church, the State, and the individual. History records that the character of any nation depends upon the noble tradition of the home founded upon marriage between one man and one woman.

Historically it is easy to demonstrate that the increase of divorce, the thawing of family morality, and the breakdown of home sanctity, have been heralds of national decay—whether it be little Judah or mighty Rome. The Roman historian Gibbon observes this lesson: "When the Roman matron became equal and voluntary companions of their lords, a new jurisprudence was established, that marriage like other partnerships, might be dissolved by the abdication of one of the associates. In just three centuries from prosperity to decay, this principle was enlarged to frequent practice and pernicious abuse."

Our own society is now similarly threatened, for today divorce is competing with death as the great dissolver of marriages. To this issue, Jesus had plain words, "From the beginning it was not so..." There was no plan in God's design for divorce. Only the sin and passions of mankind have resulted in the corruption of marriage. And on the Sermon on the Mount, He summons men back to the original plan of God. There is to be no cause for divorce (Matthew gives an excepting cause of fornication, but Mark and Luke have no excepting cause) among marriages of God's children. This is the standard of love: "love believes all things, bears all things."

This high standard of marriage can not be legislated by law to the world because "of hardness of heart." But it can be believed for by faith by God's people. Our nation depends on this standard being held high in His name.

Providing

*"But if any provide not for his own, and
specially for those of his own house, he hath denied
the faith, and is worse than an infidel."*
—*I Timothy 5:8*

The laws in our country practically insure that fathers financially provide for the needs of their families. If a man does not provide for their material needs, he can be imprisoned for non-support, and several thousand men across the country are in jails and "road camps" for that very reason today. But it would be interesting to know how many fathers are guilty of non-support in the home in God's eyes—many more I'm sure.

The childhood of Jesus illustrates what a good home was and should be. Luke 2:52 says, "And Jesus increased in wisdom and stature and in favor with God and man." That's a four-fold development...a perfect growth. He increased in *wisdom*—that means a mental development, his schooling and observation. He increased in *stature*—that means his physical growth, his play and pleasure, his love of nature. He increased in *favor with God*—that means his spiritual life, his sense of worship and moral responsibility. And finally He increased in *favor with man*— his ability to appreciate and get along with his fellowmen. This should be the objective of every home.

In each of these areas, parents hold the majority responsibility. Physically this means more than protecting them from dangers, it means playing with them—encouraging their development and physical development. Socially it means interest in and encouragement of healthy friendships. It means providing religious instruction by example as well as teaching. It means concern and involvement in what they are learning.

This sounds like work, and it is. But there is coming a day when certain children "shall rise up and call their parents blessed..." These children can be ours.

Why Believers' Children Miss The Way

"Children, obey your parents in the Lord: for this is right." —Ephesians 6:1

Some of the saddest, most tragic moments in the Bible are those when we see some of the Bible's greatest heroes looking at the fruit of their children's lives. We see Jacob wroth over the slaughter of the Shechemites produced by the wicked vengeance of his sons. We see Eli the priest mourning over the wickedness of his sons, so gross that God slayed them. We see David, the mighty king, first weeping over the death of one son by the hand of another, then fleeing for his life as another son in rebellion tries to snatch the throne from him.

Why all this heartbreak? These men had not disciplined their children. Jacob spent more time scheming in worldly affairs than in discipline. Eli's problem was that he honored his sons before his obedience to God and let them have their way. David never had a united home to minister discipline together with just one wife.

These same parental attitudes are producing similar griefs in Christian homes today. Active Christian parents are often too busy doing even "religious" things, to know where their children are and what they are doing. They defend their children, but they don't discipline them. Grief will come when they are awakened to reality.

Many share Eli's problem in spoiling their children. They do not demand implicit submission to their authority, but let the children get their own way. Without obedience to their earthly parents, there will be no learning of obedience to the heavenly Father.

Some parents try to evoke obedience from their children, but not on a united basis. The parents are divided and work against each other, and the children never receive a secure foundation. Parents must work together, or attempted correction is wasted.

Obedience to rightful authority is the greatest principle parents can teach their children. It begins with prayerful, patient, and gentle but firm discipline. God has provided ample time to parents to do this the greatest job of their lives. But it must be done.

Blind Leaders Of The Blind

*"The rod and reproof give wisdom: but a child
left to himself bringeth his Mother to shame."*
—*Proverbs 29:15*

If there is any area where Christians realize that they are in a battle with Satan, it must be over the souls and upbringing of our children. The onslaught of satanic "junk" thrust on our children is greater than ever before.

A recent example is the decision by elementary school reading textbook publishers to include profanity in their books—on the pretext that it is commonly used and normal. This is but another example of the Dr. Spock—new social order—philosophy that produced the youthful chaos and tragedy of the sixties. Nearly thirty years ago, Dr. Spock advocated, "Mild profanity is natural behavior and a good sign in youngsters of six or more. It shows they are trying their wings in a bid for needed independence." Today, that warped philosophy of "letting the child grow up in his own way" is becoming the standard of our textbooks. And we don't recognize it as from Satan?

The Bible gives clear direction in this subject; it says "train up a child in the way he should go"—it doesn't say to just let a child grow up. God's textbook puts the responsibility where it belongs: right upon the parents. There was one verse my Father quoted often and practiced more: "Withhold not correction from the child—for it thou beatest him with the rod, he shall not die." Today I do not hold that razor strap against my Dad one bit—I respect him for if and thank him for his faithfulness.

Today, the wisdom of God through Solomon is challenged on every hand. But we as believers can know the author of the challenge and know who is the Victor. We must stand in faith and prayer for our children against the adversary.

The Fifth Commandment

"Honor thy father and thy mother: that thy days may be long upon the land which the Lord thy God giveth thee."
—Exodus 20:12

The great explorer –Juan Ponce De Leon first travelled to the new world with Christopher Columbus on his second voyage to America in 1493. Several years later, he established the first Spanish settlement in Puerto Rico. While serving as Governor there, he learned from Indians of an island they called "Bimini" (Fountain of Youth), with magic springs to keep one young. For the last twelve years of his life until his death at hands of Indians, Leon searched vainly for Bimini.

Many today are still looking for the fountain of youth. The Bible tells us that the closest you'll ever come on earth is by obedience to the Fifth Commandment. A happy God-like home will lighten the load, keep one young in spirit, and guarantees a long and successful life as an extra bonus.

Why this emphasis on the home? The home was God's crowning creation! Even before creation was finished, God recognized Adam's need for companionship. After providing him a helpmate, God initiated home life with the words, "be fruitful and multiply and replenish the earth." The *state* and the *Church* were ordered only after sin had entered to corrupt mankind.

The Fifth Commandment, the first of promise, was given to restore the beauty and respect of the home. It was given mainly for the benefit of the children, "Honor..." Honor is more than obedience. It is obedience not because one has to but because one wants to. Paradoxically, honor will come only to parents who demand honor. First, they must demand it of themselves. When children see honor in action, they will appreciate it.

Honor has a way of protecting things in the home and in a nation. God plainly told the Israelites that the permancency of their nation in the land of promise was built on such home life. Even secular history subtantiates this—the long histroy of the Jews, the Chiniese, the Italians, is built on strong home life. The destiny of your home and name depend upon the same.

Youth

"It is good for a man that he bear the yoke in his youth."   *—Lamentations 3:27*

When you start talking about a yoke, young people don't get very excited. They see a big world out there and they would rather talk about liberty and adventure. But with every adventure there is a responsibility, and there is a burden for every liberty. Parents or others may now be bearing much of youth's burden. But that is only temporary.

When Jesus said, "Take My yoke upon you and learn of me," the yoke was not to be a burden, but a channel and guide. Anybody knows that a yoke is not intended to burden the ox but to make it possible for the ox to pull the load. You cannot escape the burdens of life. Even if you don't have anything to do, you will have the burden of time on your hands. One of the heaviest burdens of young people today is having nothing to do.

Now, the Bible says it's a good thing for a fellow to understand this when he is young. Children should be made to work and earn their spending money, learn to save and buy their own clothes, and pay their tithes to the church. Many youths would never get messed up in illicit drug use if they had to work for the money they use for drugs. Instead of teaching youth the blessing of work and value of money, parents have supported the "dope pusher" and then wondered how their child could use drugs.

My Bible says something about the man who is faithful in little things being given big things to do when he is needed for the big things. The fellow who has never learned the responsibility of shining his shoes, picking up his things, and making his own spending money: How do you think God could ever trust him with anything important in His kingdom?

You don't need a "tea-cup-reader" or crystal-ballgazer to read your future. You are going to be what you are now. If you are a shirker or a quitter now that's what you'll be later on. If you are dependable and thorough now, that's what you'll be later in life. The successful way to live is to put the yoke on—now.

Mother's Mother

"...the unfeigned faith that is in thee, which dwelt first in thy grandmother Lois..."
—*II Timothy 1:5*

When Mark Twain was in the heyday of his glory he came before an audience one night and said that he had just received a telegram stating that his mother-in-law had died and that he would therefore be compelled to abandon the lecture and take the first train home. The statement was greeted with tumultous applause and the reference to his mother-in-law taken as only one more of his subtle witticisms.

It is too bad that a few meddlesome mothers-in-law have made their kind an easy target for a whole raft of fun gunners. It is only proper that a mother who has made a lifetime investment in her son or daughter be interested in his or her subsequent journey. But the real reward for any mother or mother-in-law is when she becomes a grandmother. It seems that a mother's love is given double strength when it draws near the cradle of children's children.

A grandma's impact and value cannot be measured. Now, grandmas do not hold regular classes. There is no orderly routine to their curriculum, but they gets those lessons in life across just the same. Grandmothers are wonderful persons! Every child should have one living close to them. Grandmothers do more for all of us than preachers or teachers or sports coaches can do. We remember our grandma's proverbs and habits long after we have forgotten our algebra and geography.

But perhaps the greatest characteristic of grandmothers is described in our text—*unfeigned faith*. Columbus is praised for going night after night to his log book and writing "Sailed west", when all his companions wanted to turn around and sail east. That is what millions of grandmothers have done through all the ages, and they have written it with ink drawn from their own bleeding hearts. Their faith is something you can feel. It glorifies everything, its tender radiance touches and speaks more eloquently of love divine and grace sufficient than any preacher's sermon.

There was divine purpose for the eternal record of "unfeigned faith that dwelt first in thy grandmother."

The Widowed Mother

"And there was a widow in that city; and she came unto him..." —Luke 18:3

Widows are very important people in the Bible. For instance, it was a widow and her son who shared their home as God's provision for that famous Old Testament preacher Elijah. It was only the widow's mite that drew Jesus' attention in giving. The early church ordained church government to assure their provision.

The finest courage in the world and the sublimest strategy is that of widows. They are always the loyalest folk in the church. Every day, these noble queens of resourcefulness are feeding and nourising their helpless brood on less than the rich throw away.

The widow mentioned by Jesus had a great quality of not giving up. Like many others, she had an adversary, doubtless of the customary brand, "who devour widow's houses and for a pretense make long prayers." But this woman was not going to be robbed not even in spite of the handicap of a judge who feared neither God nor man, and by her persistence (confident of her need), she got justice.

But it is not in the financial realm that widowed mothers show their resplendent glory...it's in the realm of home and family affairs. Washington, the father of our country and modern democracy, was a widow's son. Moody, the great evangelist, lost his father at four and grew up on the scanty fare of a family of nine. Napoleon also lost his father at four. Garfield lost his father at three. The list goes on and on.

Then who could count the thousands and more that widows have "mothered" into the kingdom with their prayers and words of encouragement and cheer? Pure religion will always appreciate the widow.

What Is The Church?

"...the church, which is His body, the fulness of Him that filleth all in all." —Ephesians 1:23

How appropriate were the words of Paul when he spoke of "the great mystery...concerning Christ and the church". One thing is certain—it is of God and not a human institution. Its history during the past 20 centuries proves this. No man-made institution could have survived the corruptions, attacks, and tragedies it has. When it has fallen into the hands of unworthy men, again and again it has risen from its betrayal more fresh and useful in transforming human lives than before.

What church do we mean? There is no "outward marking" that clearly and totally identified the Church. But the prophet Ezekial pictured it as a river flowing from the altar of God. The Church is "a movement of the life of God." It exists wherever people together are getting the spiritual supply that comes from God and are living in it. It is where Christ is glorified and the Word of God is honored.

The Church has suffered many corruptions that threatened to cut off its flow. Under Constantine it became a state institution—gaudy, worldly, and politcal. Masses of unconverted heathens entered it because their rulers claimed conversion. Yet the scriptures have been preserved and its divine power restored time and again. Today its place is threatened with the idea that a person can be a Christian without being a part of a church.

It is true, salvation comes through Christ and not the Church. But the Church is the bride of Christ, and no one will be santified as a part of the bride without the Church.

With all its faults and "spots", we cannot overestimate the value of the Church. It keeps our souls from being stiffled with worldly cares. It admonishes us to responsibilities to God and our fellow men. It is the scene of the finest friendships, the opportunity for satisfied service, and a source of rich blessings. We are blessed in being part of this "great mystery."

Do You Love Your Church?

"...even as CHRIST ALSO LOVED THE CHURCH, and gave Himself for it."
—Ephesians 5:25

There is no quicker way to insult a man than by casting aspersion, suspicion, or ridicule upon a man's wife or sweetheart. Publicly snubbing a man's wife will bring instant anger from that husband. We almost know by intuition that it is right to treat a man's wife or bride with respect and courtesy.

Yet, many Christians do this to Christ unknowlingly when they insult the Church and weaken it with their negative attitude towards it. The apostle Paul in this letter to the Ephesians explains in detail that Christ's relationship to the Church is exactly like that of a husband to a wife. Christ's love for the Church was so great, "He gave Himself for it." He loved it so much He was willing to die a most horrible death that it might go on and live and carry His Name and bear children to His glory! Therefore, any insult to the Church is an insult to Christ.

We can belittle the Church first with our criticism of its faults and failure. But how could it have anything less when it is made up of people just like ourselves? Jesus died for us! He didn't come to call the righteous to repentance; he died for sinners. And the Church will never be perfect until Jesus presents it before His Father as a spotless bride. But we belittle the Church even more when we snub it and judge it unworthy of our time and effort—putting our own interests ahead of its needs and activities.

How did Jesus love the Church? Paul says, just as a man loves his own body: "nourisheth and cherisheth it." He gave Himself for it. His promises are for it. His intercession is for it. He is coming again for it. Let us review our attitude to the Church. Let us show how much we love and respect our Lord by honoring His bride—the Church. Let us "nourish and cherish" it with our service, encouragement, and devotion.

The Church

"...the church of the living God, the pillar and ground of the truth."   —I Timothy 3:15

About the easiest way to start a discussion these days is to tell about what kind of car you like best. Everybody has his favorite. One likes a Chevy engine—another likes a Ford. Some want body comfort, others want trunk space, and others want compactness. Some want cars with great pick-up, and others want low-operating costs and good gas mileage. No car will ever satisfy everybody.

It is not hard to see the parallel so far as many evangelical churches are concerned. Different churches meet different needs and desires. But the parallel goes one step farther. In a car, whatever make or model it is, it must have gas and oil in it. So, in the final analysis, they are dependent on the same thing to operate. Similarly, the operation of any effective church is the power of Christ and the oil of the Holy Spirit.

We have stressed church differences for too long. What is needed in the Methodist Church is needed in the Baptist Church and the Nazarene Church and on and on. The late Dr. Donald Barnhouse put it wisely: "I fellowship with all on points we can agree upon, and that's usually about 95%; then I leave the rest to God."

In addition, divisions in the Church haven't been the all-tragic thing in so many cases that we have made them out to be. The falling out between Paul and Barnabas over Mark put four missionaries on the field instead of just two. The same quarrels and divisions that have rent the Church have often broadened and multiplied the outreach of Christ.

It would be great for all churches to unite in one accord, and we pray to that end. But that is the work of the Holy Spirit. Today we still see "through a glass darkly", but the day is dawning and as the day star is rising in our hearts, we will be united as one.

What Rock The Church?

"And I say unto thee, that thou art Peter, and upon this rock I will build my church..."
—Matthew 16:18

For many years, the theological battle has raged: "Is Peter the rock upon which the Church is built?" The importance of this question is not to answer the argument, but know our foundation for the Church!

The context of our scripture is near the end of Jesus' ministry. He has been practically rejected by Israel. He was looking upon the great world of the Gentiles and was concerned that men have a correct understanding of the truth of His person. Salvation depends on right believing in Christ: "He that believeth on Him is not condemned"; "Believe on the Lord Jesus Christ, and thou shalt be saved." So Jesus questions the disciples as to His identity. Peter gives the true and great confession: "Thou are the Christ—the Son of the Living God." Jesus then praises Peter for His revelation from the Father and adds, "upon this rock (this confession and divine revelation) I will build my church."

If we still have any doubts as to whom or what the "rock" is referring, Paul lays them aside in his epistles. In I Peter 2, Peter declares that God is building a house. And the house rests on a living stone. That living stone, the chief corner stone, is Christ. The house is the Church, and the members are living stones built on this foundation.

Jesus had spoken earlier, "the wise man builds his house upon *a rock*." What rock? *Jesus*—for the man who built upon that Rock was the man who kept His sayings.

Paul used a similar analogy to Peter in his letters to Corinth and Ephesus by referring to the Church as a house upon a foundation. He writes, "For other foundation can no man lay than is laid—which is Christ Jesus...Jesus Christ, Himself, being the chief corner stone." The foundation of the Church rests squarely on our Lord Jesus Christ.

The Household Of Faith

"...let us do good unto all men, especially unto them who are of the household of faith."
—*Galatians 6:10*

In the early days of the Church, many Christians were persecuted and killed in Rome for their faith. They were brought before pagan altars and commanded by Roman officials to burn incense to the emperor as though the state were divine and its ruler a diety superior to God. It was a life and death matter.

And there were many, wishy-washy Christians who copped out. They said, "Why not? A little smoke won't harm anything. I'll continue to worship God, privately as I have always done. Surely I'm more useful to Christ alive than dead." They deemed expediency more important than the truth and fled the household of faith. Long after they turned tail, it was the blood of the martyrs that was the seed of the Church.

Everyone should have something in life for which he is willing to die, if necessary. To the early Christians, faith had a very definite meaning. In days when it was perilous to profess faith in Christ, they boldly stood together in the *household of faith*. For many, their stand cost them their lives, but they have passed on the Christian truths and principles that have become the foundation of our present day Church.

Those believers had no time for fighting each other. They were to busy fighting the devil and sin. Surely, there were differences in opinions and beliefs then and now. But they stood together in "the faith once delivered to the saints." We dare not tamper with that, but there is room for different opinions. *We must stand for something—but what we stand for must be worthy of the one whose Name we bear.*

The Body Of Christ

"and the eye cannot say unto the hand, I have no need of thee: nor again the head to the feet, I have no need of you...Now ye are the body of Christ and members in particular."
—*I Corinthians 12:21, 27*

One of the most unfortunate tendencies of American Christianity is to look upon the Church as some sort of religious club which one may join or unjoin as one's fancy dictates. This view erroneously looks at the Church as an organization rather than an organism. The Church is a body, a living unit. Understanding that fact makes all the difference in the world.

A flower does not join a plant and resign from it when it sees fit. A child does not choose a family and transfer to another blood relationship if something displeases him. Our text tells us that we are grafted into the body of Christ and become living members of the same. You can cut a flower off and the plant will live although the flower may die. A hand or foot may be severed from your body and your body will go on living even though the hand or foot can no longer function. So you can quit the Church and the Church will get along without you...but you just try and get along without your vital connection with the body of Jesus Christ!

In order to reach human beings where they live, it was necessary for our Lord to make use of a human body during His ministry among men. Likewise, in order to continue His work of redemption after His resurrection, it was necessary that He should have a visible agency through which the Holy Spirit might function. This is why He established the Church—which is "His Body." And every time we fuss and quarrel among ourselves we cripple His body and thus hinder His work on earth.

Our responsibility to the Church and fellow believers, is really to our own blessings as we are all members one of another.

The Flock Of Christ

"...Our Lord Jesus, that great shepherd of the sheep..."
—Hebrews 13:20

Flocks of sheep dotted the countryside of Palestine in Jesus' day. The work of the shepherd was an ancient profession, with well-recognized standards and duties. The shepherd always went ahead of his sheep, leading them—never driving them. He had a special call with which he summoned his own flock. His sheep would answer that call and no other.

In cool weather, he led the sheep to pasture from the morning until evening. In warm weather, he took them to the fold for safety while he took his own rest. The fold was enclosed to protect from harsh weather and fenced to keep out intruders. A guard received the sheep into the fold as the shepherds brought them and released them when the shepherds called for them.

Therefore, when Christ revealed that He was the Great Shepherd and the Church, the flock of God, his hearers understood this perfectly. He added that *all* who answer His "call" are united into one flock under one Shepherd.

Jesus carefully trained and commissioned His apostles to be "pastors", or shepherds of the flock, to carry on and extend His work, under Himself as chief "Pastor". They and we who were to come were told to lead, protect and feed His sheep, to keep them from being scattered. Human quarrels and dissensions have broken that flock and divided the sheep.

Jesus never said there would be only one fold—there are many folds, and opportunities for different groups with different emphasis. But He did say, "There shall be one *flock*, one Shepherd." Though we be of different folds, we are the same flock—supportive and protective one of another.

The Pastor

"...If a man desire the office of a bishop, he desireth a good work." —I Timothy 3:1

The apostle Paul said, "I magnify my office." In his own worth, he referred to himself as "the least," but to his office, he said, "I put great store by it. I glorify my ministry." The high calling of God drew him above his own abilities to God.

The office of the pastor is perhaps the highest calling. First, the pastor is an intermediary. He performs the work of a priest. He bears the burden of spiritual welfare for "his sheep." Like Paul, he always has the people "in his heart". And then the pastor is a guide. He leads the people to spiritual food. Shall the "blind lead the blind?" Paul would say, "Follow me!"

The pastor (or pastor-teacher as Paul declared in Ephesians 4) is charged with teaching the truth. As Jesus commanded the disciples to "teach them to observe all things whatsoever I have commanded you," the pastor's teaching will largely determine the people's testing. On occasion, he will perform the work of the prophet: "forth telling".

The pastor is his people's soul—physician. He must be an able diagnostician, but not a psychiatrist. As a shepherd, he cares for the people with his life. His words are comfort: "Speak ye comfortingly unto my people." In this the pastor is a servant, a gift to his people. He is not a bellhop or an errand boy, but perhaps the "head-waiter".

Finally, the pastor is concerned with souls. He desires a fruitful flock. He will be an example of a soul winner, keeping the passion of Christ for the lost alive in the pews.

Eternal consequences hang upon almost every utterance and act of the pastor. Everything he does affects the souls of men. The words of no other person in any office carry such eternal consequences. No wonder such high standards are commanded by Paul.

The Ministry Of Music

"...I will open my dark saying upon the harp."
—*Psalm 49:4*

The great Beethoven said in one of his letters: "Music is more than a concord of sweet sounds; it is something given from a higher world which we cannot describe, much less define; but which we have the power to invoke." Music belongs to God. He is the Author of it.

Music was one of the first arts given to man. And rightly so. No other art stirs man so deeply, so entirely, in body, mind and soul; no other sways him with such a magic spell. It is the most *sensuous* and *spiritual* of the fine arts, and therein lies its power and its peril.

Music can either unite and uplift or produce discord and tear down. It is spiritual mathematics. It moves with measured step and cannot free itself from its mathematical certainty without losing its soul. David, the great psalmist and musician, wrote: "Thy laws have become my songs in the house of my pilgrimage." He was saying the wild, glad freedom for which we hunger comes not from throwing the law away, but from obeying it perfectly. Undisciplined freedom in music produces discord and misery, even as it does in life.

Men like David have long recognized the ministry and healing quality of music. Even the Greeks used melodies to heal jangled minds. They held that music was an art which united beauty, love and truth. By its very nature, music is priestly in speaking for man to God. In the soul of every man, there are vague, mystical longings, dim stirrings of unutterable things which are ever seeking to define themselves in speech, but which no words can utter. Here music comes to our relief. It frees our imprisoned thoughts and helps us give shape to those deep yearnings of the heart, directing them upward to the source of our strength. "Sing A New Song Unto The Lord."

Worship In The Spirit

"Speaking to yourselves in psalms and hymns and SPIRITUAL SONGS, singing and making melody in your heart to the Lord."—Ephesians 5:19

Music has had a central place in the Pentecostal and Charismatic movement of our nation. The Welsh revival at the turn of the century largely resulted as ministers dared to loosen the "platform controlled" services with spontaneity and informal worship. Certain Americans went to Wales and returned to introduce spontaneous worship, testimony, choruses, and public confessions, giving great impetus to renewal in churches in America.

A young music director once approached me with the question, "Is God really concerned about which songs and choruses we sing in a service?" The honesty of the question shocked me. While the answer is obvious, in how many churches is the song service and worship led by the Spirit and Spirit-anointed just as much as the preaching and praying?

Music under the Spirit is different than music under the law: "speaking to one another in Psalms and hymns and spiritual songs." This does away with paid groups dispensing music for the entertainment of the crowd. Under the Spirit the music is mutaal and voluntary. In Old Testament law there were priests and Levites, but through the Gospel we are all priests.

Professional groups, "big names," may draw people to church but the only "artist" who can really draw the person into joyful communion with God is the Holy Spirit. No sum of gold or study course or musician's arts can adequately replace the Holy Spirit, who makes all participants and sharers of the goodness of God.

Two Mites

"Jesus...beheld how the people cast money into the treasury...and there came a certain poor widow—and she threw in two mites..."

—*Mark 12:41, 42*

The scene is Herod's magnificent Temple at Jerusalem. Jesus has brought his disciples there and He teaches them by living illustrations some lessons about true worship and hypocritical worship. Walking over to the treasury where great chests are used to receive the tithes and offerings, He and the disciples observe a pompous and self-righteous display of giving by the rich. Suddenly, a widow slips in two mites (1/10 cent), and Jesus is stirred at this generosity: "This poor widow hath given more than the rest—for she hath given all her living."

This short incident tells us much about Christian giving. First, Jesus observes our giving and considers it important. He didn't comment on the Temple music or the sermon, just the giving. God is not concerned as much with the amount, as He is in our knowing that His blessing comes in sacrificial giving: "Seek ye *first* the kingdom of God and His righteousness, and all these things shall be added unto you." Giving shows our trust of God and our love for His work.

Many of the leading companies in America have prospered so because they have put God first and honored Him with their tithe. Among these are John Kraft; Wm. Colgate, Heinz, J. C. Penney, Crosswell (Quaker Oats); Hyde, Hershey, and Baldwin (locomotives): and Kerr Canning. Time magazine recently wrote of Ruth Kerr, President of Kerr Canning: "(she) carefully watches over 'the Lord's dividend' and sees to it that out of every dollar of gain a dime is taken out for church and benevolence. Mrs. Kerr attributes the success of the company to the tithing principle. 'God has been a Partner in our business,' says Mrs. Kerr."

Our giving shows who we are really partners with in life. Giving is a great remedy against selfishness and covetousness: "we then, as workers together *with* Him." When we give to God (as the widow did), it enables us to see God work and provide. God says, "Prove Me."

Communion

"What think ye, that He will not come to the feast?..." —John 11:56

Holy communion is the grand ordinance of the body of Christ. It means coming for fellowship with each other but especially with Jesus Christ. When we come, friends and loved ones may be absent, but we need not be disappointed; for Christ will not be absent. He will come to the feast.

He will come because the feast is His. Jesus joyfully accepted fellowship. We do not recall in the Gospel that He refused an invitation to fellowship. He dined with all classes from the Pharisees to the sinners. Today he declares, "If any man will open to Me, I will come in and sup with him." And in the communion service, He comes not as *guest*, but as *host*. He invites us to drink and eat.

He will come because He loves to come. He loved cheerful, happy company. This is the Gospel record: "the Son of man came eating and drinking." Some artists and churches would have us believe He was sad, solitary, and lonely fellow, *Not our Lord*! He wants communion just as much as we do. On earth He never missed the Passover, and He will not fail us now.

Then He will come just because we are a company of sinners: "This man receiveth sinners and eateth with them." He dines with sinners! He comes to sup with us, not for our holiness, but for our need. We can approach this "friend of sinners" at the communion table with confidence that He will forgive and feed.

New life and new strength are ours today from Jesus the Bread of Life.

Memorials

"...this do in remembrance of me."
—I Corinthians 11:24

Memorials are a part of our human nature. Today our remembrances include a little faded flower in a book, scribbled notes, a picture album, a broken bit of melody, a little plot of ground with a cross on it, the granite block slab of pavement on the side of a church, and on and on. These give inspiration to our thoughts and thread our lives with significance.

Memorials are as old as the Book. When God delivered the Israel children from bondage in Egypt and slayed the Egyptian first born, He set up a yearly memorial—the Passover: "And it shall come to pass, when your children shall say unto you, what mean ye by this service?" This memorial would bring to their remembrance the guiding hand of God, sorrow for their sin, the promise of His watching love over their long pilgrimage, and His eternal faithfulness.

A second memorial was given by God in Jordan's stream—huge grey boulders set up by Joshua at Israel's passing into the Promised Land. "That this may be a sign among you, that when your children ask their fathers in time to come, saying, 'What mean ye by these stones?" That stone monument commemorated the unswerving God—how He had kept them through sorrow, conflict and hardship, unto joy and peace.

And as our suffering Savior sat down to His last meal with the disciples the memorial of all memorials was given: "Take eat...drink...in remembrance of Me." He said, "Don't forget Me. Whenever you break this bread and drink this wine, think how My body was broken on the cross and My blood was shed for you." They went forth remembering.

This memorial continues. At the communion table, we sit as guests at the banquet of the pardon of God. It is open to all: Christ died for sinners and that swings the door open. It feeds the spirit of man with food divine. It teaches that life is more than meat; the body, more than rainment—that the material can never be the measure or the substitute of the spiritual.

Most of all, it speaks: He lives! He lives for all.

Background

"...The Lord Jesus, THE SAME NIGHT IN WHICH HE WAS BETRAYED TOOK BREAD: amd when he had given thanks, he brake it, and said. Take, eat: this is my body which is broken for you..." — *I Corinthians 11:23, 24*

Background and context is so important in life. Often we cannot judge the size of an object or person unless we can relate it to a familiar background. We arrange tests to judge a product or person's performance to give a true perspective.

So it is with our Lord. We see Him against the background of life. At the *marriage feast*, He is the heightening of joy. In the *storm*, He is the Master of the situation. At the *grave*, He is weeping, making the grief bearable.

But there is one occasion where we see Christ at His best: 'The hour is come when the Son of Man should be *glorified*." It's the night of His betrayal. The world is at its worst—sin, evil, hatred, and cruelty gather to bring Him down to death. He is betrayed by His friends. Judas, who had shared Christ's secret and the intimacy of His friendship, now uses that very intimacy to betray Jesus. But Judas isn't alone in the treachery; all the disciples forsake Him and ignore the burden He carries into Gethsemane.

Against this background we see the Divine Love in action—loving, giving, sharing a last meal in compassion and tenderness, trusting the Father, enduring the treachery and shame. Can love stand in the day of adversity? Jesus shows divine love can. Moreover, it shines.

Where we would have given up, His love carried on. The gift of bread meant: "I give you my confidence; I trust you with my friendship; I put on your shoulders the greatest trust ever laid upon men: the trust of the truth the dying world needs." It was a trust of the untrustworthy, forgiving the unforgivable, and constancy in the face of man's fickleness. That is Divine Love. He loves us still.

Caesar And Christ

"...Render therefore unto Caesar the things which are Caesar's; and unto God the things that are God's" —Matthew 22:21

Every born-again Christian has a duel citizenship. We have a double loyalty: the loyalty to God and a loyalty to our country.

In Jesus' day, the Herodians, the Jewish partisans who advocated Roman rule, proclaimed the propriety of paying tribute to the Roman Emperor while the Pharisees, strict religionists, claimed the procedure was unlawful. These two opposites jointed together to trap Jesus. In baiting Him with the question: "Is it lawful to give tribute unto Caesar or not?" they figured they had Him coming or going. If He declared one way He would be accused of religious unfaithfulness; if He declared against Caesar, He could be prosecuted for treason.

What ability our Lord had to push aside nonessentials and get to the heart of the problem. His answer (our text) sets forth the unchanging principle of Christian responsibility to (1) the world of government and (2) the kingdom of God. This is the way of peace. When both Church and State remember this principle of Christ they work along harmoniously.

The United States was perhaps the first country founded on this principle. Our forefathers endeavored to break the Old World fetter with its *State Church*, where corrupt rulers and corrupt churches working together brought untold misery on the people.

Men like Jefferson and Franklin recognized that the state should be subject *only* to the beneficent influences of religion and never bound by religious dogma. And the church should never be contaminated by the patronage of the state. The church, to maintain its "salt", its "savor", must deal primarily with the state of the soul. When it begins to function in the realm of the state, it loses its saving qualities. The church's power is the Holy Spirit; the power of the state is law.

In the state, a man's home is his castle, and the king may not enter unbidden. In religion, a man's soul is kept inviolate by his God, and even the Lord stands seeking admittance—but only by invitation. Thus, no church or authority can police the human soul. These principles must be kept close to our heart in a day when freedom is challenged even in America.

The Freedom Train

"Righteousness exalteth a nation: but sin is a reproach to any people." —*Proverbs 14:34*

As we passed the two hundredth birthday of our nation, we heard much about the "spirit of '76" and talked much about our founding in terms of Christian faith and principles.

The United States has been a favored people, not because we have always been godly, but because as a nation we were founded by God-fearing people with godly ideals. The faith of these founding fathers is seen in the Virginia Charter, declaring therein their purpose of "propagating the Christian religion to such people as yet live in darkness and miserable ignorance of the true knowledge and worship of God." The first legislature assembled on the soil of America (in Virginia) enacted the law that "all persons whatsover upon the Sabbath days shall frequent Divine services both forenoon and afternoon." We would rebel today against legislation in behalf of religion, but it demonstrates the faith and God-fearing ideals of the people who founded our nation.

Today, our nation faces uncertain times. There is no doubt that our nation was founded on the Rock. The big question we face is, *Are We Still On That Foundation*? The answer lies to a great degree with the church. Will we encourage the people to return to godliness and stand as the prophets of old fulfilling the command of God who said, "I have set thee a watchman"?

We must not be like the spider who, living high upon a cliff in the darkness, one day spun a silver thread to the sunlight at the entrance of the cave. There he wove a magnificent web. He caught flies, feasted and soon forget his former existence. One day, travelling about his web, he noticed the silver thread reaching to the ledge above. In a spirit of arrogance, he said, "What is this? I do not know where it goes and have no need of it here. Therefore I will cut it." And he did. His web immediately collapsed and he was destroyed. "Contend for the Faith."

A Time For Decision

"...as for me and my house, we will serve the Lord."   *—Joshua 24:15*

Our nation recently came out of one of the saddest, most miserable wars in our history. We fared badly. Why? Our nation entered a war without fully weighing the cost. It had not as a people come to a united decision. The Bible warned us many many years ago that this kind of action would only end in failure.

General Joshua, captain of Israel's host, realized that *decision* comes before action. He called the nation to a decision. He would not move forward to battle with a bunch of nampy-pampies. He would have committed men in his charge with strong spirits and backbones. He laid his own decision on the line as an example: "As for me and my house, *WE WILL...!*"

In the final analysis the only man who will stand for the cause of freedom (or truth or God) is the man who wants to be free (and have truth and God) more than he wants anything else in the world. Paul warned the Romans: "Let every man be persuaded in his own mind."

Fortunately, today we are not faced with war. Yet our nation faces many critical decisions—in morality, in foreign policy, in the economy, in education. To not decide is to flounder and let the evil forces bring disorder and decision. Let us pray that our President and leaders will stand even as Joshua, and call our nation to a righteous decision.

Book Burning

"Many of them also which used curious arts brought their books together, and burned them before all men: and they counted the price of them, and found it fifty thousand pieces of silver."
—Acts 19:19

This revival brought about quite an expensive bonfire. Those fifty thousand pieces of silver were worth about fifty thousand dollars in our money. And the figures are accurate because they are in the Bible. Expensive, yes, but a mere pittance in ratio to the harvest of righteousness that fire produced. Listen to the result: "So mightily grew the word of God and prevailed."

Righteousness for a community or a nation is never cheap. Many lives were sacrificed to establish this nation in faith and righteousness. And many more lives have been given to help protect that righteousness. To establish and maintain our democracy, our forefathers sacrificed much. Today, we are in danger of becoming deceived into thinking we can continue our democracy without any sacrifice: to please a few we allow untold amounts of pornography to corrupt our youth; we portray gross "filth" on our movie screens; we maintain thousands who would rather not work on our welfare rolls; we kill thousands of unborn babies—all in the name of liberty and democracy.

Jesus had some plain words about all this. He said, "if your right eye offend thee, pluck it out, and if your right hand offend thee, cut it off—for it is profitable for thee that one of thy members should perish and not that thy whole body should be cast into hell." None of us like to "offend" another's desires. But if our nation is to be kept from floundering into hell, it must have standards of righteousness. Those standards may cost us something. In fact, they may cost much in prayer, in contending for faith, in choosing Godly leaders, but then *we will prevail*!

NOVEMBER:
Witnessing to a Lost World

"But ye shall receive power, after that the Holy Ghost is come upon you: and ye shall be witnesses unto me both in Jerusalem, and in all Judea, and in Samaria, and unto the uttermost part of the earth." —Acts 1:8

Not Ashamed

"For I am not ashamed of the gospel of Christ: for it is the power of God unto salvation to everyone that believeth; to the Jew first, and also to the Greek." —Romans 1:16

I, like many grew up in a Christian home. I knew from the time I was a small boy that I was supposed to preach. I even used to preach to my pillows in my bedroom. But it was another thing to preach fearlessly before men. However, when I discovered the power of this verse — "not to be ashamed", it set me free.

I find it works all the time now. When I stand up for the Gospel and its power, God honors that stand. We never need to shrink back or give excuse for being a Christian even when we fail. The Gospel is man's life-line, so we need never to be ashamed of it.

Mark Buntain
Missionary to India

Honesty

*"For if I have boasted any thing to him of you,
I am not ashamed; but as we spoke all things to you
in truth, even so our boasting which I made before
Titus, is found a truth." —II Corinthians 7:14*

Peter Marshall
Author, Pastor

This verse is a plan for life. If we live truthfully, we need never to be ashamed. If we are tempted to boast, let it be of the good of others. "Love believes the best of others."

I see in Paul's life and his writing an openness and unashamedness for his beliefs and abilities, and even his inabilities. This encourages me and causes me to seek to be open and unashamed with my peers, the family and the world. I believe this is freedom and true life in Christ.

Evangelism

"He must increase, and I must decrease."
—John 3:30

All of us want to be successful, especially in our service to Christ. But I have realized after many years of ministry that there is nothing in Lowell Lundstrum that can bless anyone. (Fifteen thousands souls are won to Christ yearly through the Lundstrum ministry). As an evangelist, I'm just one beggar telling another beggar where to find bread.

The only good in me is that Christ lives in me. Therefore, it only makes sense to let Him control more and more of me. The flesh profits nothing: Jesus is worth everything.

Lowell Lundstrum
Music Artist

The Holy Spirit Bears Witness To Jesus Christ

"But when the Comforter is come...he shall testify of me." —John 15:26

When the Holy Spirit came upon the disciples at Pentecost, they were changed. They knew they received a new power, a new strength and purpose; their words were no longer their own. So when Peter and the other disciples were strictly commanded by the Jewish council not to teach in the name of Jesus, they gave credit: "We are witnesses of these things, and so is also the Holy Ghost."

Until the Holy Spirit bore witness of Christ in their hearts, they were weak and afraid. This is our case today: we need the work of the Holy Spirit in our lives to be effective witnesses. And receivers, as well! Many times we have sat down with a friend or loved one and explained to them Jesus, the Savior atoning for the guilt of sin and the Savior resurrected from the power of sin. We can go over it from Scripture until we're blue in the face, but they cannot see it. Why? Because the Holy Spirit has not enlightened them. Then with another friend, we simply explain it and they see it and accept Jesus right off. Because the Holy Spirit has borne witness.

The difference is that when a person surrenders His will to God, he puts himself in a position where the Holy Spirit can do His work. As Jesus said in John 7:17, "If any man wills to do His will, he shall know of the teaching, whether it be of God or whether I speak from myself." All God asks for is a chance. If you are not sure of God or His work in your life, seek for yourself the testimony of the Holy Spirit regarding Jesus. Respond to God in obedience, and the Holy Spirit will enlighten and bear witness, and you will soon know you serve a real God. The Holy Spirit will do the convincing.

By This Shall All Men Know

"By this shall all men know that ye are my disciples, if ye have love one to another."
—*John 13:35*

Almost every other man one meets nowadays wears some sort of insignia: a badge, a pin, or some emblem. Even most Christian organizations have their own particular emblem they offer. These identify and unify people of like interest. But in some cases they can divide even as groups of diverse interests can divide.

Our text gives us the official emblem of a Christian, the "Christian's badge." Jesus gave the disciples this identification on the night before His crucifixion after He had washed and wiped their feet. He was concerned that the disciples have an identification to keep them together but not divisive. What would it be?

Jesus told them "a new commandment...by *love*." Love them—not any peculiarity of dress or wearing the hair or beard; not any dogma or doctrine: love—an active, unselfish, Christ-like love. This is the badge of Christian discipleship. Paul adds to put on this badge, to "put on love." John adds that love is the acid test: "by this we know...that we love the brethren." And Peter concludes, "Be fervent in your love among yourselves." This is the badge that identifies the believer and unifies all no matter what their color, religious background, culture, or intelligence level. All these fade in the background at the manifestation of love.

Jesus in the same discourse goes on to say that by this same love, the world will identify the reality of Christ and faith. Do we want to be a better witness? Let us love!

What Brings The Victory

"...and the power of the Lord was present to heal..."   —Luke 5:17

Madison Avenue tells us the secret to a successful product is creating the desire—the "want to" for it. Early in American history, the "want to" was for land; then came the "gold rush"; and then "industrial revolution" with technology and science; and recently the "wonders" of medical science. But in our text, the "want to" was to get to Jesus!

The context of our scripture is the familiar story of the paralyzed man with palsy whose friends brought him to Jesus. When they couldn't get him in the house where Jesus taught because of the crowd, they lowered him through the roof. Like many oppressed and depressed today, this man could not get to Jesus himself. He needed help. The key was (and is) to get to Jesus and get Jesus to the people.

Even as the friends of the man with palsy had the compassion to find a way through the obstacles, so do we need divine compassion, to bring others to Jesus. James declared, "Pray one for another that ye may be healed." This is our responsibility as Christians. And *compassion* gives us the "want to". The compassion of the daughter of Pharoah saved Moses' life. The compassion of Moses saved Israel from God's Wrath. The compassion of Jesus healed the blind, cast out the evil spirit, and comforted the disciples. Each met plenty of blockades, but compassion urged them forward to victory.

Compassion goes beyond the conventional. How the "doctors of the law" listening to Jesus' teaching must have reacted when the dust and chips from the roof came falling down on them! But Jesus approved of it! The purpose of His teaching was to build faith. Here was faith in action! These men had brought their neighbor to Jesus—the rest was up to Him. When the man gets to Jesus, the victory is won. Jesus simply says, "Arise", and the man is healed.

Compassion brought the palsied to Jesus. Is there a needy one you know who needs help to get to Jesus?

What Are We Waiting For?

*"And now, Lord, what wait I for? My hope is
in thee."* —*Psalm 39:7*

Americans are a hopeful people. Daily we reach hungrily for the newspaper. We faithfully watch the television news. We go eagerly to the mailbox, always looking for something. We go back time and again hoping, hoping. What are we waiting for?

Almost daily we read the same news: crime...tragedies...scandals...investigations...inflation...fighting...world flareups...accidents ...divorces...immorality. What are we waiting for?

The psalmist David asked this question after God had chastened him for his sin with Bathsheba. He had failed God greatly and was mourning about his own sinfulness as much as anything. But what was he to do now? Things were not going to get better by his moping about. His hope was in God, and God had given David a job to do. It was now time to get up and do it.

How we as Christians need to heed the same advice! It is so easy to get discouraged at all the evil in our world. But things will not get better by our discouragement. What are we waiting for?

God promises that "if my people (that is we Christians) will humble themselves and pray, and seek my face and turn from their wicked ways; then will I hear from heaven, and will forgive their sin, and heal their land". God has given us a job to do. If indeed, our hope is in Him, we will get up and with joy go about doing it. There is no need to wait. Today is the day of salvation.

The Corridors Of Our Lives

"...Edom refused to give Israel passage through his border..." —*Numbers 20:21*

Our text concerns the wilderness travels of Israel toward the land God had given them—Palestine. In their migration, they asked permission to travel through the land of Edom, promising to pay their way. This request was refused.

Edom was afraid that this marching army of several million men and women would tear up her cultivated fields and destroy her national produce. She didn't want to be bothered with anything outside her little sphere of interest.

How like our world today. All along, the world has been refusing to let Christ through. Man reserves the inn and says "no room." The world closes it border—it's not interested in His destiny. They fear that this man Jesus may do "a little tearing up." They are afraid that if Jesus got too near them, He might compel them to live "unnatural" lives and destroy their human instincts. While in reality, one is never so natural as when he is a Christian, Christ does "tear" up some things. He helps put an end to our selfish, choosy living. He opens our borders to those who pass our way.

Like Edom, every day we encounter those whose journey we can make easier. Their path leads through our time and interests. What will we do? Will we lock the gates of mercy and understanding and turn some soul back into its "wilderness wanderings" again? Will we be a stumbling block in their way or a stepping stone? Responding in love and concern may make a little change in our plans. But if we refuse them help, "Israel" may not pass our way again, asking a favor. The next time they may come in judgment.

Healing Hands

"...they shall lay hands on the sick and they shall recover."   *—Mark 16:18*

Hands are the instruments of God's love. Listen to this report of the medical profession: "Of all human acts, few can match the quiet slendor of the moment when the pale and tremulous fingers of the sick are grasped in the firm, reasuring hands of a compassionate physician. When pain and fear make a sick person feel that all is lost, the laying on of hands brings solace and hope. Their strength can even turn the tide of illness and amplify the curative effect of the strongest wonder drug. The laying on of hands remains today as it has always been, man's oldest medical miracle."

The body of Christ can rediscover much in these statements for her service as God's instrument of love to a needy world. There never will be a satisfactory substitute for the human touch motivated by a heart filled with divine compassion. It alone carries the message to the sick or dying: "somebody cares for me."

Some time ago a pastor told how he was sitting at his desk working when he heard the door creak. Suddenly there was a sharp cry of pain. Looking up he saw his little daughter. She had started to enter his study, but her fingers caught in the door. He jumped to his feet and called his wife. The mother came and, taking the child, said tenderly, "Doesn't it hurt so dreadfully?" 'Oh, it hurts", said the child, "but the worst thing is that Daddy didn't even say, Oh!!" Jesus has sent us forth with that kind of mission. He said that hands ministering to others will set healing forces at work that will redeem lives and make those we touch better for such a touch.

"They shall lay hands on the sick." The initiative is here. The credentials are here. The authority is here. We are to attack sickness just as we are to attack sin. Every Christian hand is the hand of an evangelist, a channel for that stream of life flowing to us from God.

The Danger Of A Great Experience

"...It is good for us to be here: and let us make three tabernacles..."   —Luke 9:33

For Peter, James and John, what they saw on the "Mount of Transfiguration" was a fantastic experience. They saw the heavens opened, and they caught a glimpse into the unseen glory of the spirit world. How could such a wonderful experience be anything but good?

As the reflection of glory shone on them, it completely absorbed them so that they could not speak afterwards. The outside world, with its troubles and tragedies was so remote that for the time being it was forgotten. Herein lies our first danger. It was so thrilling, Peter wanted to camp out there. He didn't know what he was saying, but he was advocating isolating himself from the needs of life on our earthly plain. Jesus, rather, used this experience to lead him more deeply and tenderly into the needs of the world about Him. As He came down, as many as touched Him were healed, such was His pity and radiance of power. So we should use our "high" spiritual experiences.

The second danger is to lose strength. The greater the altitude, the more difficult it is to exert energy. It is a physical as well as a spiritual impossibility to stay long at a great elevation. The test of the reality of an experience is its touch with actuality—what its effect is on human need through God's love for men.

Finally, building a tabernacle or glorifying one certain experience tempts us to settle down. And that is fatal to the Christian life. When the missionary spirit dies, we die. Christianity is always only one generation from extinction. Life is fluid and if we are not moving forward, we are slipping backward.

Undoubtedly this was the greatest experience the disciples had had until then and perhaps the greatest they thought they would ever encounter. But they came into even greater power after Pentecost. They went from experience to experience, from power to power, from grace to grace.

There is no limit to what God can do if we are willing to go all the way with Him and not settle down and make tents when we think we've gone far enough.

No Man Cared For My Soul

"I looked on my right hand, and beheld, but there was no man that would know me: refuge failed me, no man cared for my soul." —Psalms 142:4

It has been said of D. L. Moody that he was the only man of his day who had a right to preach on Hell, because he did it with a sob in his voice and tears in his heart. *He had a passion for souls.*

D. L. Moody had it because he received it from the great Soul Winner: Christ had a passion for the souls of all men. When he saw the multitudes, he was moved with compassion and prayed for more laborers for the souls of men. Everywhere Jesus went He was in the business of leading men to God. Even on the Cross, He had time to win a soul. There was a great "must" in the Master's heart. Day and night he strove to reach men. It is the same "must" of all soul winners. Paul wrote: "three years I ceased not to warn every one night and day with tears..."

A reporter approached Billy Sunday in his hotel room and said, "Mr. Sunday, will you tell us the secret of your marvelous success in getting men to God—in getting men saved?" Billy walked to the window, looked down at the throng of humanity in the street, and said, "They are going to Eternity—those folks down there are going to Eternity!" He believed that men are lost, and he loved the souls of men and tried to help them. His passion was a borrowed one—it was Christ in Him reaching out to a lost world.

It is the same Christ in us who will give us the same burden for the lost. Are we willing to weep for the lost? If we see their need, we will weep like Jeremiah: "Oh, that my head were waters, and mine eyes a fountain of tears, that I might weep night and day for the slain of the daughter of my people." People all around us are going into eternity. If we do not warn them, God will require their blood at our hand.

A Second Chance

*"And the word of the Lord came unto Jonah
the second time..."*   *—Jonah 3:1*

When John and Charles Wesley met and heard General James Oglethrope, Governor of Georgia, speak about life in America, the Indians and pioneers, they determined in their hearts, that they would go and bring the Gospel to this new land. They sailed, and they failed. Charles, who went as the Governor's secretary, fell ill. John, who went to preach, fared even worse. The whites did not take kindly to his preaching and mannerisms and the Indians listened stolidly and were not convinced.

The brothers returned to England, sadder but wiser men, failures,the both of them. They should have been crushed, but instead their vision had been narrowed and sharpened. They returned to a debased and degenerated society. Every sixth house in London was a saloon. Drunkeness, child abandonment, bands of ruffians, and crime prevailed. The country was alive with crime with 160 crimes punishable by hanging. The church had grown cold with its fox-hunting parsons. Religion had lost its warmth and power: the upper classes laughed at it and the lower ignored it.

How the land needed the fiery preaching of the Wesleys, though again and again they were greeted with boos and pelted with stones, mud, and rotten eggs. John literally leaped into the saddle, travelling to and fro through the land. He preached from two to five sermons a day for over fifty years. His message to the rich and poor was "Repent ye, for" and *"Now* is the day of salvation..." He made faith in Christ a living reality, and brought people to believe that the condition of the worst of us was the fault of the best of us. The nation was stirred. He aroused society to help widows, orphans, the illiterate and prisoners. Among his converts was Robert Raikes, who awakened to the need of abandoned children and formed the first Sunday School, which spread like wildfire throughout the country and abroad. A spiritually awakened England became a socially awakened England.

Wesley's converts did finally bring the message of faith to America. The circuit riding Methodists sparked a flame that established our nation in faith. Out of failure, came the second chance with sharper vision and determined faith.

Christianity Means Service

"If any man will come after me, let him deny himself and take up his cross, and follow Me."
—Matthew 16:24

A young girl sixteen had been left to bring up a family and run a home early in life, because her mother died when the youngest was born. She was left to care for her father, clean house, prepare the meals, and see to the younger children. Now she was dying of tuberculosis in a hospital because she was worn out. A lady church worker approached her and asked her perfunctorily if she was confirmed or baptized or in Sunday School. To each unfeelingly asked question came the quiet answer, "No", until the worker smugly inquired, "What are you going to say to God when you have to tell Him that?" This saintly lass weakly raised her hands and said: "I shall show Him my hands"—work-stained, honorable hands.

This lass had taken up the cross, and every cross of ours is a part of His cross. Paul wrote, "That I might know Him in the fellowship of His sufferings." To Paul that meant striving for and against the same things as Christ. It meant expending energy, praying as if all depended on God, but working as if all depended on Paul. To this end, he writes that he would "fill up that which is behind in the afflictions of Christ."

What is lacking in the sufferings of Christ? Did He not pay the full penalty on the Cross? Charles Peace, a notorious criminal, told the prison chaplain prior to His execution, "Sir, if I believed about Jesus Christ what you profess to believe, I would walk with my bare feet on broken glass to the ends of the earth to tell people about him." The price is paid in full but unless the Good News is communicated to others so they may too receive, it is paid in vain.

When Lincoln was asked by friends whether he thought God was on his side, he replied, "I don't much trouble about that, but I am concerned that I be on God's side." A life concerned only about self is starved, but when we get rid of "self", we begin to live. The cross of Christ means "I" crossed out. "To me to live is Christ."

Working For Him

"Servants, be subject to your masters with all fear; not only to the good and gentle, but also to the froward."
—I Peter 2:18

The servants of Peter's day composed a large part of that society. There were as many as sixty million slaves in the Roman Empire at that time. And with no union or working condition rules, it is not surprising that the Gospel appealed to them. You can imagine how these "underprivileged" revelled in their spiritual freedom and liberty in Christ.

However, there was immediately the temptation to throw off all restraint and responsibility and openly rebel against the unfair conditions. *"Not so,"* says the Apostle Peter. He suggests the Christian way is respect for law and order, endurance and patience, waiting for the proper opportunity to secure a greater measure of freedom. How much that says to many of us today!

Peter speaks not only to the actions of the workingman, but also to his attitude toward his employer. Peter asks the servants to be peacemakers and go the second mile. He adds, "if you suffer for Jesus' sake, this is thankworthy", or literally, "God says thank you." It means if some underpaid and mistreated servant will, for God's sake, check the impassionate outburst of indignation, endure grief, or suffer wrongfully, there is a thrill of delight started through the very heart of God as He lovingly stoops to say, *"Thank You"*.

A pastor friend was opposed by a certain group in his church who spread many false stories about him. He never responded to these, but continued lovingly and earnestly to preach the Gospel. God honored his preaching with many new souls, but the group was finally able to have him removed from the pulpit. He quietly submitted and moved to the next door God opened. Years later, a businessman from that town traveled to meet him saying, "Your influence of peace and love saturates the whole community. You seem to be still living in their midst, influencing them to be true Christians by the life you lived there when so many wrongs were done against you." Your task and suffering may seem thankless, but God says thank you.

The Inner Circle

*"And He suffered no man to follow Him,
save Peter, and James, and John the brother of
James."* —Mark 5:37

When Jesus began His ministry, He drew about Him a vast multitude of followers. From this throng He selected twelve as His ambassadors. Then, from the twelve He chose an inner circle of three who were destined to become His intimate and confidential friends.

Peter, James, and John—three fishermen, unlettered and from the humble walk of life—were Jesus' intimates. Peter, impulsive by nature, blundering and brash, was a loyal soul. In a moment of weakness he faltered, but spent the remainder of his life confessing Christ and died witnessing for the truth. We know not a lot about James except that he died a martyr to the faith early in Church history by the order of Herod Agrippa. His character was fiery and bold. He was likely older than his brother, John. John loved Jesus with an intensity and passion unequaled among the disciples. He was closest to Jesus and wrote the most intimate biography of our Lord. So we have Peter, the intrepid; James, the undistinquished; and John, the rare.

Where does Jesus take this inner circle in our text? To a house of mourning. The little daughter of Jairus had been delirious and expired. But Jesus says "only believe" and takes the inner circle to the room where the child lay. He speaks the word of faith and the child is well. What does all this mean? Those who would follow Jesus closely will often go to the "place of mourning", the home of want and of trouble.

Visiting the sick and lonely, comforting the bereaved and disheartened, is a large part of a Christian's duty. Jesus' ministry was full of healing. He went about doing good. Like Christ, the business of a Christian is to help somebody else. Therefore, he will be found in the house of the financially needy, with those with family troubles, with old folk, those who cannot read, the underprivileged—lending a helping hand.

Many can be found in Church, but the inner circle is found doing Jesus' will.

Some Youthful Advice

"...I have written unto you, young men,
because ye are strong..."　　　　　*—I John 2:14*

Young manhood will always be the symbol of strength. But the man who writes these words is no longer young, but nearly 100 years of age. As he writes, he thinks back on a full life of excitement and miracles, now quiet and mellow in eventide. He recalls his youthful strength and how it was tempered by the conscious and sheltering presence of a Love which had never failed him through all the years.

In his last days, his favorite greeting was: "Little children, love one another." Who would have guessed this from one who was in his youth so wild and tempestuous. Until gentled by the Master, this fiery and untamed spirit had been "a son of thunder." Hot-headed and quick-tempered, he was born with a willingness to fight at the drop of the hat. The Zebedee family must have been an electric household with not just one like this but two—James and John. No wonder Dad Zebedee went fishing most of the time. These were the boys that Jesus found one day along the Galilee coast and said, "Come, follow me!"

Under His wise and patient discipline, all this tremendous energy was transformed into sweetness and service. What a *transformer Jesus Is*—like a great power plant converting the rage of fire in the furnace into a gracious radiance that fills our home with gentle light. That's what Jesus is doing in millions of lives today. James and John were transformed by the Master into so gracious a tenderness that James was among the first martyrs who willingly laid down his life for the Lord, while John is remembered best as the apostle of love.

So it's easy to understand both the appeal and concern of John for the young men of strength. He knows that this youthful zeal can be harnessed for the work of Christ. *Link up with God!* This is John's message.

Pass It On!

"Wherefore, sirs, be of good cheer: for I believe God..." —Acts 27:25

A popular conception today which is just an old lie of the devil says that what a man believes should be of no concern of anyone else—that it is his own affair. Let a man be honest, industrious and straight, and it does not socially matter what his creed is. Others are not the better for his faith, nor worse for his lack of it.

A man's beliefs and faith will either inspire others or depress them. The story from which our text comes gives living proof of this. On their voyage to Rome, the ship in which Paul travelled encountered a storm for many days. The crew had given up hope of survival. So Paul's faith made him intensely and practically useful to the others. In the hour when things were the darkest, Paul was the most useful man on board because he believed in God. And who would question the practical usefulness of Jesus' faith in God? He filled the fishermen's nets, fed the thousands of hungry folk, healed the blind and deaf, restored the withered arm, and cheered the home at Bethany. We help people by what we do, but we help them more by what we are.

Paul's faith calmed the fears of his shipmates and brought new hope to everyone on board. They had not seen sun nor stars for days, so Paul's faith was a glimmer of hope. Afterwards, things were just as dark as before. But the sailors' attitude was different—faith mattered a lot. Faith is contagious; it radiates. Faith in God can outlive the storm and give us strength and peace when others cry in terror.

And Paul's faith brought cheer. Paul believed God, so he could smile. What power a smile can have in the midst of terror or strife. Paul could simply give thanks and take his breakfast. His faith gave the men "heart" again.

It is never wrong to "live" your faith out before others. Don't keep it to yourself.

The Gospel

"...this Gospel...shall be preached."
—Matthew 24:14

In our generation we have seen an outpouring of the Holy Spirit un-paralled since the day of Pentecost. It has brought together Catholics with Baptists, Pentecostals with Presbyterians, and Mennonites with Methodists, all united in one Gospel. Why? Because the rain of the Holy Spirit overflowed each of their little puddles, and they found themselves in one great pond as the scriptures prophesy: "For the earth shall be filled with the knowledge of the glory of the Lord, as the waters cover the sea."

It is interesting to see where this interdenominational renewal move-ment started. It did not start in any human ecumenical discussion, for salvation is of God and not of men. Rather it started largely among the missionaries, in prayer conferences. As missionaries faced devil-powers in pagan mission fields and human needs greater than any social program could possibly undertake, they gathered to cry out to God for His help, and denominational barriers easily toppled under their united prayers. And God's blessing poured out on Catholic and Protestant alike, and that blessing has spilled over all the world in recent decades.

There is only one sure way that this outpouring of the Holy Spirit will continue and grow in our midst: if we continue to maintain a missionary spirit and seek out the need for the Holy Spirit's blessing on the lost and those reaching the lost. "This Gospel...shall be preached.!" This only is the challenge of the Church: that there will be only two types of people—the preaching and the preached to.

With God, One Is A Majority

"...and there went with him a band of men,
whose hearts God had touched." —I Samuel 10:26

In the first book of Samuel we find Israel, which for 400 years needed no king, clamouring for a king. It was not so much that they needed a king as because the surrounding nations had kings, and they aspired to be like their neighbors.

They had lost a sense of their history. For four hundred years Israel had been under the peculiar guidance of the King of Kings. In times of danger, deliverance had come through some such genious as Gideon or Deborah. God was their great defender—but God is never without some human agent to accomplish his will among men. In one age God chose Cyrus, and in another age Charles Martel; in one age Gustavus Adolphus, and in another William of Prage; in one age a Washington, and in another a Lincoln. It seems God always has timber growing in his forest wherewith to make a vessel's keel or form a battering ram.

There have been little Gideon's bands to deliver his people all through history. A little band of men in Europe whose hearts God had touched brought about the Reformation, men like Savonarola, Zwingli, Erasmus, Luther and Wycliffe. In England, as the Church grew cold and corruption reigned, a little group of students whose hearts God had touched gathered for prayer and Bible study. Out of this little group came Whitefield and the Wesleys to redeem England from a reign of terror. In America, at Williams College another little band touched God with a longing for world evangelization, and out of that group flowed missionaries and revivals in Africa, India, South America, and Burma, and inspiration for tens of others who followed them.

God still touches hearts. He can still raise up deliverers for his people. We are among His vessels. Let us not cry out out for what the world has when we have the King of Kings to lead and guide.

Mass Evangelism

"Teaching them to observe all things what-soever I have commanded you: and, lo, I am with you alway, even unto the end of the world. Amen."
—Matthew 28:20

The word evangelism means a "proclamation of good news," especially the news of a battle or victory won. In the Christian sense, it is the proclamation of our wonderful Savior. Now, many have narrow ideas about what evangelism is. But the public preaching of the pastor is evangelism. The explanation of the Gospel by the Sunday School teacher is evangelism. The testimony of every Christian, the printed page, tracts, and missionary work are all in the service of evangelism. It is a fundamental work of all Christians everywhere.

Now, mass evangelism goes just one step further. It is grouping together as a church or community to proclaim the Good News over a broad area. It is really going out after the harvest and getting us out into the open in a big, unashamed way. Moses specialized in mass evangelism. Elijah magnified it. Jesus was the supreme Master of it. Peter exalted it. And the names of Whitfield, Wesley, Finney, Moody, Sunday, and Graham are synonymous with it. These men have been the life blood of the body of Christ in giving their lives to bringing in new souls for God's kingdom.

In these last days God has given us new weapons in evangelism: the electronic mediums of radio and television. Literally millions can see and hear the Gospel at once via television. Yet the foundation for mass evangelism has not changed. There still must be prayer. We will not see anyone saved until we have first prayed for them. We must pray for the ministries sharing the Gospel and pray for others needing salvation. And then we must organize and encourage. No person is ever totally whole in Christ until He is brought into a local fellowship of believers—in union, there is strength. And then we must be vehicles of love providing that environment where new souls can receive and grow.

These are all parts of the Church's greatest job—evangelism.

A Final Audit

"So then every one of us shall give account of himself to God."   —Romans 14:12

Perhaps the reason most people fear speaking before a crowd more than any other fear is that it suggests an accounting of oneself before one's peers. Many of us do not want that and would gladly forget that each of us must eventually stand or fall before a higher tribunal than man's. Moffatt translates our text: "All of us have to stand before the court of God...each of us then will have to answer for himself to God."

Modernization, urbanization, and computerization have brought many advantages but they have also weakened our sense of individual responsibility. Social programs add to this thinking. Yet it was strong individual responsibility that built our nation and it is individual effort that makes the Church, a body. The worldly excuses for lack of personal effort such as heredity, lack of education, handicaps, or injustices hold no water in the Church (or before God). Each person has a job to do to make the Body complete.

Each person is first responsible for his own *conscience*. Our consciences must be cultivated and balanced in recognition of both Christian liberty and Christian responsibility. It is fine to have a liberal conscience (not on dogma but matters of form and custom) as long as that liberty is combined with a sense responsibility. We must shoulder the load of how what we eat, drink, dress and behave not only affects our attitude about ourselves but how it affects others.

Every one of us is responsible for the opportunities that come our way. "To whom much is given, much is required." That is why no worldly excuses will work, for there is no accounting for that which we haven't been given. But what we have, we must use responsibly.

How have we handled the Good News given to us? Have we shared it? Are we utilizing the blessing of health, intelligence, and prosperity? These are personal questions between you and God, and avoid them as we may, answer them we must, before Him.

Colors

"Go ye therefore, and teach all nations, baptizing them in the name of the Father and of the Son, and of the Holy Ghost."   —Matthew 28:19

A local fellowship was having a beautiful church built, and they decided to put a colored stain glass window over the choir. They wanted the picture to be about little children; so they hired an artist to paint it.

The artist painted and painted until he thought it was perfect...for there was Jesus, and all around Him the clearest, loveliest, happiest children you can imagine, singing as they stood around the Savior. When it was finished, he called the church committee to come examine it the next morning. But that night in bed the artist thought for sure he heard a noise in the studio, so he got up and hurried in to find a stranger painting on his picture.

The artist rushed up, crying: "Oh, stop! What are you doing?" The stranger calmly said: "I'm correcting your painting. You have five colors on your palette—why did you use only one for the faces of the children? Who told you their faces were all White in heaven?" The artist shook his shoulders in question. So the stranger added, "I have simply used the other colors and made some of the faces yellow, some black, some red, and some brown, for these little ones have come from many lands in answer to My call."

"What call?" asked the artist. To which he heard the familiar words: 'Suffer the children to come unto me, and forbid them not, for such is the Kingdom of Heaven." Surely the Stranger was the Lord Himself, but as he looked up, he awakened to find the sun shining in the window. His meeting had been a dream but still it was truth. He ran to his studio and diligently worked to correct the painting just as the stranger had said. And when the committee arrived, they saw it too: "Why, it's Gods' family at home with Him, isn't it? This is just what we'd hoped."

Many churches have left the picture all white. But the Master put colors in it. The great commission He has given says: "into all the world" and "to every creature." What are we doing to add color to God's kingdom?

He Who Led Paul To Christ

"There was a certain disciple at Damacus, nam-
ed Ananias.."   *—Acts 9:10*

The Lord had a tiger by the tail in Saul! Who would He choose to tame him? Would it be one of the apostles, a great preacher, or a prophet? No, as is so much like our God, He chose one amid the ordinary circumstances of work-a-day life to fill this important task. The Lord seems to take pleasure in those who are faithful over a *few* things, by giving them much.

Ananias is only mentioned twice in Scripture but some radiant characteristics gleam forth. His readiness is portrayed by his description as "a disciple" and "a devout man according to the law." He lived according to principle, so he could be counted on to *act* according to those principles. Also, he had "a good report *of all the Jews* that dwelt there." He was a man whose character was such that even his enemies respected him.

"Ananias went his way." He was willing to obey. How many of us would not have argued with God if he'd sent us to minister to our most bitter persecutor? Like when God sent liberal Senator Hughes to bring God's love and encouragement to former Nixon "hatchet man" Chuck Colson. Ananias' faithfulness is seen in his loving attitude toward Saul: "Brother Saul." He graciously put his hands on Saul with no trace of resentment. And he confessed the root of his brotherliness, loyalty to Christ. "The Lord, even Jesus...hath sent me." He did not obtrude himself into the message but humbly kept himself in the background.

Ananias shows us some great qualities for Christian workers. It is not always what we do for Christ, but what we allow Him to do through us. Five words in obedience can do more than five thousand words of our own. If we glorify God today just where we are, there is no telling how He may glorify us tomorrow!

Faith In The Soul

"So is the kingdom of God, as if a man should cast seed into the ground; and should sleep, and rise night and day, and the seed should spring and grow up, he knoweth not how...But when the fruit is brought forth, immediately he putteth in the sickle, because the harvest is come."　　—Mark 4:26-29

What makes a great soul winner? So many churches have soul winning classes, yet few become faithful soul winners. What does it take? Our text suggests the answer is *faith*. The true soul winner must have faith in God, faith in the message of life, and faith in those to whom he carries the message; or in the words of the parable, faith in the Lord of harvest, faith in the good seed, and faith in the soil.

Our parable deals with good seed (the Gospel) falling into an honest heart, the place of God's kingdom. In sowing the seed, the greatest needs are forbearance and faith in the soil. Just as God created the soil, He created the human heart. The soil, with its millions of germs and bacteria, acts on the seed to produce life. So the human heart with its needs and desires acts on the implanted Word to produce life. Just as God made all kinds of soil from Jersey loam to Carolina clay, there are different conditions of the human heart. As the process of the seed springing to life occurs in the dark, and no man can fully explain it, so in the human heart is the transformation effected by the Word of God. The sower scatters the seed, God does the rest, and in His own way.

Without patience, children often try to tear up the soil to check the progress of the seed. So it is with some and God's word. All great soul winners have loved men and women and have had faith that they would receive the word and bear fruit. This is the secret of personal evangelism. To see in every one you meet a plot of soil for the good seed of the Gospel. And to keep on sowing.

How does the fruit come? "The earth bringeth fruit to herself." The good heart just as the good soil will produce the fruit for God's harvest. If we want to share in the harvest, let us join in the sowing.

Human Hands

*"Whatsoever thy hand findeth to do, do it with
thy might..."*   —Ecclesiastes 9:10

Did you ever stop to consider how many things we do with our hands? "Hands up," says the robber. "Hands off!" says the merchant. "Give me a hand-out," says the panhandler. "Shake hands," says the host. "Here's my hand," says the friend. "Give me a hand," says the neighbor in need. "Hand it to me," says mother, teacher, or fellow worker. "Hold up your hand," says the clerk of the court. And perhaps the loveliest and best remembered gesture, taking hands in marriage, "to have and to hold."

Human hands—all the skills of life, its masterpieces of industry and commerce, science and art, are fabricated by human hands. Next to the human face, the human hand is the most unique and beautiful thing in the world, despite its gnarled, blunt finger ends, its sometimes twisted muscles and bent bones.

My question today is personal—what has your hand found to do? What is in your hand? There may be many things that you want to have in your hand: money, power, a new car, this person. But what *is* in your hand now?

Hands are there to reach and mold and use. You are the master; your hands are only your faithful and tireless servants. In your hands may be a book to brighten or bring new vision to your life, or the Book to strengthen and guide. There may be a child in your hand: his or her future depends on how you mold them—will it be for faith or greed? There may be a service, a skill, an instrument to glorify God, needing your hands in disciplined practice, trained to be of use to help others. There may be a friend or stranger at your hand who needs that hand of friendship and kindness. Our hands today can be the hands of Jesus, reaching out in love.

Say So

"Let the redeemed of the Lord say so..."
—*Psalm 107:2*

Our text this day concerns, one of the great, lost arts of human behavior: expressing thankfulness and appreciation. Now, I'm not saying that people aren't grateful. I don't think I've met a dozen really beastly, unthoughtful, and ungrateful people in my life. But many of us have either forgotten or haven't learned how to "say so."

If somebody does you a good turn, don't let him dream that it made you glad—"say so!" If somebody has shown rare courage or devotion, and you were present to see it, it's up to you to "say so." In fact, Christian people, the way I see it, ought to be a pretty noisy people. One of our big troubles today is that we're too quiet. We sit on the sidelines and let the destructive and wicked elements run away with the ball. We hide our light and live in the shadows. We need to speak up for good and cheer for the moral victories that are won. For too long we've let the world have all the "say so." This is why Christian television is such a blessing; finally good Christians are standing up and "saying so."

But we also need to "say so" in our homes. When our wives make that great pie and we stuff ourselves with the second piece, before we head for the garage or flop in the big chair, we need to "say so"—with all our heart. Our children will soon be grown and gone—do we notice the things they make or what they bring home from school? If you are a Christian Mother or Dad—get into the habit of "saying so." It will create a new atmosphere in your home.

The difference between a stagnant pool and a bubbling spring is that one always keeps what it gets while the other is passing it on. One is speechless—the other has learned the art of "say so." It is the mark of a redeemed man when words of praise and gratitude come easily.

Giving

"Heal the sick, cleanse the lepers, raise the dead, cast out devils: FREELY YE HAVE RECEIV-ED, FREELY GIVE." —*Matthew 10:8*

Perhaps the greatest threat to our nation of America today is *greed*. Our nation was blessed and prospered under a Christian giving and missionary spirit. And today in the height of luxury, she is threatened by greed. The newspapers tell us of a tire company that knowingly marketed a structurally defective tire that may have maimed thousands, just to keep up profits. An oil company buys up a cheaper energy source to keep it off the market. Food manufacturers can legally add poisionous substances to their products in order to lengthen product life and provide more profit. Into this type of world, Jesus says, "freely you have received, freely give."

In a day when Americans have more material goods than any generation in history, there are more cries for rights than ever before—black rights, white rights, labor rights, gay rights, women's rights, rights of the product and the consumer, rights of the tenants and landlords, rights of the farmers, railworkers, miners, and who ever else. Into this world, Jesus says, "freely you have received, freely give."These words first came to the disciples in Jesus' instructions about communicating the Gospel. Jesus was particular about the spirit in which they were to go forth. It was not to be doled out to men in proportion to their merit. It is to be as free as the sunlight, and as unbought as the rain.

If we think about the meaningful things in our lives, we will see that most of them were freely given us. Let us give in that same spirit.

A Feast In Preparation

"But when thou makest a feast, call the poor, the maimed, the lame, the blind: And thou shalt be blessed; for they cannot recompense thee: for thou shalt be recompensed at the resurrection of the just."
—Luke 14:13-14

Sometime very soon, even now, God is planning a feast above all feasts. It is going to be one gigantic humdinger of a meal with the best food and fellowship that one could possibly imagine. This supper is going to be a fun and thrilling time. Like the grandest of all school sports banquets with the Lamb as host, it will give crowning honor to man's generosity and compassion to his fellowman.

God wants each of us to be there, but will we be worthy of this honor? In the verse before our text, Jesus warns his followers of catering only to their friends, relatives, and wealthy neighbors who can and will return the favor. This fellowship is rewarded on earth and establishes no credit for the coming divine feast.

But when we invite the poor and handicapped and unfortunate to dinner, those that cannot return the favor, we bless these needy people. We give them hope and illustrate to them the care and compassion that the Father wants to give them. When we do this, God takes this on as a debt to us and will reward us with interest at the resurrection: "shall receive a hundred fold and shall inherit everlasting life."

Do we want to lay up riches in heaven? Let us "mind men of low estate." There's more than a feast awaiting as our reward.

God Hates Littleness

"...a DWARF...shall not come nigh to offer the bread of his God." —*Leviticus 21:20, 21*

Years ago as a young evangelist, I lodged in the home of a very godly woman whose husband owned and operated a fleet of taxis. Not only did this man hate his wife's religion and resent every moment his wife spent with her God and her church—but he charged her full taxi fare out of her household expense money every time she requested him to take her to church. This man was huge physically but in his heart, he was a dwarf. This is the kind of person our text speaks of.

God hates a miserly spirit, whether it is toward Him or our fellowman. And usually you don't have to look farther than a person's church giving to see how big or small his attitude is toward God. God accepts our giving by our attitude. Says Paul: "For it there be first a willing mind, it is accepted according to that a man hath, not according to that he hath not." God loves a cheerful giver, for he will be one who gives liberally.

I heard a man complain to his pastor that he had always given his ten percent in church and never gotten rewarded as the pastor had promised. His pastor pointed out the problem: "You can give even your body to be burned, but *if you have not* love, it profits you nothing." Love must be our motivation in giving; and love is not small minded. "God *so*—loved the world that He *gave*." May we *so* love that we give.

You cannot be big in your attitude toward God and small to others. Jesus told the dramatic story of the man forgiven of the large debt to his lord only to be unmerciful to the little debt of his fellow man. He showed his unworthiness of that grace and thereby lost it. So will we if we withhold from our fellowman—whether it be forgiveness or help in need.

There are no bargain days with God. You can't get the same thing cheaper somewhere else. Calvary is big enough to cover *all* your sins and meet *all* your needs. In return, God expects *all* your love.

Real Co-operation

"They helped every one his neighbor; and EVERY ONE said to his brother, 'Be of good courage.' So the Carpenter encouraged the goldsmith, and he that smootheth with the hammer him that smote the anvil..." —Isaiah 41:6, 7

The key to the coming together of the body of Christ in these days is cooperation. Some people think that to have unity, you must have uniformity. God never intended that. He does intend that members of the Body cooperate—so much more can be accomplished by cooperation than competition.

In this age of specialization, we see we're not all cut out for the same thing. One man can perform with ease and skill a task which another would bungle. I find that out anytime I try to mess with my own repairing of appliances or the car. But each of us has a place to fill and a task to do that can be satisfying. In this way, work need not be a curse but rather a blessing.

Our text gives a key to cooperation. It suggests that each man was finding pleasure and enough to do in his own job, but that all of them, as busy as they were, *took time to pat the other fellow on the back and encourage him.* If we come to be too busy to say a cheery word to the other guy, we're just too busy. We all need a word of admiration and appreciation. It strengthens a man's soul. Its power cannot be overestimated.

An encouraging word is contagious. It gathers the body. The words went from the carpenter to the goldsmith to the blacksmith and on and on. Encouragement not only strengthens each but bears the burdens of all and breeds inspiration—to do the best for the sake of all.

Every day we have opportunities to encourage and compliment others. Are we making their task easier and more effective with words of good cheer? Jesus does.

DECEMBER:
Preparing for Christ's Return

"Looking for that blessed hope, and the glorious appearing of the great God and our Saviour Jesus Christ;" —Titus 2:13

Fulfillment in Life

"For a day in thy courts is better than a thousand. I had rather be a doorkeeper in the house of God, than to dwell in the tents of wickedness."
—*Psalms 84:10*

Roger McDuff
Singer

It is such a joy to be a Christian. God's people are the best! The rewards of success in the world are meager. Jesus is coming soon and evil is all about us in the world. To be "in" or even a leader among the wicked, is to have nothing. So many of the Hollywood and Nashville stars, find fame fleeting at best, and often empty and lonely when the lights go out.

There is nothing to compare with the comfort of God and the love of God's people. And to know that what I am doing is of service to God and a blessing to others, makes life all worthwhile.

Death and Resurrection

"Verily, verily, I say unto you, Except a corn of wheat fall into the ground and die, it abideth alone: but if it die, it bringeth forth much fruit."

—John 12:24

When my first book, Run Baby Run, was published I griped to the Lord that my name on the dust jacket was in tiny letters. God reminded me that his name didn't appear at all. So I felt guilty and prayed John 12:24.

When my second book, God Can Do It Again, which I ghost wrote for Kathryn Kuhlman appeared, God and Kathryn made it in big letters. And I was omitted completely.

Jamie Bucklingham
Pastor, Author

All of which proves that some prayers are more dangerous than others. But that prayer is still "bringing forth much fruit." And will as long as I don't try to kick off the dirt.

Life Is Important

"For to him that is joined to all the living there is hope; for a living dog is better than a dead lion."
—*Eccleasiastes 9:4*

Doug Wead
Author

At a time of discouragement and inferiority God gave a me a marvelous scripture. I have been reading the life of Winston Churchill. I thought that a diversion might help but when I finished the Churchill story I was more depressed than ever. Why was I born? What could I ever hope to achieve?

I took the Bible and began reading. Deep in my heart I was crying out to God for help. I read in Eccleasiastes, "A live dog is better than a dead lion." Even though the writer, Solomon, was expressing a pessimistic unspiritual philosophy, a God inspired thought burst forth. I stood up, pointed at an inmaginary figure and said, "Winston Churchill, you are a dead lion! But I am a live dog!"

Yes Sir, no matter how far you have fallen or who you have hurt or what you have lost, you may be a dog, but as long as you can still breathe one prayer you are better off than Elijah or Moses because you can still change things. Don't stop living until God takes you. Keep believing, keep praying, and keep trying. Are you alive? Okay, then quit feeling sorry for yourself and get busy!

The Hope Of The Second Coming

"Blessed be the God and Father of our Lord Jesus Christ which according to His abundant mercy hath begotten us again unto a LIVELY HOPE by the resurrection of Jesus Christ from the dead."

—I Peter 1:3

Every generation of Christians since the ascension of Jesus has looked for His return. The apostle Paul believed in His soon return and told the believers in Thessalonica to comfort one another with this hope. Yet in our generation this is a hope and expectancy of Christ's return as perhaps never before. Recent fulfillment of prophecy and movies, books and contemporary music about His coming have stimulated this.

The "blessed hope" of being reunited with loved ones and meeting our Savior must have a sound basis. First, the Second Coming is part of God's eternal decree for man's destiny: "It is appointed unto man *once* to die." Death fixes character and destiny; so does the return of Christ:"we shall not all sleep, but we *shall* all *be changed*." God's decree will be upheld in that there will be no more opportunity to again compensate for wrongs.

Even as it is appointed for man to die once, it is also appointed for man to live again: "For as in Adam *all* die, even so in Christ shall *all* be made alive." Christ's return will bring the resurrection of the dead "in Him" to spiritual life and the wicked to spiritual death: "He that overcometh shall not be hurt of the second death." The second stands in relation to the first physical death. There is no release from the second death.

The Second Coming is necessary for the fulfillment of the divine judgment, "after death, the judgment." The Bible indicates that after Jesus is established on the throne of His glory "before Him shall be gathered all nations and He shall separate them one from another as a shepherd divideth his sheep from the goats." Judgment follows death. It results in penalty for evil deeds done in the body or reward for good motives, thoughts, and works experienced and accomplished in this life for Christ's sake.

The divine decree declares that there should be reward for the offering of Christ's body for sin once and for all. The second advent cannot fail because the determinate counsel of God fixed and settled it for both Christ and the earth before the foundation of the world!

The Second Coming

"And Enoch also, the seventh from Adam, pro-
phesied of these, saying, Behold, the Lord cometh
with ten thousands of his saints..."   Jude 14

From the time of Enoch till today, believers who have walked with God have found hope in the Lord's coming. The blessed hope of Christ's Second Coming brings great strength to the Church.

First, it energizes and vitalizes the Church. Jesus warned that because the bridegroom tarried longer than was expected, there were bridesmaids who slumbered and slept. Asleep, they were dead to the world and inactive to the duties delegated to them as bridesmaids, until the cry went forth, "He cometh." That cry awakened, quickened and energized them so that they arose, trimmed their lamps and went forth to greet Him. Such is the message of His Coming to the Church today.

Second, it separates the Church from ungodliness. The Church is the Bride of Christ. What bride does not bathe and dress in her finest garments when she goes to meet her bridegroom? So the Church in anticipation of the return of Christ will purify herself through the blood of Christ and put on her finest robes of righteousness.

Third, this hope exerts a transforming influence on lives and character. For every believer, there is a goal and purpose filled with certainty. It straightens our walk and gives us direction, unlike the person without goals or knowledge who just staggers about from one lustful pleasure to another. A firm belief that Christ may return at any time has a sobering influence on our lives.

Fourth, this hope has a restraining influence on the Church. Jesus told the story of the employee who left his business in the hands of two of his servants, telling them that he might return at any time. The first servant never wavered from his appointed tasks, knowing his Master might return at that moment. This uncertainity restrained him from any idleness, cruelty or irresponsibility. So should the return of Christ affect our lives. When He returns, we will be rewarded even as was the faithful servant

The Second Coming of Christ (II)

"For the Lord Himself shall descend from heaven with a shout, with the voice of the archangel, and with the trump of God: and the dead in Christ shall rise first." —I Thessalonians 4:16

We have talked about the vitalizing and sanctifying influences of the Second Coming of Christ on the Church. But it exerts consoling and evangelical influences, also.

Jesus Himself spoke of the consoling influence before He left: "Let not your heart be troubled...I will come again." This is the best and most comforting news to any believer facing the difficulties of life. The church at Thessalonica faced as many persecutions and fiery trials as any church in history. Paul's message to them? "Jesus is coming again; therefore, comfort one another with this hope." One day, all trials for the believer will be over forever "in the twinkling of an eye."

Second, the truth of Christ's soon Coming exerts an evangelical influence on every true believer. Jesus said, "This Gospel of the kingdom shall be preached in all the world for a witness unto all nations; and then shall the end come." Every new tribe entered and lingual barrier broken by the missionaries of the cross hastens the coming again of Jesus Christ. From the time of Christ's ascension, when the angel encouraged the disciples of Christ's return, believers have gone forth under the power of the Holy Spirit to evangelize the world. They certainly wouldn't have done it had they believed that Jesus would never come back—that He was gone for good. They worked for and in the light of, His soon coming!

Finally, this hope was stabilizing influence on the Church. It keeps the Christian moving forward and encouraged. James writes, "Be patient therefore, brethren, until the coming of the Lord." Many times, life seems unfulfilling, almost hopeless. But no, life is not at an end: Jesus is coming back in victory—for us to share!

Looking To His Return

"Looking for that blessed hope, and the glorious appearing of the great God and our Savior Jesus Christ..."　　　　　　　　　—Titus 2:13

The hope of our Lord's return is one of the great doctrines of the Church and the Bible. Every time a believer partakes of Holy Communion he is reminded of our Lord's return: "Ye proclaim the Lord's death till He come." Our Lord's Prayer reminds us of His return. The Church creeds speak of His coming. When we attend a funeral, we hear in the service for burial of the blessed hope. When we read our Bible, over and over again the Holy Spirit bears testimony. In every book of the New Testament except Philemon, we find reference to His appearing.

Yet to many believers it is still merely doctrine. It has not pierced their hearts so as to be integrated into their lifestyles. This was not the case of the early Church. They even laid aside individual ownership for the common good in Christian community. Why? Because they believed they would soon not need their belongings, since Jesus was soon to return. So today it would be good for some of God's children to loosen their tight grasp of worldly goods and property if they truly believe Jesus is coming soon. How are we using our resources to speed His return?

There are many today who are saying just what the Bible predicted: "Where is the promise of His coming?" They are content to go with business as usual. Jesus speaks of these as like those in the days of Noah: "eating, drinking and marrying." Ignoring God's call, they will also be caught in God's judgment—not by water but by fire.

Jesus used stories to teach His followers not to be caught napping at His appearing. There will be no time to get ready then. Our preparation must be now in our lives:'Therefore be ye also ready—for in such an hour as ye think not the Son of man cometh."

Packing Our Bags

"Beloved, now are we the sons of God, and it doth not yet appear what we shall be: but we know that, when He shall appear, we shall be like Him; for we shall see Him as He is."　　　—I John 3:2

If we want to be like Jesus when He comes again, we will want to be like Him now. Our hearts must be purified now, for there can be no change in attitude after He comes. The Bible tells us five things that every believer should be found doing when Jesus comes—and now.

The first is to *"Look Up!"* As our redemption draws nearer we should be looking up to Jesus for strength, victory, and deliverance: "Seek ye first the kingdom of God." If our interests are God's, we will be engaged in prayer and intercession, especially while the spiritual battle for God's kingdom heightens as the end nears.

The Second, is to *"occupy till He comes."* God's concern is for His kingdom to come on earth as it is in heaven. That, then too, should be our concern, to welcome His kingdom in our hearts and endeavor to share with all others about. The believer will overcome and not just escape.

Then, believers will *comfort one another* and *forsake not the assembling of ourselves together.* The devil is so pouring out his wrath and deceit even as the coming of Christ nears, the strength of the believer must be in fellowship with one another and common encouragement. No Christian will stand as an island but must find his place in the Body of Christ.

Finally, the believers with this hope will *"purify themselves."* The Christian walk is fluid. Not to move forward is to fall backward. The evil force of this world stands against faith, but "greater is He that is in us." This is the believer's victory.

Predictive Prophecy

"But the prophet, which shall presume to speak
a word in my name, which I have not commanded
him to speak, or that shall speak in the name of
other gods, even that prophet shall die."
—*Deuteronomy 18:20*

Among the people of Israel, it was not a light thing to speak forth in the name of the Lord. To serve as a prophet for God's people meant that one's life was on the line. If one prophecied falsely and incorrectly, it meant death. This partly explains the hesitancy of prophets like Isaiah and Jeremiah to respond to God's calling.

It was under this stringent law that the prophetic utterances of the scriptures came. Yet, the Bible is filled with predictive prophecy. Nearly every book of the Bible contains a measure of it. God's eternal plan for man's redemption in the light of human history is described prophetically. And we are living in an age now when much predictive prophecy from both the Old and New Testaments is being fulfilled.

In considering predictive prophecy, there are three laws governing its validity. First, the prediction must be beyond the power of human foresight and wisdom. Second, the prediction must contain sufficient number of details to preclude guesswork. And third, a sufficient time must elapse between the prediction and its fulfillment to preclude any agency of the prophet or his contemporaries in bringing about a result.

The biblical record of prophecies concerning Israel miraculously withstands this test. Their settling of the Promised Land, their blessing, their captivity, the desolation of Jerusalem, their return, the rebuilding of the Temple, the advent of Christ, His crucifixion and resurrection, the scattering of Israel, the grafting of the Gentiles to the Church, all are fulfillment of predictive prophecy. Current events of the restoration of Israel, their recovery of Jerusalem, the signs of the end-times, the preparation for the Second Coming of Christ are all found prophetically in Scripture.

The significance of predictive prophecy is for all God's people. God has promised that He would not do anything without first warning His people. "The testimony of Jesus is the spirit of prophecy."

Seventy Weeks

"SEVENTY WEEKS are determined upon thy people and upon thy Holy City, to finish the transgression, to make an end of sins, and to make reconciliaiton for iniquity..." —Daniel 9:24

The predictive prophecies in the ninth chapter of the book of Daniel are as important as any in the Bible. In these 450 years before the birth of Christ, Daniel accurately predicted the exact time of the advent of Christ, His sacrificial death, and the later destruction of Jerusalem.

The circumstances under which the prophecy of Daniel was given are significant. Daniel and all Israel had been carried away captive unto the land of Babylon. The armies of Nebuchandnezzar had utterly destroyed the city of Jerusalem. Uncovering God's sentence of 70 years of captivity and desolation for Israel in Jeremiah's writings (which time was about complete), Daniel sought God about the return of Israel to Jerusalem and the future of the Holy City. God's answer came—Israel would return, and Jerusalem be rebuilt in troubled times, and the Messiah would come in 69 weeks. Translating the weeks into days and taking the days as years, the 69 weeks find perfect fulfillment in history's record of Jesus' sacrificial death on Calvary in 32 A.D.—483 years after the commandment of Darius for Israel to return to rebuild Jerusalem.

Daniel went on to predict that "in the midst of the (last) week, He shall cause the sacrifice and the oblation to cease." This was fulfilled in the rent veil and the later total desolation of the temple by Titus' armies in 70 A.D. In both the Gospel records of Mark and Matthew, Jesus speaks of this prophecy of Daniel in referring to the coming desolation of Jerusalem by Titus. Yet even as all great events cast a shadow on future happenings, Daniel saw as he recorded of the seventieth week the present restoration of Israel and the mounting conflict that shall precede the return of Christ.

This prophecy has an immense evidential value as a witness to the truth of Scripture. It is accurate to the very year—only God could have foretold some 500 years in advance the very day on which the Messiah would ride in Jerusalem and present Himself as the "Prince" of Israel. Daniel looking to Jerusalem and Israel also speaks to our day, and this prophecy gives these messages further support. God has given us a perfect record to trust.

The Mystery Of Modern Iniquity

"But we speak the wisdom of God in a mystery, even the hidden wisdom, which God ordained before the world unto our glory."
—I Corinthians 2:7

When our prisoners of war were returned home after the Vietnam conflict, many of them were appalled at the growing immorality and decline of righteousness during the just few years they were gone. People ask, "Why has all this evil come into our generation, and can it be stopped?" Today the foundations are gone. People need a stabilizing word in this hour. Where can it come from? The answer is—*From the Church of God and its ministry.*

God reminds us that we who are believers are "stewards of the mysteries of God." He does not want His children to be ignorant of His program in the world. He tells us much in Scripture about these last days—the wars, the fear, the iniquity, immorality and lust, the Middle East tension, the lawlessness and the decay of righteousness. The Bible also tells us the reason behind all the lawlessness and decay in the world today: the fallen state of man. The world is blind to this and goes on blindly trying to apply its useless human remedies, but to the man who knows God's word it is no mystery—it is plainly written in the Bible.

God's word also tells the believer in plain language what to do in these evil, perilous days: (1) He is to stand fast (II Thessalonians 2:15). He must so believe the Word of God that he cannot be shaken. (2) He is to comfort his heart and the hearts of others (II Thessalonians 2:17). He is to be concerned but not alarmed at world conditions. (3) He is to hold his ground in spite of opposition. "Be not weary in well doing" (II Thessalonians 3:13). We are not to let up. We are to keep worshipping and working for God. We will not close up shop until the moment we are caught away.

There is a spiritual attack by the Prince of the Power of the Air, who knows his time is short today, but thank God there is a blessed counterattack coming in the air—the return of the King of Kings and Lord of Lords. Let us be steadfast 'til He comes.

The End Of The World

"But the day of the Lord will come as a thief in the night; in the which the heavens shall pass away with a great noise, and the elements shall melt with fervent heat, the earth also and the works that are therein shall be burned up." II Peter 3:10

Somebody is always predicting "the end of the world." It used to be that the doomsday prophets could get some attention, whether from the newspapers or area officials. But they became so common, today no one will even listen.

Believers and religionists alike have been trying to fix a date on the return of Christ and the end of the world. As early as the second and third centuries, Papias and Justin Martyr and other early church fathers predicted 2000 A.D. as the date of Jesus' return. Believers around the year 700 A.D., a year which signaled the completion of a cycle of time, thought the end was near. Others felt the same when the year 1000 A.D. approached. Then, not until the 1800's were renewed predictions emphasized. Many proclaimed dates in the 1800's or early 1900's including C. J. Russell, from whom the Jehovah Witness cult gets much of its doctrine. The predictions have continued with greater momentum until today.

But as to the date and hour, Jesus said, "But of that day and that hour knoweth *no man*." The certainty of Christ's coming is sure; His timing is uncertain. Jesus warns us of the unexpected suddenness of His return: "For in such an hour as ye think not the Son of man cometh."

It will be a surprise. Even the angels in heaven do not know when Christ will return. It will be a sad surprise to some who have ignored God and His love, but to those who are saved and look to His appearing it will be a gladsome time of rejoicing. The homecoming of soldiers from war will hold no candle to this great reunion for believers with their Lord. The closing saluation of our Lord in the scriptures says, "Surely I come quickly" to which John adds a hearty, "Amen, Even so, come, Lord Jesus!" This is the cry and echo of our hearts, too, today.

As It Was

"...As it was in the days of Lot...even thus shall it be in the day when the Son of man is revealed."
—Luke 17:28, 30

Jesus says that the days of His Second Coming would be typified as in the days of Noah (with eating, drinking and marrying) and as in the days of Lot. In relation to the days of Noah, there are pressures of earthly circumstances upon human life over which an individual has no control—eating, drinking, homebuilding and wage earning—which each of us is engaged in. None of these things need hinder us from service to God or preparing for His return. But there are circumstances which are in our control. Such was the situation with Lot.

When Abraham obeyed the call of God, nephew Lot went right along beside him. Lot worked hard, and he and Abraham became so properous that their possessions crowded in upon them. A spreading out was necessary. Lot knew of the bad reputation of the plain, but he chose wholly upon worldly advantage, leaving God out of his choice. God again warned Lot when thieves confiscated his holdings and Abraham had to rescue him. But again Lot turned back to Sodom. So when the noise of Sodom's iniquity reached God's ears, and He determined to bring judgment, where was Lot? Was he interceding for God's mercy like Uncle Abraham? No, he was dwelling with the wicked and could hardly convince his own family to obey the warning of God's angels.

We cannot escape the necessity of daily choices. But we can keep two things in mind that will protect us from Lot's situation. First, we must *be wary of covetousness*. Wealth does not keep one from serving God—Abraham was rich; it was the greed of riches that was Lot's downfall. Second, we must *be wary of luxury*. Over and over, history warns us that "soft living" is the presursor to national and individual decay, just as it was with Lot's family.

Where will Christ find us when He comes? Dragging out of the smoldering plains or climbing, moving mountains in faith?

Perplexity

"And there shall be signs in the sun, and in the moon, and in the stars; and upon the earth distress of nations, with perplexity; the sea and waves roaring..."
—Luke 21:25

The dictionary defines perplexity as "a condition of bewilderment" and how accurately that pictures much of our world today. In our "age of Aquarius", we have experienced the signs of the heavens—both as man has travelled out into space, and as "signs" from space have come upon us. It is no coincidence that the phobias of "Star Wars" and "Close Encounters" are the interest of youth. God said there would be signs and perplexity.

But much of man's perplexity has to do with things on earth: "distress of nations, sea and waves roaring." It seems this is no longer the age of wholesale war but rather of terrorism. Nations are in fear and distress as terrorists spread their destruction and bloodshed, and seemingly little can be done. The sea, which in the Bible is symbolic of sin, is roaring. Crime and immorality continue to grow, and who can control them? Only the love of God. The waves speak of our economy and government. Are they not roaring, bobbing up and down with inflation and uncertainty?

In these days, the only one who can be sure is the believer in Christ. When these things happen, Jesus says, "Look up for your redemption is soon." If there was ever a time to know Jesus as Savior and Friend, the time is now. That knowledge and relationship is about to pay off.

Treason

*"This know also, that in the last days perilous
times shall come. For men shall be...TRAITORS..."*
—II Timothy 3:1, 2, & 4

Traitors and treachery are a sure sign that we are now in the last days. Only 25 years ago, people were sentenced to death for treachery to our nation. Today, not only America but around the world, nations are continually plagued with traitors who discredit the nation, stir up strife, and breed terrorism against governments.

The world has always had its traitors, but never before in world history have they been the order of the day, nor reached the scale of our present-day treachery. Men seem ready to betray everything that is sacred and worthwhile. Yet the Bible condemns treachery. It was the crowning sin against our Lord. So we ask, "What is this sin that gets into people?" There is never much money involved. The great traitors of the world have sold out for pitifully small sums. There is no honor connected with treachery. The names of Judas, Quisling, Arnold, and Rosenburg are ruined forever. What do people think they will profit?

The best explanation may be found in the words of Jesus, who said to Judas: "Satan entered into thine heart." The devil is the arch traitor. He betrayed God's sacred trust and his high office. And he seeks continually to lead others in the same path of treachery. God seems to have respect for out and out sinners like Paul, Manassah and Matthew—but only contempt for those who "betray with a kiss."

For a little longer, Satan is still on the loose, and he desires to enter each of our hearts to twist and corrupt with his evil designs. But we need not be a stooge, when under God we can be a saint!

Scoffers

"For this they willingly are ignorant of, that by
the word of God the heavens were of old, and the
earth standing out of the water and in the water:
Whereby the world that then was, being overflowed
with water, perished."   *—II Peter 3:5 & 6*

It seems that today there are fewer jokes and laughter by smart alecks about Noah and the Ark with his strange cargo. Scientific and archeological discoveries have so verified the truth of the Biblical record of the Great Flood, it is God's people who are having the last laugh. God has allowed the story of the Deluge to be written on the face of Mother Earth.

In our text, Peter describes the impact of the flood: *"the world that then was."* It must have been a beautiful world; our dramatists still try to describe it, and men still look for what they call Atlantis. But it came to an end with savage fury as all the haughty scorn for God of men could not save it. God's divine verdict on the world reads: "the wickedness of man was great in the earth and that every imagination of the thoughts of his heart was only evil continually...it repenteth me that I have made them."

Here was the tragedy: "every imagination of the thoughts of his heart was only evil." Man's inventive genius is the wonderful faculty that separates him from the beasts of the field. How it hurt the heart of God to see this marvelous genius being misused to produce only horror and destruction.

God's feelings have not changed and, unfortunately man's attitude has not largely changed. Scoffers today are "willingly ignorant" not to learn this great warning of history, as they still use their genius for lust, greed, and war. So this world is hasting unto a new day of judgment: "Wherein the heavens being on fire will be dissolved and elements on earth shall melt with fervent heat."

Peter concludes that, "Knowing this, what manner of persons ought ye to be in all holy conversation and godliness?" This is a day of preparation and warning as we anticipate our Lord's return.

Wars

"But when ye shall hear of wars and commotions, be not terrified: for these things must first come to pass..."
       —Luke 21:9

We are no doubt living in the most exciting times of fulfillment of Biblical prophecy in history. The eyes of the world are fixed upon the Middle East—exactly where God said the drama preceding the return of Christ would occur. Already we have seen the fulfillment of the gathering of the Jews from being scattered among all nations to be established in their nation, the miraculous restoration of their holy city of Jerusalem, and the blessing of God upon their land.

In more than thirty centuries of Israel's history, no other nation has had a more tumultous existence, and with good reason. Satan knows better than anyone that God's purposes of world redemption are wrapped up in Israel's being settled in their land. He knows that his kingdom of darkness and cruelty is in jeopardy when this peculiar nation of destiny is in its God-ordained place of blessing and power. He will resist in any way possible.

The prophet Zechariah was one of the greatest preachers of the Second Coming in all time. In the last three chapters of his prophecy, he lists eight outstanding events connected with it:
(1) The gathering of the nations for combat against Israel (12:3).
(2) The seige of aliens against Jerusalem (14:2).
(3) The battle of Armageddon and the deliverance by the Lord (14:3).
(4) The outpouring of the Holy Spirit upon Israel (12:10).
(5) Israel's godly sorrow for crucifying Prince of Glory (12:12-14).
(6) The foundation of cleansing that will be opened for the nation (13:1).
(7) The return of the Lord Jesus Christ on Mount Olivet (14:4).
(8) The setting up of His kingdom and the millenial blessings (14:9-21).

These eight events are on God's time-table, and we see them readily approaching. Despite hopes for lasting peace, pressure will only increase rather than lessen. The gathering of the Arab league, Russia, and the Common Market of Europe have found their place in Bible prophecy. The current time of peace is for Israel's strengthening and the preparation for God's outpouring on His nation, but the final conflict is inevitable: the last stand of the foes of hell, and the greatest victory of Christ and His people.

Ghost Riders In The Sky

"...Tell us, when shall these things be? and
what shall be the sign of thy coming, and of the end
of the world."   —Matthew 24:3

The great historian Arnold Toynbee writes that the events of history are racing to a climax in our century. Believers and agnostics alike are haunted today by the inescapable conviction that certain events over and above us are gathering speed and compelling the human race to gather by a will greater than their own toward a "rendezvous with destiny."

There is the sign of apostasy: "for the day of the Lord will not come unless the apostasy comes first." Apostasy means to turn one's back on God in repudiation. This is a sign of our age, as around the world, men have turned to socialism, materialism, Satanism, Communism, and all the other "isms" to replace the rightful place of God's rule in their hearts.

There is the sign of Israel: "The house of Israel shall come out to the north country, and from all the countries whither I had driven them; and they shall dwell in their own land." This year Israel has celebrated the thirtieth anniversary of the First National Assembly of the re-established State of Israel. Her growth and prosperity is every bit as great a miracle as was her establishment. Christ said, "that when his branch is yet tender and putteth forth leaves," His return would be imminent, "even at the doors."

Then there is the sign of lawlessness. Paul gives Timothy a view of the last days (and other times): "lovers of their own selves, covetous, boasters, blasphemers, disobedient to parents, unholy without natural affection, high minded, lovers of pleasure..." A moral lawlessness has perverted the land despite the Spirit of renewal in the Church. But then, it is even as the Lord said, "the righteous are more righteous and the filthy, filthier."

Even modern "miracles" are talked about in the scriptures. Bombing planes: "Like the noise of chariots on the tops of the mountains as they leap—like the noise of a flame of fire that devoureth the stubble, as a strong people set in battle array." Atomic Bomb: "And men were scorched with great heat." United Nations: "to gather the nations that I may assemble the kingdoms." There are also the failures of columnists, judgment on nations, overthrowing of sinful leaders, and seeking of supernatural signs. The Pharisees also sought a sign from heaven, to which Jesus responded, "Can ye not discern the signs of the times?" Can we?

The Remaining Things

"...Now He hath promised, saying YET ONCE MORE,....signifieth the removing of those things that are shaken—that those things which cannot be shaken may remain." —Hebrews 12:26-27

All things are *changing*. As Alvin Toffler tells us in *Future Shock*, things are now changing at a more rapid pace than ever in history. We sense convulsions everywhere. That which has been dormant is erupting again. The words of our text magnificently communicate this. They fit exactly into ten words of the prophet Hosea: "He (Christ) shall come unto us as the rain—as the latter and former rain unto the earth (harvest time)."

We are rapidly approaching the threshold of another "millenium"—the significant date of 2,000 A.D., surely a significant date in human history, as it closes a complete cycle of 6,000 years. Many of God's people are asking: "Will the next millenium start God's millenium?" To that question, we have only the conviction of our hearts as we see the signs and the witness of the Holy Spirit to that conviction.

Surely this last century of the second millenium after Christ is finishing just as the first millenium began. The current outpouring of the Holy Spirit is going around the world to accomplish that which began with the first Spirit outpouring in Jerusalem and the surrounding region. That first outpouring shook the foundations of the Roman world. Even the enemies of Christ declared, "They have turned the world upside down." Why? So that those things which are sure and true would remain and be uncovered and apparent.

The same thing is happening today as the renewal in the Holy Spirit sweeps every denomination and country, shaking away the dead chaff and revealing the Truth. The "Yet Once More" is happening and gaining momentum for the soon return of our Lord and King.

Harvest Time

"Let both grow together until the harvest: and in the time of harvest I will say to the reapers, 'Gather ye together first the tares, and bind them in bundles to burn them: but gather the wheat into my barn."
—Matthew 13:30

Our text gives the conclusion of Jesus' parable likening God's kingdom to the farmer who sowed his field with seed. By and by the enemy came and sowed tares among the wheat. The servants of the farmer asked him how to rid the field of the tares. This parable explains that which has existed in our world for nearly 20 centuries—namely, the mixed state of affairs. The "field" represents the religious world in which the True and False "grow together."

The only way the farmer could rid his field of tares without harming the wheat was to wait until harvest time when the difference would be apparent. Such is God's way of ridding this world of evil. As we steadily approach the day of *Harvest*, when the angels will put in their sickles to reap, the difference between good and evil is becoming easier to see.

Notice in our text the order—tares are gathered into "bundles" *before* the wheat is actually garnered: "*gather* ye together first the tares and bind them *in bundles* to burn." The removal and burning comes afterward. But first, there is the separation of the tares *in* the field in order to leave the wheat "distinct" and ready for garnering. This gathering into "bundles" is one of the signs of the times. Men are having to choose their identification: there is the commercial bundle, the social, the political, the ecclesiastical. What a horrible end lies ahead for the wicked, the bundled tares: "And shall cast them into a furnace of fire...Then shall the righteous shine forth as the sun in the kingdom of their Father."

The "weeds" and "tares" of this world, Jesus said, would grow right until harvest time. Rather than wasting our time on reform movements to cultivate the tares, we must preach the Gospel that men may bear fruit unto righteousness: "Every branch that beareth not fruit he taketh away."

The Jew

"Thus saith the Lord, which giveth the sun for a light by day, and the ordinances of the moon and of the stars for a light by night...If those ordinances depart from before me, saith the Lord, then the seed of Israel also shall cease from being a nation before me forever." —Jeremiah 31:35-36

Mark Twain had this observation of the Jew: "He could be vain of himself and be excused for it. The Egyptian, Babylonian, and the Persian rose, filled the planet with sound and splendor, then faded to dream stuff and passed away. The Greek and Roman followed and made a vast noise, and they are gone. Other people have sprung up and held the torch high for a time, but it burned out, and they sit in the twilight, if at all. The Jew saw them all, beat them all, and is now what he always was, exhibiting no decadence or old age or slowness of energy or dullness of mind. All things are mortal but the Jew—all other forces pass but he remains. What is the secret?"

In this age of roots, none can hold a candle to the Jew. He is a person of covenant; it was he to whom the Gospel was first presented. He is God's oldest testimony on earth. His covenant will be kept at all cost. Both the Old Testament and the New Testament have declared a spiritual future for the Jew. Isaiah declares: "Israel shall blossom and bud—and they shall fill the face of the world with fruit." And Paul writes that when "the fulness of the Gentiles be come in—and so all Israel shall be saved."

The millenium can not and will not occur without the coming to Jesus and the cooperation of the Jews: "God is able to graft them (the Jewish branches) in again." God has promised the land of Palestine to Israel: "I will give thee and thy seed...all the land of Canaan for an everlasting possession." God has today prospered the Jews in Israel in accordance with His timetable for the revelation of the Man of Sin and the Great Tribulation. The Jews will be purged and will confess their rejection of the Messiah and return to Jesus. When they look on Him "whom they have pierced," they shall mourn "as one mourneth for his only son." They will then be established in righteousness—forever.

Ishmael and Isaac

"And as for Ishmael, I have heard thee. Behold, I have blessed him, and will make him fruitful, and will multiply him exceedingly; twelve princes shall he beget, and I will make him a great nation. But my covenant will I establish with Isaac..."
—Genesis 17:20-21

In recent decades, people have assumed that the great conflict of the age would pit Russia, the bulwark of communism, with America, the stalwart of capitalism and personal freedom. But that is not in God's plan. In His providence, He has seen that the world's great energy resources of oil would be concentrated in the area of the Middle East. Today the world's attention is focused in the world's birthplace—the home of the Arab and the Jew.

Satan has long suceeded in maintaining strife been the descendants of these stepbrothers Ishmael (Arab) and Isaac (Jew). He knows that when their alienation is over, so is his time on earth. In recent years, the devil has inspired Russia to stir strife between the Arabs and Jews with the idea that Russia would establish a needed sea outlet in the Arab world. Today the Arabs are recognizing Russia's selfish interest, and Russia's foothold is greatly weakened.

The possibilities of peace between Israel and the Arab world through the negotiations of Sadat and Begin are increasing. We must pray toward that end. God has called Israel to be the keystone upon which will hinge the great consummate events of Christ's Second Coming. No one, including Russia, is going to upset God's plan or God's schedule. Therefore, this effort to pit Ishmael against Isaac will come to naught. God's hand will intervene. Watch closely the development of these events and then lift up your heads, for your redcemption draweth nigh.

Omar or Zion?

*"Pray for the peace of Jerusalem: they shall
prosper that love thee."* —Psalm 122:6

A temple or a Mosque? Islam's crescent or David's Star? What is
history's destiny for Jerusalem? This Middle East city has been the center of
more of the world's struggles and has incurred more seiges, 28 in all, that
any city in the world.

Jerusalem means "possession of peace." It was taken by David from
the Jebusites a thousand years before Christ. Ever since, it has become the
city of David and more significantly, God's city: 'The Lord said, In
Jerusalem will I put My Name." Therefore, God promises a blessing to all
that pray for her.

It was over Jerusalem (and only that city) that Jesus wept. And it was
in Jerusalem that the Church was founded and from which it spread
abroad. More that any other city of the world, it is a city of prophecy. God
promises to "establish Jerusalem as a praise in the earth;" "shall Jerusalem
be holy;" "the kingdom shall come to the daughter of Jerusalem." "And the
Lord...shall choose Jerusalem again;" "All the nations that come up against
Jerusalem;" "a fountain opened to...Jerusalem;" "And His feet shall stand
in that day upon the Mount of Olives which is before Jerusalem."

Surely, God's eyes are fixed upon Jerusalem. It is the only city on
earth after which a city in heaven is named. The New Jerusalem is God's
heavenly city out of which flows from the throne of God and shall come
down to bring eternal peace on earth at the Second coming of Christ.

Many thousands of men have died in siege trying to "purchase"
Jerusalem. But it is God's city. It belongs to God and His people. It is here
that Christ, who paid the supreme price for God's people, will place His
feet at the Second Coming and rule forever more.

The Tribulation

*"For then shall be great tribulation, such as was
not since the beginning of the world to this time, no,
nor ever shall be."* —Matt. 24:21

When we think of all that has transpired during the history of
humanity, we can only shudder as we see that none of its bloody pages can
be compared with the coming Great Tribulation. There have surely been
tribulations: Carthage's fall before Rome, when nine days of fire and
sword wiped out every living thing; In Titus' conquest of Jerusalem, when
the suffering was so terrible that mothers frantic from hunger ate their own
sucklings; the Black Plague of London, which left that city as a graveyard;
the French Revolution; the atom bomb over Hiroshima—all terrifying and
revolting, but miniature in comparison to the Great Tribulation.

The difference is that all tribulations until now have been *local*. This
one will cover the whole earth; no spot will escape this coming visitation.
The reason for the Tribulation is a chastisement from the Lord for tran-
sgressions of His laws: "The Lord cometh out of His place to punish the inhabitants of the earth for their iniquity." God's laws are "holy, just and
good," and nations have utterly disregarded them. Sins of nations as well
as individual sins must be dealt with. God's love is balanced with judgment, and if nations won't repent, they will be punished.

The destruction of the Great Tribulation will be devastating: "The
earth shall disclose her blood." Bloodshed will be so rampant, the living
will not take time or have the desire to bury the dead: "No more cover her
dead." It will come to the point that death would be a gracious relief, "but
they shall not find it" and therefore, will suffer on.

Great physical disturbances affecting the whole world will cause
paroxysms of fear. "The earth shall reel to and fro like a drunkard." Man's
magnificient achievements and his marvelous civilization will be torn to
shreds as God deals with man's pride of life: his mind. Those that pro-
crastinated their day of salvation and the scorners who rejected Christ, will
face this day.

But even in the Great Tribulation, the call of salvation will not be
altogether hushed, as God will have two witnesses in the midst. All who
are saved and who come out of the midst of the Tribulation will seal their
salvation in martyrdom: "As many as would not worship the image of the
beast should be killed. In Christ, we can escape this coming tribulation."

The Antichrist

"And every spirit that confesseth not that Jesus Christ is come in the flesh is not of God: and this is that SPIRIT OF ANTICHRIST, whereof ye have heard that it should come; and even now already is it in the world." —I John 4:3

The prophets as well as Jesus and His apostles tell us of a coming one who will lead the inhabitants of the earth into a idolatrous revolt against God. His reign will plunge the world into a series of indescribable horrors. Paul calls him the *man of sin* and the *son of perdition*. John calls him the *antichrist* and the *beast*. Daniel calls him the *little horn* and the *king*, "who shall do according to his will"—a *dictator*.

This great final world—figure is a person. All systems and movements opposed to God and Christ head up in him: "the lawless one, even he, whose coming is according to the working of Satan with all power and signs and lying wonders." Not a local dictator, he will see to it that he is the only object of worship in the whole world.

Our text says that even in John's day there was personalization of rebellion and arrogance. There have been many since, but not on the world scale that will come about when God's people are raptured from this world and Satan is confined to earth with the knowledge that "he hath but a short time." At this time, he will energize his "son of perdition" and give him "power, throne, and great authority." Just as the devil has always been a liar and murderer, this Antichrist will blaspheme God and enforce an avalanche of persecution unequalled by anything in history.

Though the Church will be gone, this Antichrist with his blasphemy and desecration of everything that speaks of God will provoke enmity towards any who will believe in a living God. These will be persecuted and martyred for their faith, but they will be saved. The return of Christ to establish His eternal kingdom on earth will mark the defeat and death of the Antichrist and the binding of Satan for the Millenium.

Freedom from the Antichrist and his spirit of lies is ours today in the truth of Jesus Christ.

Superman

"And he doeth great wonders, so that he maketh fire come down from heaven on the earth in the sight of men." —*Revelation 13:13*

As we look upon the actitivies of the soon coming Antichrist in the thirteenth chapter of the book of Revelation, it reads like many of the superhero cartoons they show on TV on Saturday mornings. But this great world leader and "Superman" will be for real, and he will deceive those on earth so that they will set up an image of him and worship it. And those who will not worship the image of the beast will be killed.

This "Superman" will grasp the attention and rulership of the entire world. It is hard to think that America would succumb to such leadership and regimentation of idolatry. But Jesus gives a hint to the reason: "Men's hearts failing from *fear*." Fear can paralize and cause desperation. People will submit to the only thing left to try—world government. But eventually the "Superman's" remedy will be the same remedy man has always tried—not love, but force. For this reason, the Bible calls this world leader, without God and bereft of spiritual instinct, a beast. He will be responsible for great crime and bloodshed.

What hinders his appearing now? The Bible tells us in Second Thessalonians: "and now ye know what with holdeth that he (the Antichrist) might be revealed in his time...only he who now preventeth will continue to prevent, until he be taken out of the way." It is the Holy Spirit of God that works truth and prevents the devil's agents from enslaving men. But that same Spirit will be removed with the Church in the rapture. When He is gone, the world will be like our cities when the police go on strike. Men's souls will have no protection and will be looted by the devil; so that men's only hope will be martyrdom. Such will be the lot of men who now ignore the remedy of God in Christ.

When Jesus Reigns On Earth

"And in the days of these kings shall the God of heaven set up a kingdom, which shall never be destroyed: and the kingdom shall not be left to other people, but it shall break in pieces and consume all these kingdoms, and it shall stand for ever."   —Daniel 2:44

For nearly 2000 years the Church has prayed, "Thy kingdom come, thy will be done in earth, as it is in Heaven." This is a God-given prayer, so it must be answered. And there will soon come a time when it will never have to be offered again. Man has had his day trying to set up his own kingdom. So, it will soon be God's turn.

When Christ returns to reign, there will be many changes on earth. First, Christ will sieze and bind the true enemy of man—the devil: "He laid hold on the dragon, which is the devil, and bound him a thousand years. There can be no Millenium as long as Satan is at liberty. The day is coming when the great accuser will be rendered powerless.

Christ will establish true justice on earth: "A King shall reign in righteousnes." In righteousness, the earth will become fruitful and plenteous. "The land that was desolate is become like the Garden of Eden." Even animals will respond in kind: "The wolf and lamb shall feed together." Perfect safety will be available for all: "and none shall make them afraid." None "shall hurt or destroy in all God's holy mountain." War shall be gone forever: "They will beat their swords into plowshares," and there shall be long life for all.

The world will all know the love of Christ: "All shall know me, from the least to the greatest." So every nation and tongue will have a full knowledge of God and be united. No more will oppression reign, for it will be God's saints that rule. Israel will shine, and Jerusalem will be the center of worship with our Lord Christ enthroned as King. The voice of "sorrow and mourning shall flee away.." and "everlasting joy shall be upon their heads." Should we not look for His appearing?

Resurrection Of The Body

"For if we have been planted together in the likeness of His death, we shall be also in the likeness of His resurrection."
—Romans 6:5

Do you believe in the resurrection of the body? We must if we are to believe the scriptures. It was a favorite message of the apostles, not just that Christ arose, but that He arose in the same body wherein He lived on earth. He was easily recognizable; the nailprints in His hands and the scars in His body were part of His resurrected body.

What is the significance of the resurrection of the body in which you now live? It is that the identity of the body is supremely important to personality. No one will argue that one cannot read character in a person's face. The cast of the countenance is determined by the shape of the soul. The two are interlocked. Many who knew nothing of me have pegged me as a preacher right off. Why? Because that which is inside is shaping and controlling that which is outside. The body is only the outer expression of the soul and takes its individuality absolutely from that source. That's why dead bodies don't mean so much to us—the source is gone. But this soul of ours needs the body through which to express itself. Therefore, the resurrection of the body is a necessity.

There are those who don't want to be resurrected in the body they now live in because of their age, physical limitations, or infirmities. What is their hope? The Bible says that the resurrection will conquer all death; the body that will rise again will be relieved of every trace of death. So all effects of death, direct or indirect, will be destroyed utterly and forevermore. The wrinkles, the gray hairs, the defects, these are of death. When *all* death is abolished then all these will be gone, too. The good news is "the corruptible must put on incorruption."

Assurance

"...if it were not so, I would have told you..."
—John 14:2

We live in an age of insurance. People desire protection from all sorts of ills with insurance. But for the believer, someone has rightly suggested, "We need more *assurance* than *insurance*." Assurance is the best remedy. The shield of God today gives two certainties for that assurance: Christ is coming again, and heaven is His eternal home.

Jesus spoke our text to His disciples just before His betrayal, after Judas left. The disciples were to face the fiery trial but have Christ's promise upon which to cling. Godset translates the verse: "If our separation were to be eternal, I would have forewarned you." It is Christ's promise, and His word validates it.

Even as Joshua's word opened the way for Israel's passage to the promised land, Jesus opened our way to heaven. He said, "I am *the way!*" His precious death in our stead has made the way for us to live eternally with Him. Even today, Christ's priestly presence sustains heaven for us. He is what makes heaven attractive to us. As the little boy said, 'There is no hell where Jesus is."

Jesus, then, is God's testimony to heaven. He said that there was a heaven and we would be with him there. So if David could cheer on his men to capture earthly Jerusalem with the assurance that there he would dwell and they should have abodes with him, we too should be encouraged to press on to obtain our mansion with Christ in heaven.

Jesus is soon coming for His own—for those who look to His promise. Believers will soon be caught up in the clouds. Are your bags packed?

Looking To Heaven

"We are confident, I say, and willing rather to be absent from the body, and to be present with the Lord." —II Corinthians 5:8

The surest thing we know about heaven is that it is awaiting those who believe. Jesus will be there, so it will be wonderful. What we will do in heaven is not altogether clear from Scripture, but we are confident that we are preparing for that life even now.

It was the belief and tradition of the early Church leaders that the saints who went on before continued in Christian service even in heaven. Origen wrote: "All souls who have departed this life still retaining their love for those who are in the world concern themselves for their salvation and aid them by their prayers and meditation with God. It is my opinion that all those fathers who have fallen asleep before us fight on our side and aid us by their prayers."

St. Jerome, who gave us the Vulgate Bible, adds: "If the apostles and martyrs while still in the body are able to pray for others...how much more may they do so now...one man, Moses, obtains from God pardon for 600,000 men in arms; and Stephen, the imitator of his Lord, begs forgiveness for his persecutors...shall their power be less after they have begun to be with Christ?"

It is a pity that the Church has largely ignored this aspect of heaven. Certainly the doctrine of the prayers of the saints was taken into excess and abuse before the Reformation. But in ridding the abuse, we largely ignored this truth—that not only Christ ever lives to make intercession for the saints but we are encompassed by a cloud of witnesses, saints who have gone on before, who continue to pray and urge us on to gain the victory. We can appreciate the prayers of those who have gone before—they can bring comfort and strength.

Life In Heaven

"...and His servants shall serve Him."
—Revelation 22:3

With all the keen interest about heaven today, the scriptures are strangely brief in the description about life in heaven, and a lot of what they do tell us is given in poetic language. For example, they suggest that there will be harps in the hands of everyone. This seems to convey the thought that over yonder, utterance shall be music. Music can express what speech never can, and up there we'll be able to express ourselves perfectly.

Then we read that in heaven there will be no temple. No one will have to go to church at certain hours. Why? Because we'll live in an attitude of worship all the time; going to church will be unnecessary. We are also told that there will be many mansions. Individuality will be preserved: a place for us will be prepared there even as it was here.

And in our text, we find the most significant quality of life continuing in heaven. The ruling passion of one's life on earth will be the ruling passion of the life beyond. A true believer is a man who serves, and heaven will be filled with them. Jesus Himself took the form of a servant, and even as Christ has received His reward, we shall enter heaven to discover that the reward of service is a larger service. There will be service for the saints above, even as Christ ever lives to make intercession for (and serves) the believers today.

Because self mingles in what we do, here our finest service is imperfect. We are at best unprofitable servants. In heaven there will be no limitation of ignorance, no need for shortcuts, no infirmity to man, or devil to tempt. With knowledge perfected and the tireless zest of eternal morning, at last His servants shall serve Him fully, according to His inestimable worth!